THE EMPIRE IS MARCHING

Glen St. J. Barclay

THE EMPIRE IS MARCHING

A STUDY OF THE MILITARY EFFORT OF THE BRITISH EMPIRE
1800–1945

WEIDENFELD AND NICOLSON   LONDON

ISBN 0 297 77125 6

Printed and bound in Great Britain by
Morrison & Gibb Ltd, London and Edinburgh

Contents

Acknowledgements

I should like to express my indebtedness to my former students Mrs Caroline A. O'Brien and Mr Michael Birgan for their assistance and encouragement, as well as for their own trailblazing work in the area of Australian foreign relations; to my colleague Dr Joseph M. Siracusa for his invaluable assistance in directing me to new areas of research and scholarship; to Dr Denis J. Murphy for sharing with me his specialized knowledge of the Australian experience in two world wars; to Mr Christopher Falkus of Weidenfeld (Publishers) Ltd for suggesting the topic in the first place; to the staffs of the National Archives of New Zealand and the Australian Archives for their unfailingly prompt and generous assistance; and especially to Dr Dean C. Allard, Head of the Operational Archives Division, Department of the Navy, Washington, for his great services to the study of military and diplomatic history.

Illustrations

Maps

Look north! Look south!
We're strong and unafraid;
Look east! Look west!
We're marching in the Great Crusade:

From Bengal to the Rockies,
From the Rand to Mandalay,
The Empire is marching
Towards The Day.

Second World War Song

'A great Empire and little minds go ill together.'

Edmund Burke

1 We could afford to lose a place like Sydney (1800–85)

The nineteenth century had been in many ways the century of Britain. There were ample grounds in 1899 for believing that the next hundred years would be the century of the British Empire. No power in the history of mankind had ever seemed to hold in its hands such capacity to influence the destiny of the human race. British authority was extended in some form or another over 11.25 million square miles of territory, with approximately 400 million inhabitants. By comparison Rome at its zenith had counted only 2.5 million square miles, with 132 million subjects. Nor was British predominance merely a matter of numbers and real estate. The Royal Navy was the one admittedly supreme fighting force in the world. Its battle force of twenty-eight capital ships was almost equal to the combined strength of the next two most powerful navies, the French and Russian. British primacy at sea was even more overwhelming in the commercial sphere: over 49 per cent of the world's merchant shipping flew the Red Ensign at the turn of the century.

This tremendous commercial dynamism indeed seemed to have provided the Empire with a new expansionary thrust, comparatively lacking in previous decades. Henry James had rather apprehensively expressed the wish in 1877 that 'England would *do* something – something striking and powerful, which should be at once characteristic and unexpected'. He asks himself what she can do, and he remembers that this greatness of England which he so much admires was formerly much exemplified in her 'taking' something. Can't she 'take' something now? There is the *Spectator*, who wants her to occupy Egypt: can't she occupy Egypt?[1] He was soon to be reassured. Egypt was occupied. Indeed 3 million square miles and 232 million subjects were occupied in the second half of the nineteenth century alone. Nor could this possibly be the end: the Orange Free State and the Transvaal were clearly in the category of unfinished business, which would be taken care of at the appropriate time.

Even the obvious anomalies and contradictions in the structure of the Empire seemed to be improving. The British race itself was for example becoming more evenly spread over its possessions: in 1837 only 1.5 million persons of British ethnic origin lived in the colonies, or about 5.2 per cent of the whole; by 1897 this proportion had risen to 21 per cent, representing 10.5 million out of a total of 50 million, although admittedly the proportion of ethnic British in the total population of the Empire had fallen in the same period – from 17.3 to 12.5 per cent. The Empire had in practice become clearly divided between the mainly or wholly British-inhabited areas and the almost wholly non-British. There was a bright side to this, however. The huge territories of Canada and Australasia should be able to support enormous British populations in the future. Confident estimates forecast 100 million each for Canada and the Australian continent, and another 20 million for New Zealand. This would give the British race ample numbers to overwhelm the Germans and at least match the Americans and Russians, even without the help of India or Africa north of the Zambesi.

The long-term prospects for the British people in the contest for world power were thus encouraging. The short-term prospects were less so. The basic cause for concern here was economic. There were indeed grave reasons for believing that the whole future of the British Empire might depend on whether the productive capacity of the over-seas territories could be expanded quickly enough to compensate for the economic decline of Britain itself. The reality of that decline could not be doubted: in 1870 Britain had produced 29 per cent of the world's steel, 49 per cent of its pig-iron, and 49 per cent of its coal; by 1900 the relative figures were 18 per cent, 22 per cent and 27 per cent. The United Kingdom had been overtaken by the United States as a pro-ducer of steel in 1880, in iron production in 1890, and in coal production in 1900. It had been overtaken by Germany in steel production in 1895, and would soon be overtaken in iron production as well.

It was of course easier to note the fact of this decline in economic power than to define why it had come about. What was obvious was that there had been a striking retardation in the rate of technical pro-gress and innovation in the United Kingdom, especially compared with the new industrial powers of the United States and Germany. Initially this may have stemmed from the slackening in consumer demand during the interminable 'long depressions' of 1873–85 and 1891–6. The lack of demand for new technology to satisfy sluggish or over-supplied markets further exacerbated what Corelli Barnett has identified as one of the major factors contributing to the decline of British power, the failure of the British educational system to produce technicians and business administrators in numbers to match those graduating in the United States and Germany. By the beginning of the twentieth century there were thirteen universities and university colleges in Great Britain. Germany had twenty-one, with three times as many students. Perhaps more relevantly, nearly five times as many Germans as British citizens were receiving advanced technical education.[2] It is of course difficult to gauge the actual impact of this educational disparity. Dr Richardson argues that differences in efficiency 'were probably very small' between Britain and its competitors, and claims that there 'is no aggregate statistical evidence to support the view that technical progress in Britain was much lower . . . '.[3] This however might mean only that the full effects of the educational lag were yet to be experienced. For example Dr Kindleberger has shown that the very high level of comparative efficiency still being maintained in certain vital British industries such as shipbuilding 'was achieved through the great craftsmanship of the British worker, through an enormous amount of specialisation and in spite of comparatively backward equipment. Shipyards lacked electric lighting on the ways, electric motors, pneumatic tools. But the degree of specialisation was carried further than anywhere else.'[4] British industry in other words was subsisting on the accumulated and diminishing capital of past technical and organizational achievements.

More serious still was the lack of real concern to develop new skills and techniques to match those of the Americans and Germans. Here imperial expansion played a direct and malignant role. The fact that traditional British industries could gain assured and preferential markets within the colonies made it superficially less essential for them to compete in foreign markets with the new generation of manufactured products being exported by the Americans and Germans. The proportion of British exports going to the Empire had indeed declined from 35 per cent in the late 1850s to 25 per cent in the early 1870s. However it had risen again to a peak of 38.5 per cent by the beginning of the twentieth century. Similarly the proportion of exports going to agricultural countries, including the colonies, rose from 56.3 per cent in the middle 1850s to nearly 69 per cent by the end of the century.[5] In other

words British entrepreneurs and investors were actually neglecting the
new sophisticated growth industries in which they would have to meet
American and European competition, in favour of less sophisticated
traditional industries that could continue to exploit the captive markets
of the Empire. One consequence was an ominous deterioration in the
British balance of payments position at the turn of the century.[6] The
fact remained none the less that 'expansion in old-fashioned exports
meant that the old industries appeared relatively more attractive than
the new to the domestic investor. . . . In order for there to have been
less overseas investment and a more intensive development of the new
industries, the pre-1914 generation would have had to make real
sacrifices in terms of current income . . . of possible investment outlets
of the time new industries *appeared* to be the least profitable.'[7]

A more perfect formula for economic and probably moral decline
could not have been devised. Disaster for the Empire was inevitable
unless new-generation growth industries could be developed in the
colonies to compensate for the decline in British performance due to the
diversion of investment capital to old-generation industries. This was
the more urgent in that decline in industrial technology was certain to
mean a decline in military efficiency, at a time when chemistry, metal-
lurgy and engineering were all beginning to change military tactics.
The pursuit of short-term capital gains had put the British Empire on
the block.

In this situation the ability of the Empire to defend itself with its own
resources became vital. Here again the picture was unclear. The Royal
Navy was by far the biggest in the world, as we have seen. However it
had not fought a fleet action since Trafalgar, unless one could count the
extermination of the Turks at Navarino in 1827. Neither indeed had any
of its potential European rivals, except for the Italians and Austrians,
who had fought at Lissa in 1866 using techniques of ramming, which
had not been employed seriously since Roman times and were not likely
ever to be employed again. On the other hand the Americans had fought
the first battles of the new technological era against fellow Americans in
the Civil War, and had recently enjoyed battle practice against Spain.
So had the Japanese against the Chinese navy in Korean waters.

The state of the British army was still more serious. Here the problem
was not lack of battle experience: the British had enjoyed more action
of this kind than anybody else, thanks to their never-ending colonial

wars. They had also fought another European army in 1854–6 in the Crimea, in a war that was admittedly a carnival of negligence in the High Command and incompetence in the field. The trouble was that since then they had had too much of the wrong kind of experience: as the official German history of the war in South Africa later put it politely:

The insufficient tactical training of the English Army is partly explained by the peculiar conditions under which it is called upon to fight; it must be ready to meet an enemy, trained and armed in Europe, or, on the border mountains of India, an adversary most skilful in taking cover and who, even with an antiquated fire-arm, makes remarkably good practice. In the Sudan it had to expect an assault by fanatics, who saw their salvation in the use of cold steel; at one time skirmishing is necessary; at another troops must be massed together. It is, therefore, conceivable that the experiences of one war could hardly be assimilated for the general military good; it had, therefore, been left to the troops to find out the most suitable formation, and this knowledge was almost invariably very dearly purchased.[8]

There was however a simpler ingredient for disaster in the colonial experience of the British army: it was that a tradition of deploying minute forces of professional soldiers in the most underdeveloped parts of the world, against enemies always ill-disciplined, ill-organized and hopelessly ill-equipped, was the most likely one possible to encourage methods totally inappropriate for war against another modern great power. This had been shown clearly enough in 1881, in the struggle with the tiny army of the Republic of the Transvaal. The Boers had no artillery, the numbers on both sides had been miniscule, and the terrain was as colonial as nature could make it. The Boers were however militarily literate, and armed with the most modern infantry weapons. The British had been totally outmanoeuvred and outfought in every engagement, and had been virtually compelled to make terms. If the war of 1881 was a fair index of the readiness of the British army for modern war, then the survival of the Empire might well depend on the contribution that the colonies would be ready and willing to make to the defence of the mother country. What this contribution might amount to was the most intriguing unanswered military question of the nineteenth century. The military history of the British colonies provided no clues to the effectiveness or magnitude of any help they might provide. It was a long history. Local defence forces had been developed in the earliest days of every colony, for protection against either foreign invasion or local uprisings. A volunteer force had been raised in Canada as early as 1763 to cope with the Indian rising of Pontiac. The Australian colonies had been equally prompt to look to their own defence. In 1800 the Loyal Parramatta and Sydney Association was approved by the Governor of New South Wales 'to deal with any disturbance which might arise from the influence of Irish rebels who had been transported' there.[9] They were in fact used to put down an Irish convict rebellion in March 1804, and were mobilized again in November of that year when two unknown ships appeared in Botany Bay. These proved only to be an armed English whaler and its Dutch prize, so Australia's second invasion scare passed off painlessly.[10] In the absence of any more panics the association became officially defunct in 1809. It had never numbered more than ninety-two all ranks at its strongest. By contrast the Canadians had been compelled to develop a large militia of their own, to cope with an invasion from the United States in 1812. These volunteers were however disbanded after hostilities ended, and rapidly degenerated into a rabble apparently totally devoid of any military qualities, armed for the most part with sticks and umbrellas. A Militia Act was introduced in 1846 in an attempt to revitalize the local defence organizations, but the Canadians appeared quite simply to have lost interest in military matters.[11]

In Australia, by contrast, interest in local defence was rising at the mid-century. While the Canadians were naturally concerned to avoid any kind of military preparations that might be construed as provocative by the United States, the Australians on the other hand were trying to prepare themselves in the face of open provocation by France. The governments of the Restoration seemed to have transferred Napoleon's territorial ambitions from Europe to the world outside. French armies had invaded Spain and North Africa; French naval squadrons had seized Vera Cruz and blockaded Buenos Aires; and in July 1828 the frigate *Artémise* was sent to the Pacific to warn the chiefs of Hawaii and Tahiti 'to conduct themselves in such a manner as not to incur the wrath of France'. James Busby was hastily despatched from New South Wales to the Bay of Islands in New Zealand, in an attempt to forestall any notion the French might have of annexing those islands, after the eccentric Baron Charles de Thierry had appointed himself Sovereign

Chief of New Zealand. (The islands were in fact secured for Britain in 1840.)

However the French terror continued unabated. In 1838 the corvettes *L'Astrolabe* and *La Zelée* had carried out a punitive expedition against Fiji, landing and burning a village in retribution for the massacre of the crew of a French vessel four years before. Another expeditionary force compelled Kamehameha III of Hawaii to pay an indemnity and virtually grant diplomatic immunity to French citizens, as well as extending preferred treatment to French imports. In May 1842 a French squadron from Valparaiso seized the Marquesas. Four months later Tahiti became a French protectorate. In November 1842 Captain La Ferrière in *La Bucéphale* induced fourteen local chiefs in New Caledonia to acknowledge the sovereignty of Louis-Philippe. It was not surprising that the government of New South Wales should have urgently remonstrated with the British against the policy of transferring British regulars from their colony to New Zealand for local defence against Maori discontent. The French were closer to Sydney than the Maoris, far more dangerous and infinitely more mobile.

Paradoxically the most powerful stimulus yet to colonial self-defence came with the outbreak of the Crimean War, in which Britain and France actually fought as allies against Russia. The Crimea might have seemed a long way away. Russian seamen had however been ranging the Pacific since the turn of the century. The Australians did not waste any time. War was declared by Queen Victoria on 27 March 1854. On 6 June a Bill was introduced in the Legislative Council of New South Wales for the formation of a volunteer and yeomanry corps. Fears were expressed at first that the volunteers might collect by night in public houses after parade, and possibly start shooting each other instead of the enemy. It could only be hoped that the police would be able to cope with what would after all hardly be a new side of life in New South Wales. The risk had to be taken in any event: the Adjutant-General of the colony, Colonel MacArthur, while agreeing that 'native courage and undisciplined valour, eagerly and zealously pressing forward in defence of the country, would not, it is true, be ever lacking in time of danger', none the less was sure that the time had come 'when the establishment of a Militia or Fencible Force in New South Wales ought no longer to be delayed'.[12] In fact it was delayed. The Australians decided on second thoughts that their first line of defence ought to be the sea. The

Volunteer Force was therefore allowed to languish, but in 1855 New South Wales built its first warship, a 60-ton armed sloop named *Spitfire*. It was the beginning of the Royal Australian Navy. Effective use of the resources of the Empire in wartime would obviously require some kind of effective organization and co-ordination. What was all too clear at the time was that anything like the basis for a reasonable system of imperial defence simply did not exist. The House of Commons learned on 22 May 1859 that there was not a single colony of the British Empire in a state of adequate defence and security in the event of war breaking out.[13]

Queensland was however first among the Australasian colonies actually doing something seriously about its own land defence: troops of mounted riflemen were enrolled in March 1860 under the terms of the Act approved in New South Wales, but not yet implemented in the parent colony.[14]

It was a singularly timely move. The inauguration of the Queensland Force barely anticipated the report of the Select Committee of the British Parliament, chaired by Arthur Mills, which proposed to divide the Empire for the purposes of defence into 'military posts . . . in which for objects altogether independent of and distinct from the defence of particular countries in which they are situated the Imperial Government thinks it necessary to maintain garrisons'; and the rest, including Canada and the Australasian colonies, which could be expected to bear the main cost of their own defence.[15] This did not necessarily imply that any part of the Empire was to be regarded as indefensible, or even ex- pendable. At the same time, Robert Lowe told the committee frankly that he should have hoped that in the event of Britain itself being threatened by France, 'the government today would be inclined to keep every man in England and even bring troops from the colonies. We should think we could afford to lose a place like Sydney, but London we could not afford to lose from the Imperial point of view.'[16] One could hardly dispute the order of priorities, even admitting that Sydney had been the main centre of European settlement and commerce in the South Pacific since the beginning of the century. It was however a point of view that could only seem more compelling above the line of the Equator, rather than below it. Australia could not afford to lose a place like Sydney. Nor was this kind of analysis really compatible with what might be termed the true imperial spirit: one could well ask what kind of a British Empire would be left once places like Sydney had been lost to it.

It was at this critical stage in the evolution of imperial defence that the Australasian colonies received the greatest incentive they could well have known, short of an actual attack. A Russian Far Eastern squadron of six ships had been formed in the Pacific in 1857, after the Crimean War. In 1862 the powerful new frigate *Svetlana* visited Melbourne. The Victorian authorities were impressed by the armament and style of the Russian ship. They were even more impressed by the fact that their defence batteries at Port Philip Bay had been unable to respond to the visitor's salute, apparently through lack of ammunition. In 1863 the even newer and more formidable corvette *Bogatyr* arrived. Again the port batteries remained silent. Concern escalated when British newspapers brought reports of the Polish insurrection of 1863, and of an alleged Russian plot for a naval swoop on Melbourne if war were to break out again with Britain.[17] Nothing in fact seems to have been further from the minds of the officers of *Bogatyr*. Their reports were filled with accounts of the delights of Melbourne and Sydney. The Russians were particularly impressed, like other visitors after them, by the athletic charms of the Australian girls, who 'sat unceremoniously in the captain's cabin and played his piano and sang', and clambered around the spars and rigging of the ship, undeterred by their crinolines.[18] It must have been a memorable show.

The Victorian government did not however realize where the Russians' interests really lay. They urgently requested the British Admiralty to provide one of the new monitors, or any other suitable ship that could be reconstructed as a floating battery to remedy Melbourne's vulnerability. The British replied by passing the Colonial Naval Defence Act, authorizing the colonies to raise and maintain their own naval forces, 'under such conditions and for such purposes as Her Majesty in Council from time to time approved. . . .'[19] It was time for a new move in the development of Australian defence – the Queensland Defence Force had finally become defunct, after the entire strength of the Volunteer Artillery quitted the parade ground to get drunk at the nearest hotel.[20] Their loss was however amply compensated: Victoria acquired a formidable iron-clad monitor, *Cerberus*, with four 18-ton guns; South Australia introduced its own Volunteer Act; and New South Wales proceeded to implement in 1867 the Volunteer Force provided for in the Act of 1854.

Australia was beginning to fit itself to play some part in a system of collective imperial defence.

The Canadians were in fact doing far more. For one thing they were acquiring unwillingly a tradition of actual combat experience, as well as practice in the deployment of quite large bodies of men, with both of which the Australians were utterly unfamiliar. Canada had already fought for its life against the United States in the War of Independence, and again in 1812. In 1866 no less than 20,000 militia were called out to contain raids by the Fenians across the United States border into Ontario. The Canadians were forced to retreat three times before superior Fenian forces, veterans of the most formidable army in the world, Grant's Grand Army of the Republic. They succeeded however in totally routing a second invasion the following year. Again in 1870, 771 militia with accompanying guides and *voyageurs* assisted 373 imperial troops in a movement from central Canada to Manitoba, to contain the rebellious activities of Louis Riel. A further 300 militia were despatched to Manitoba in 1872. In 1876 they were called out again to keep order on the railroad. The Canadians were undoubtedly seeing action at frequent intervals, and on long and arduous campaigns, while other colonial volunteers were parading for the ladies or getting drunk.

In August 1877 General Sir William Jervois, Governor of South Australia 1877–83, Governor of New Zealand 1883–9 and former Secretary to the Duke of Cambridge's Defence Committee, together with Colonel Peter Scratchley, who had served with distinction in the Indian Mutiny, had arrived in Australia to advise and report on the condition of local defences.[21] Their opinion, after detailed observations, was that in general local defences were absolutely useless against any serious attack.[22] This view was delivered to the Queensland government just as a thoroughly demoralizing cable arrived from London, warning the colonials that the Royal Navy could not be expected to guarantee all parts of the Empire against attack at the same time.[23] New Zealand continued unperturbed to allow its militia 'to exist only on paper'. Australia accepted the news less complacently. South Australia hastened to pass a Rifle Companies Act, and New South Wales began to build up its defence capability to the quite impressive level of 319 permanent force troops and 1,800 militia.

The Scratchley–Jervois report moved even Disraeli in October 1879 to set up a new committee to investigate the defences of the more important colonial ports and coaling stations.[24] The situation was discussed further at the Australasian Intercolonial Conference in 1881, at which South Australia proposed that the Imperial Government should keep a vastly increased fleet in Australian waters, the cost to be paid half by the colonies and half by the Imperial Government itself.[25] This was understandably not well received by the British. The proposal was accordingly shelved, but the colonists at least agreed among themselves to use all legitimate endeavours to procure the effective fortification and land defence of their ports at their own cost.

A consistent pattern was beginning to emerge in imperial relationships: the British government would not hesitate to enlist colonial support in British concerns, but it was generally far from willing to commit British support for colonial concerns. Quite obviously it preferred not to hear about them. It was of course true that the bleats from the Australasian capitals tended to arrive at the most inconvenient times. There was nothing that the British government could have wanted less at the present juncture than trouble with another European power. General Charles Gordon had been sent to the Sudan in January 1884, on the rather improbable mission of supervising the withdrawal of the remaining Egyptian garrisons there. In March London learned that he was himself besieged by the forces of the Mahdi in Khartoum. The decision to extricate him was finally taken in August, after prolonged and agonizing debate. The appeals from Melbourne arrived in the critical stages of the deliberations. Some petulance on the part of the British was not surprising. Lord Derby sneered in the Commons at Australasian fears of attack from 'nobody knew what power, nobody knew what part . . .'.[26] This was merely being dishonest. Everybody knew exactly what power the Victorians were concerned about at the time, and also the geographical location of their fears. But their alarms were as remote from London as they were unwelcome there. It none the less did not inevitably follow that London should not have treated them as seriously as it was prepared to treat the imbroglio in the Sudan. Complications of this type were part of the price of Empire; and it was not unreasonable to suggest that it might have been even more rewarding for the British government to concentrate its resources and energies on developing and protecting British settlements in the huge colonies of Canada and Australasia, instead of extricating the Egyptians from the heart of Africa.

On this count the Victorians showed themselves more genuinely imperial-minded than the British. Their vision was not entirely clouded by the spectre of *récidivistes* in the Hebrides. Ignoring Derby's clowning, they decided to make a generous offer of military co-operation. *Victoria* and *Albert* were in the Mediterranean at the time, *en route* to Port Philip Bay. The government in Melbourne offered their services to the British, for use in the coming campaign to rescue Gordon. The offer was tentatively accepted, and the gunboats put in at Suakin, the port on the Red Sea which the British were using as a base. They were then told that they would not be wanted, because their status as coast defence vessels did not qualify them for use as warships on the high seas. The British government indeed did not seem willing to grant them any kind of legal status at all. HM Customs refused to clear them as merchant ships. The Admiralty refused to recognize them as warships. Undefined, unappreciated and for the time being unemployed, the little ships with their enormous guns waddled on to Port Philip Bay.

Commander G. Hermon Gill, the historian of the Royal Australian Navy, has commented on this episode:

The incident is of note as establishing a precedent which Australia never failed to follow: then at the time of the Sudan War; later in the Boxer Rebellion in China; in the First World War; in the Abyssinian trouble in 1935; in China and in the Solomons also during those years; in the Second World War, and since. Thus the Australian Navy has always been in the forefront of Britain's 'interdependent' friends with practical help in an emergency.[27]

It was no more than the truth. Admittedly nobody can tell, the first time that anything happens, whether a precedent has been established or not. But it might at best have appeared that colonial governments were prone to be more ready to offer military co-operation than the British were to accept it. There was disconcertingly little evidence of a meeting of minds across the oceans.

News of Gordon's death reached Britain and Canada about 8 February. On 10 February Canadian Prime Minister Sir John MacDonald suggested to the Governor-General's military secretary, Lord Melgund, that it might be possible to raise a second battalion of the 100th Regiment to take part in the Sudan campaign, enlisting the men as regulars and not as militia.[28] Landsdowne passed the proposal on to London, affirming that Canada was ready to raise a military contingent. Canadian militia and permanent force officers were indeed beginning to volunteer in their hundreds. Meanwhile the news of Gordon's death was published in the *Sydney Morning Herald* on 11 February. By noon on the following day the Acting Premier of New South Wales, William Dalley, had cabled to his Agent-General in London, offering the British government 'two batteries of the Permanent Field Artillery with ten 16 pound guns, properly horsed, also an effective and disciplined battalion of infantry 500 strong', undertaking to land the force at Suakin within thirty days from embarkation.[29] Victoria, Queensland and South Australia also offered troops, after learning of the New South Wales *démarche*. First come was however first served. On 15 February a cable was received in Sydney accepting the colony's 'splendid offer', but declining one of the two batteries. Canada and the other colonies were informed that their offers would have to be rejected, as their contingents would probably arrive too late.

This was not to say that the British saw no advantage to be gained from the colonies in the way of military assistance. General Lord Wolseley, who had been given command of the rescue expedition, had been involved in the movement of some 1,200 troops to Manitoba in 1870, along the water route from Thunder Bay to Fort Garry.[30] He now suggested to Lord Derby that the Canadian *voyageurs* who had demonstrated their skills in that campaign might have just the kind of expertise needed to get the British army safely down the Nile to Khartoum. Derby accordingly asked the Governor-General of Canada, Lord Landsdowne, on 21 August, to supply 300 *voyageurs* for the Sudan. Recruiting began almost immediately: 386 *voyageurs* and their officers sailed from Quebec on 15 September, followed by eight steamer pilots in October. There was of course no question of this being any kind of military expedition. The *voyageurs* and pilots were explicitly non-combatants. Nor did they suffer any casualties from enemy action, although no less than fourteen were drowned or died of sickness in Africa, and another died on the voyage home. Their services were coolly evaluated by the British authorities: the Colonial Office reported to Landsdowne that not more than 7 per cent of the men had shown themselves to be completely useless, and that only 45 of the 394 were really unsuitable material.[31] Their expedition was however too long delayed: two steamers that reached Khartoum on 5 February reported that the city was in the hands of the Mahdists.

On 3 March 800 men and 224 horses had sailed from Sydney for
Suakin on the *Iberia*, taking with them as gifts from the people of New
South Wales biscuits, tea, pipes, 20,000 cigarettes, 100 cases of wine,
20 cases, 600 bottles and 576 flasks of whisky, 30 cases of rum and 50
dozen bottles of New Zealand Herb Extract for Dysentery. It was the
first time that the colonial troops of the British Empire had left their own
territory to fight in a foreign war.

The auspices were not favourable. The *Iberia* collided with the dread-
fully appropriately-named sightseeing steamer *Nemesis* as it moved into
the stream, killing two women; the volunteers were already being
denounced for drunkenness and lack of discipline before they had even
embarked; the horse slings had been embarked on the wrong ship, the
officers' revolvers usually jammed and the contingent was generally sea-
sick. Far more seriously, on 29 March, the day on which the Australians
landed in Suakin, Russian forces drove out the Afghan garrison on the
oasis of Penj-deh. It was at least possible that all the available forces of
the Empire might well be required on another front than the Sudan, to
face the challenge of an enormously more resourceful opponent than the
Mahdi. Meanwhile the rebellion of Louis Riel was forcing the allegedly
ill-trained and ill-disciplined Canadians into a substantial military operation over some 1,600 miles of territory. Prime Minister Sir John
MacDonald wrote furiously to High Commissioner Sir Charles Tupper
on the day before the Australians came under fire for the first time:
'We do not stand at all in the same position as Australasia. . . . The Suez
Canal is nothing to us, and we do not ask England to quarrel with France
or Germany for our sake. . . . Our men and money would therefore be
sacrificed to get Gladstone & Co. out of the hole they have plunged
themselves into by their own imbecillity [sic].'[32]

The Canadians had no cause to be dismayed. They had carried
through a far more impressive military enterprise than the Australians,
and carried it through successfully. By the time the *Métis* had been
suppressed and Louis Riel brought to trial, Canada had deployed 4,919
militia in the field, losing nine dead and thirty wounded in actual
combat.[33] Ironically the non-combatant *voyageurs* had given far more
lives to the cause of Empire than either their fellow Canadians of the
militia, or than the adventurers of the Australian military contingent,
who sailed home on 17 May, arriving in Sydney in pouring rain on
1 July, to march through almost empty streets, breakfastless and soaked

to the skin. Their enterprise had not been glorious. They had failed to reach Khartoum, and had suffered three of their number wounded in action and six dead from dysentery, for a total bag of two Arabs taken prisoner.

Their demonstration had however not been wholly without effect. The British troops had been suitably impressed by the sheer physical size of the Australians; General Sir Gerald Graham congratulated the colonials on their soldierly spirit and endurance; Queen Victoria asked Dalley's Agent-General to convey 'her warm thanks and great gratification that her Colonial Forces have served side by side with British troops in the field';[34] and perhaps most significantly recruiting had been stimulated in New South Wales to such an extent that the armed forces of the colony had risen from 1,500 after the departure of the contingent to 3,600 by the time of its return. All this certainly helped to mitigate some of the sense of futility arising from the fact that the government of India had sent a larger contingent of native troops to parade in Sydney on the ninety-seventh anniversary of the founding of the city, than New South Wales had sent a few months later to the Sudan. The historian of Australia's early military efforts has described the episode of the Sudan contingent as 'ludicrous' and 'pitiful'.[35] It was not entirely so. It was in any event the last time as it was also the first that such terms could be applied to the colonial military effort of the British Empire.

The 800 all ranks who sailed in the *Iberia*, so amply supplied with tobacco, alcohol and Herb Extract, were the advance guard of one of the great military phenomena of the twentieth century, the British colonial fighting men, the furies in slouch hats who were to be accepted by competent judges in two world wars, along with the United States Marines and the crack regiments of Germany, as probably the most formidable infantry in the world.[36]

2 The sea is wide, the coming nights long and dark (1885–98)

In the meantime some principles for co-operation among the pro-liferating colonial defence forces had to be established. Even as the New South Wales contingent prepared to leave for Suakin, Admiral Sir George Tryon, Commander-in-Chief of the Australia Station, had approached Governor Loch of Victoria in the hope of rationalizing the defence programmes of the Australasian colonies. Tryon was blessed with a persuasive manner and a superb eighteenth-century prose style. Even more unusual among British admirals, he was at least able to understand what the colonials were actually worried about: as he admitted to Loch: 'History is apt to repeat itself; squadrons and fleets have escaped the most vigilant admirals, and the most skilful strategists failed in days of old so to order our fleets as to prevent this . . .'.[1] How-ever Tryon then attempted to argue that the very geographic and demo-graphic features that gave the Australians most cause for concern could be regarded as a source of legitimate comfort, properly viewed. On the one hand the enormous distances of the Australian continent made it difficult for the main centres of population and production to give sup-port to one another. But it also meant that they could not be attacked simultaneously by an aggressor. Tryon was however forced to concede that they might be attacked consecutively, if they did not hasten to combine in common defence. This indeed was exactly the problem. But the outlook was better than the Australians imagined: a hostile fleet could not really do much damage to cities the size of Melbourne or Sydney, even if it were to expend all its ammunition bombarding them. Raids by fast, light cruisers were what Australia had most cause to fear, but raiding cruisers and unarmoured ships could do little against even small local defences.

Tryon's solution was accordingly that the Royal Navy should con-tinue to provide the basic defence for the colonies on the high seas. However, the colonies should continue to maintain their own forces of coastal defence vessels, to act under the orders of the Commander-in-Chief Australia Squadron, who would undertake not to remove them from Australian waters without the approval of the colonial governments concerned. Tryon described the concept as one of 'navy by contract', for which he found historical precedents in the reign of Henry IV. The Australians were not wholly convinced. New South Wales Premier Dalley wrote to New Zealand Prime Minister Sir Robert Stout, agreeing that the whole seagoing naval force for the defence of the Australasian colonies should be placed under one control, but insisting that the most effective arrangement would be for the British government simply to treble the strength of the Australia Squadron.[2] Tryon, concerned not to cost the British taxpayer more money, insisted to Dalley on the absolute importance of adequate local forces to supplement the seagoing strike capacity of the Royal Navy: on the one hand, as he had told Governor Loch himself, Australia was in the favourable position that its great centres of wealth, of trade and commerce were 1,400 miles apart and could not all be attacked at the same time; on the other, 'the sea is wide, the coming nights long and dark, and the ships cannot be everywhere . . .'.[3]

Meanwhile the New Zealand government had made up its mind to obtain an 'Esmeralda' class cruiser specifically for the defence of New Zealand, by offering to pay the interest on the purchase and the cost of maintenance.[4] The Queensland Premier, Sir Samuel Griffith, agreed with Dalley that there should be combined action on defence by all the colonies, but wanted the British to begin by building six fast cruisers to form a separate Australian fleet for the defence of Australia alone. Colonial Secretary Lord Derby complained in reply that the whole object of the present exercise was to 'seek closer harmony with the Royal Navy'.[5] On Christmas Eve 1885 Tryon circulated a carefully worded memorandum to all the Australasian governments. His proposal now was that the local defence naval forces should remain essentially on their present footing. However any seagoing vessels that might be acquired by the colonies would be manned by the Admiralty and accorded the same status as Her Majesty's Ships of the Australia Station. Ships actually provided at the expense of the colonies would be retained within Australian waters, unless otherwise agreed to by the appropriate colonial governments.[6]

It was hoped that this arrangement might endure for the next ten years. It should in any event be discussed at an intercolonial conference, whose theme should be the 'union and harmony of purpose' in defence policy.[7] Dalley warned grimly that so far 'nothing of value has come from intercolonial conferences', and that there was no need to expect better results from the next one.[8] Two things were however becoming clear. In the first place imperial naval defence was apparently almost exclusively a problem for Britain itself and the Australasian colonies: Canada's maritime horizons did not yet extend beyond the Great Lakes, and it could be presumed that the Royal Navy could cover the approaches to South Africa for as long as it could cover the Home Islands. Only Australia and New Zealand were involved in the issue of naval co-operation. Secondly the question of Australasian naval defence was necessarily involved with that of Australasian federation: Tryon's idea of concentrating local defence forces for mutual support could not be legally viable so long as the continent's military capacity was divided among separate colonial establishments, formally unable to operate outside their own frontiers. It was not the kind of obstacle that would cause much concern in a real crisis, but it was as well to get it out of the way while there was still time.

Some kind of co-ordinated effort was foreshadowed by the establishment of the Colonial Defence Committee, which began to despatch memoranda to the Australasian governments in 1886, advising them on technical matters such as the protection of telegraph cables, lookout stations, entrenchments and the management of the civilian population in the event of bombardment or invasion.[9] The colonies had however other problems, on which the Colonial Defence Committee was scarcely competent to advise them. For example, Queensland's naval defences had been temporarily paralyzed by the criminal careers of the captains of its two gunboats. The Commander of *Paluma* had been found to be embezzling government money, and was dismissed from the Service by an Admiralty Board. He went quietly. However the Premier then decided to dismiss the commander of his other gunboat, *Gayundah*, for continued bankruptcy, unauthorized appropriation of funds, fiddling of mess bills and refusal to make payment on demand. The commander thereupon threatened to hoist the White Ensign of the Royal Navy instead of the Blue Ensign of the colony, and steam off to Sydney. When the Premier proposed to have him taken off by the police, the commander in turn threatened to open fire on Parliament House, while the arresting officers ducked for cover behind the poincianas in the Brisbane Botanical Gardens. He too submitted in the end, but it was a situation that Sharkey or Kidd would have been more at home in dealing with than their Lordships of the Admiralty.

Absurdities of this kind had an obvious message. Divided authority was not effective. It was intolerable that ships paid for by the colonies could at the same time be regarded legally as property of the Royal Navy. It was also clear, as the Governor of Queensland hastened to point out, that ships badly officered and worse manned did not contribute to anybody's security. He accordingly suggested that Britain should provide the officers and the men, while the colonies provided the ships and the money to maintain them.[10] The obvious objection to this was that the colonies were likely to get unpromising defenders, as only those officers would be sent to them who were unable to get appointments elsewhere, 'like the erring members of the aristocracy [sent] to rehabilitate their damaged reputations in our purifying atmosphere'.[11] It was also feared that the development of a separate fleet subsidized by the colonies might be used by the British government as an excuse to reduce the overall naval strength of the Empire. Tryon had been emphatic that a mere subsidized force could not be a solution to the problems of Australasian defence. But this was exactly what the new Australasian Naval Defence Act produced. Five light cruisers and two torpedo gunboats of the Royal Navy were to come to Australia. The colonies were to pay 5 per cent interest on the prime cost of the ships and to bear the full cost of their maintenance. In return the ships would be retained within the limits of the Australia Station, and would be removed out of them only with the prior consent of the colonial governments.

This was at least a stopgap. Meanwhile the colonies could see about improving their own defence establishments. In April 1887 the colonial governments agreed unanimously to ask the Colonial Office to arrange to have their local defence forces inspected from time to time by a British general officer. The Colonial Secretary expressed his 'sense of gratification' to the Victorian government for forwarding the request to him.[12] By the beginning of 1889 the Victorians felt that the time had come for a further review of their defence capacity. Exciting prospects were being conjured up: the Victorian commandant assured his Premier that 'a time will come when these Colonies . . . will initiate such operations as may make the enemies of the Empire in the Pacific and China Seas and Indian Ocean look after their own possessions. . . . A war of offence is far less costly, irritating and injurious commercially than a war of defence.'[13]

The Victorian government had indeed already contemplated this possibility. Their inner Cabinet had resolved to improve on Queensland's attempted annexation of New Guinea, by sending units of the Victorian Defence Forces to the New Hebrides 'in a swift steamer with orders to hoist the British flag and keep it flying', in the event of any move by the French to seize the islands.[14] The flag was not to be hauled down 'except upon express instructions from the Home Government'.[15] The adventure was abandoned at the last hour, when it was thought that the French had given up their intention of annexing the group. There was however no doubt that the concept of offensive defence envisaged by the Victorians would need a radical change in the structure of Australian defence. The armed forces of the various colonies would first of all have to acquire the right under international law to operate outside their own frontiers. They would also need a genuine oceangoing navy, instead of having to count on being able to requisition any police launch or 'fast steamer' that happened to be available. In April the other colonies accordingly agreed to a Victorian proposal to invite Major-General Edwards, British Officer-in-Command, China, to give his views on Australia's defence capabilities.[16] Edwards was apparently impressed by the enthusiasm and even by the size of the Australasian forces. However he also appreciated that their effectiveness as a deterrent would be increased very greatly if they could combine their 30,000 to 40,000 men to meet an attack against any one of their chief cities. The knowledge that such a united force was available for their defence would also, he hoped, bring an end to the unseemly scares that took place in the colonies whenever British relations with a foreign power became strained.[17]

This in practice meant federation. But the Colonial Defence Committee did not altogether endorse General Edwards's proposals. The problems of Australian security were not considered serious enough to warrant urgent attention. The committee went so far as to affirm that: 'On account of their geographical position, and of the now considerable population in all these colonies except Western Australia, there is no British territory so little liable to aggression as Australia.' These factors, along with the size of the armed forces maintained and the strong spirit that animated them, seemed to reduce the danger of attacks upon the Australian littoral to occasional raids by hostile cruisers, as Tryon had predicted. Here too the committee saw little cause for apprehension: Vladivostok was 4,900 miles away and was closed by ice for three months of the year, and Noumea was unsuitable as a base for naval action.[18] Australia could apparently rest in peace behind the shield of the Royal Navy.

The Australian commandants themselves were prepared to accept the provisions of the Naval Agreement as providing adequate cover for the prescribed ten years.[19] Deteriorating economic conditions in the colonies in any case discouraged any ambitious defence programmes. However it was precisely at this time that the British government began to be convinced of the advantages of persuading the colonists to make a more substantial contribution to imperial defence as a whole. The Colonial Office was still prepared to sneer at the myth of 'the Russian Man-of-War . . . that phantom ship', which had terrorized the Australians since the 1850s; but Sydenham Clarke, the Secretary of the Colonial Defence Committee, observed on 20 March 1891 that the Naval Defence Agreement could really be 'a matter far bigger than the Admiralty have ever realised. France, Russia and Co., struggle to compete with us for naval supremacy. Let them once realise that they no longer compete with the British taxpayer, but with those of all the Great Colonies, and they will abandon the competition as hopeless.'[20]

London at the same time had apprehensions about possible colonial behaviour in international relations. New Zealand's ambitions in the Pacific appeared to be bounded only by the Equator; Victoria and Queensland had both apparently been prepared to contemplate acts of aggression far outside colonial waters; and the last day of 1895 brought the most blatant and embarrassing of colonial enterprises, the Jameson Raid across the border of the Transvaal, precipitating yet another cheap military victory for the Boers at the expense of the British. Four hundred and seventy mounted riflemen and Cape Police with two field guns and two machine guns were outmanoeuvred and besieged by the Boers and forced to surrender in the field, having lost sixteen dead and fifty-five wounded. Boer losses were five dead and three wounded.

In this situation it was perhaps reasonable for the British authorities to emphasize the virtues of an imperial strategy based essentially on action by the Royal Navy, under wholly British command, with the colonies providing mainly increased finance and perhaps expeditionary forces on request.[21] Even the latter contribution appeared to the Admiralty to have its dangers, as it was at least doubtful whether the Australians would be likely to remain within their own 3-mile limit in wartime, until the British government chose to unleash them. The Victorian commandant's enthusiasm for wars of offence admittedly gave some justification for these fears. It was accordingly felt safer to drop the notion of 'using Australian troops, under general Imperial control, for the capture of places which might be made hostile bases against the Australian colonies . . .'.[22]

London still did not realize that different parts of the Empire presented quite different ways of viewing the problem of imperial defence. One indeed could scarcely talk reasonably of an overall Empire problem. Canada was likely to be threatened only by the United States, and it was not in the power of Canada, and increasingly less so in that of Britain, to provide any convincing defence against such a threat; South Africa was threatened primarily by land, internally by the native tribes and externally by the Boers, and would have to rely upon British command of the seas for reinforcements against either; Australia was comparatively free from any threat of invasion or insurrection, but was vulnerable to every imaginable form of hostile action by sea.

These problems in their turn suggested different implications. Canada could expect rationally to gain little if anything from collective defence with the rest of the Empire, and could therefore be expected to contribute relatively little, except from the complex motivations of patriotism, domestic political exigencies, and a desire to avoid too obvious a dependence on the United States. South Africa could be counted on to identify itself with Britain completely, at least for as long as the Boers presented any kind of threat, especially since the kind of aid South Africa counted upon was the kind that Britain could most certainly provide: if the Royal Navy could not guard the sea lanes to the Cape, it would probably not be able to guard the Home Islands either. But the situation of the Australasian colonies was different from either. These territories had the most convincing of all reasons for identifying themselves militarily with Britain, since only Britain could provide the kind of maritime security they needed. But the fact was that the maritime strategy endorsed by the British Admiralty could not provide that kind of security either.

The situation had indeed changed over the years. In 1878 the British China Squadron outnumbered the Russian Pacific Fleet by about four to one. However by 1897 the combined Eastern fleets of Russia and France, allies since 1894, matched British naval power in the region. Far more serious still were the implications of the rise of Japan as a naval power. As Creswell warned on 27 January 1897: 'Recent changes in the East, the rise of Japan as a naval power and her well-known aspirations, the establishment of Russia at Port Arthur may have in the future an effect which will be undesirable for Australasia; the "New Hebrides" question of the next generation may be one much more threatening to our well-being. . . .'[23] Already the Japanese navy outmatched the forces of the British China, Australia and Pacific stations by five battleships to three, even though the British could still deploy twenty-two cruisers against sixteen. Reinforcements could presumably be sent from the Home and Mediterranean fleets, but these in their turn would then hardly be able to contain the Russians and French.

Britain, with its relatively declining economic power not yet adequately supplemented by the production of the colonies, could hardly construct a fleet to confront a hostile world. At the same time it was extremely difficult to determine abstractly what lesser order of construction would meet the needs of the still-expanding Empire. No attempt was ever made to resolve the problem. The Select Committee on Naval Estimates reported to the House of Commons in August 1888 that 'no complete scheme had ever been laid before the Admiralty, showing apart from the financial limits laid down by the Cabinet, what, in opinion of naval experts, the strength of the fleet should be'.[24] In December 1888 the Secretary to the Admiralty had suggested a possible formula to Parliament: the British navy should be 'of larger strength than that of any other two European countries'.[25] This was easy to understand, and had indeed the compelling attraction of having already been realized in practice. It was however a purely European viewpoint, and the problems of imperial defence were no longer wholly European. This complication may indeed have been recognized by the First Lord of the Admiralty, Lord George Hamilton, when he told Parliament in 1889 that the leading idea was 'that our establishment should be on such a scale that it should at least be equal to the naval strength of any two other countries'.[26]

Some members of the Opposition actually argued that this standard might well be inadequate, as Britain might well be involved in quarrels with more than two other powers, in widely dispersed parts of the world. Nor was this the only weakness. The enormous navy that sailed in review in five columns for five hours in honour of Queen Victoria's Jubilee was already lagging qualitatively far behind many of its rivals. Its deficiencies were incredible. Professor Marder notes that the training of officers was neglected, there was scanty knowledge of the tactics and strategy of the new era of naval warfare; there was no staff or war college to instruct future commanders in the relevance of such matters as armour-plating, steam propulsion, torpedoes or long-range ordnance, or wireless; there was no reasonably detailed plan of action in the event of war; gunnery practice was limited to 2,000 yards, 'little greater than in the time of Nelson'; and it was still thought appropriate that seamen should eat with their fingers.[27]

Any improvement in the situation was obviously going to cost money. Colonial Secretary Chamberlain pointed out to the assembled Premiers that: 'If we had no empire, there is no doubt that our naval and military resources would not require to be maintained at anything like their present level.'[28] This was however hardly a compelling argument: the British would presumably be prepared to go on paying the cost of imperial defence, for as long as they considered it worth their while to keep an empire that they had to defend. The situation accordingly remained virtually unchanged: the Canadian Laurier spoke in terms of vehement patriotism,[29] but was utterly unresponsive to suggestions that Canada should consider making any contribution to imperial naval capacity, despite the fact that Canada made no contribution to that area of collective defence at all, and indeed expended less on defence of any kind per head than any other recorded country in the world;[30] and the British were forced to accept the existing Naval Agreement with the Australasian colonies, when they failed in a new attempt to take control of the Auxiliary Squadron completely out of Australian hands.[31]

It was the familiar impasse. First Lord of the Admiralty Goschen continued to insist that British policy in time of war had to be aggressive, seeking out the enemy on the high seas; and completely centralized control of the navy was essential if such a policy were to be implemented effectively. He delivered this argument in a speech to the House of Commons, affirming 'the immense advantages possessed by a single Power wielding a single fleet with one system of organisation, with the same signals, and with the confidence inspired by constantly working together. . . .'[32] But the fact was that Tryon's words were now truer than ever: the ships of a single British fleet simply could not be every-where. There were not going to be enough of them, for a start: the United States had already embarked on a programme of battleship construction, following the call of Senator Beveridge of Indiana to 'build a navy to the measure of our greatness . . . the trade of the world must and shall be ours'.[33] The American programme was matched by the French. Russia also began to rearm at sea, doubling its naval estimates of 1890. Germany had founded a naval league and begun construction of a high seas fleet. The race for sea supremacy was on again. Among the stakes was the survival of the British Empire.

The problem could have been approached in various ways. The British might simply have decided to spend more on their navy. Britain was indeed already spending more on defence, both per head and in actual figures, than any other European power except France. However, because of its comparative prosperity, it actually spent a lower proportion of its national income on defence than any. The strain would no doubt become more painful as states like Germany and eventually Russia overtook Britain economically, but it was not obviously necessary to assume continued British economic deterioration. It was also at least singular that Britain was still spending far more on its army than on its navy, even though the British navy was by far the largest in the world, and the total armed land forces of the British Empire, including every imaginable variety of police, militia and members of rifle clubs, amounted to barely one million, or about a quarter of the equivalent capacity of any of the European great powers.[34] Defence policy could hardly be entirely a matter of cost accounting; but it would certainly appear that money spent on the British army would bring in a far higher return in power terms if diverted to the British navy.

The question of how much Britain should spend on arms was necessarily in part a question of whom Britain should be arming against. Allies could very well prove a convenient substitute for increased expenditure – if they could be found. The British began looking, for the first time in more than eighty years. In January Prime Minister Salisbury approached the Russian Tsar Nicholas II, apparently to seek Russian agreement to a partition of China and Turkey, in terms of spheres of influence rather than simple territorial divisions, 'a partition of preponderance'.[35] The Russians were unresponsive, however. The next move was made on 29 March by Colonial Secretary Chamberlain, who flatly offered the German Ambassador von Hatzfeld proposals for an alliance, suggesting that a treaty of agreement should be arranged between their two countries for a period of years, and that 'it should be of a defensive character based upon a mutual understanding as to policy in China and elsewhere'.[36] German Foreign Secretary Bülow was however convinced that negotiations with the British were unnecessary, as the pressure of events would sooner or later force Britain to Germany's side, on Germany's own terms.[37] Kaiser Wilhelm himself viewed the alliance with apparent enthusiasm, and hoped that it would be concluded soon. However, Bülow instructed von Hatzfeld to tell Chamberlain that it was doubtful if public opinion in either country was yet fully prepared for the responsibilities that such a treaty would involve.

They were not the only ones who could sense the hostile forces massing outside the enormous frontier that London did not seem to know how to defend. As the last year of the British century drew to its close the Australian naval commandants presented a documented analysis of the defence problems of the Empire, which had all the elements of a horror story:

In the event of a European combination of such strength as to require the attention of the British Fleet, the continuance of a policy which in no way advances Australian ability for sea defence might have disastrous consequences. . . . Within the last half-dozen years the keen attention of the political world has been concentrated on the Pacific. There is every indication that it will play the part of the Mediterranean in the past century as the arena of national contending forces. France, America, Japan have established naval bases and possess powerful fleets in the north of the Pacific. Nearly every other European power has effected a lodgment in the seas to the north.[38]

The Empire had more than enough to worry about. But the gloomiest Cassandra could hardly have foretold what the new year was to bring. Within a year the German calculations were to seem more than justified. The British Empire would be at war, and British troops in retreat or facing encirclement along a front of 1,500 miles, from Ladysmith to Mafeking.

3 Fat damned lot of wasters (1899–1902)

The first great imperial war of the British Empire in the twentieth century was one of the most anomalous struggles ever fought. The three-year contest with the Boer republics almost baffles analysis. It was, for example, a war in which both armies employed the latest modern technology, including quick-firing cannon, of a kind typical of the Second World War rather than the First. On the other hand the symbolic figure of the conflict, the mounted rifleman, was to play virtually no part at all in wars between modern powers thereafter. Again, the Boers had developed probably the most sophisticated and rational system of modern infantry and cavalry tactics known to any army in the world. But they had done this without the assistance of any General Staff in the conventional sense, and without even any experience of modern warfare, except briefly against the British in 1881. They also managed to combine all the pre-eminent physical and moral qualities of a warrior race with a complete absence of traditional military values.

They were arguably the toughest and most indomitable people on earth, but their sense of the importance of a white man's life in Africa repeatedly led them to abandon perfectly defensible positions rather than incur serious bloodshed. In the same way, they fought on undeterred for two years after their cause had become obviously hopeless, but they were also capable of simply riding away from the battle zone whenever they felt entitled to enjoy the two weeks' leave back on the farm, which every burgher was by custom entitled to after three months' service. They consistently outmanoeuvred the British, employing the most original and complex cavalry tactics,[1] yet their most informed and sympathetic critics, the German General Staff, judged that their overall conduct of the war showed 'a complete lack of tactical training', that they 'dispensed with all direction of fire', that they knew nothing about 'a distribution of troops for the combat', and that they furthermore had 'a complete lack of discipline'.[2] Finally, they repeatedly surprised and overwhelmed British detachments in the open field, introducing a system of offensive tactics in which physical shock was replaced by fire-effect; but they never succeeded in the whole course of the war 'in carrying through victoriously such an attack against a well-entrenched adversary . . .'.[3]

In April 1889 the Uitlanders in the Transvaal petitioned the British government for assistance. Only two weeks later the Mayor of Adelaide called a meeting to consider the implications of the British decision to support the Uitlanders. The forty citizens present passed a resolution approving British policy. Their convictions were soon to be tested. The British Commander-in-Chief suggested to War Secretary Landsdowne on 8 June that it 'would create an excellent feeling if each of the Australian colonies, Tasmania, and New Zealand, furnished contingents of mounted troops and that Canada should furnish two battalions of foot'.[4] The proposal did not have unanimous support in London. General Sir Redvers Buller, who had been appointed to command the force being assembled for South Africa, preferred to recruit irregulars from among Uitlanders expelled from the Boer republics, fearing problems of discipline if he employed other colonials. He was however prepared to consider attaching small units of colonial infantry to the British regiments.[5]

Chamberlain on the other hand was enthusiastic: on 3 July he asked Canadian Governor-General Lord Minto if Canada would volunteer troops for a campaign in South Africa, 'without the application of "external pressure or suggestion" '.[6] Once again the Canadians temporized, in the face of certain opposition from Quebec. Once again the Australians were the first in the field. While negotiations were still in train between Chamberlain and President Kruger, the government of Queensland offered 250 men and a machine-gun detachment to the British government on 11 July, as a 'proof of practical sympathy . . .'.[7] The following day the commander of the South Australian Machine Gun Corps informed his men on parade that he intended, if they were agreeable, to offer the services of the corps in the Transvaal if war broke out.[8] On 17 July the Malay states came to the party with the offer of 300 Guides. Nigeria followed the next day with a donation of 300 Housas. These last offers were however declined by the British government, which decided on 28 July that only whites should be used in any coming conflict in South Africa. By the end of the month Queensland had still made the only acceptable offer of assistance.

The other colonies were becoming concerned at the absence of any kind of directive from London. The Victorians thought that the commandants of the military forces of the Australian colonies should meet in Melbourne to prepare plans for the despatch of a unified Australian force.[9] Meanwhile the colonel commanding the Royal Australian Artillery at the Victoria Barracks, Sydney, offered the services of his entire unit.[10] The New Zealanders were also stirring: they had been unable to make any contribution to the Sudan, although they had promised the services of a thousand men if war with Russia ensued,[11] and they were not going to miss out again: on 28 September Prime Minister Seddon recommended the despatch of a contingent of mounted riflemen for South Africa.

On 2 October a new development occurred. In 1885 New South Wales had formed its own squadron of Lancers. The unit had assembled just in time to see the New South Wales contingent leave for the Sudan. On 3 March 1899 the Lancers had sailed to England for six months' training at Aldershot. They were at sea again on the return voyage in September. On 2 October the New South Wales government learned that the Lancers had arrived at Cape Town and had volunteered their services. New South Wales had won the race again.

On 3 October Chamberlain moved deliberately to force the hands of the colonial governments. He despatched cables to all the governors, thanking them for their offers of help and requesting that colonial troops should be organized in infantry units of not more than 125 men each. Queensland was still the only colony that had actually made an acceptable offer, although the presence of the seventy New South Wales Lancers in Cape Town could be taken as proof of that colony's goodwill. The most embarrassed colonial government was of course that of Canada, which had again been the first to be asked, and had again failed to make any response. Prime Minister Laurier qualified this position a little later, arguing that the war in South Africa would be 'a petty tribal conflict in which the aid of the Dominions would not be required', but promising that 'he would put all the resources of Canada at the service of the mother country in any great war for the security and integrity of the Empire'.[12] Meanwhile the Australian commandants had decided to offer a united force of 2,023 all ranks, made up of 745 from New South Wales, 543 from Victoria, 275 from Queensland, 160 each from Tasmania and Western Australia, and 140 from South Australia, the whole to be preserved 'intact and distinct' from other imperial forces in the field.[13] On 14 October the Canadian government at last agreed to undertake 'to equip a certain number of volunteers, not exceeding 1,000 men . . .' .[14] The Empire was on the march, even if hardly in step.

So were the Boers. On 11 October General Joubert led an army of 18,000 men with 14 guns across the border of Natal, in three widely separated columns. Opposing him were the British forces of Sir George White, with 15,000 men and 78 guns. For the first and only time the Boers actually enjoyed a numerical preponderance along the whole front. The total number of burghers under arms possibly amounted to 40,000, including police and railroad guards, against some 28,000 in the British Field Army. However the technological superiority of the British should have been overwhelming even at the start. The British had 173 guns in all against the Boers' total of 41, and 65 machine guns against 37. The only weapon in which the Boers had a conspicuous advantage was in their virtual monopoly of quick-firing cannon, of which they had 28. It was not surprising that the first engagement of the war should have been a British victory. On 20 October a British force of 3,800 including 500 cavalry, with 18 guns, attacked the invaders at Talana Hill, where they had established themselves with about 3,300 men, 4 guns and 4 quick-firers. The overwhelming superiority of the British artillery and an enthusiastic charge of the cavalry brought victory after repeated but unsuccessful attacks by the British infantry against hidden Boer marksmen. It would have been a most promising start were it not for the fact that British casualties numbered 500 against a Boer loss of 142. It was at the same time inappropriate to describe it as a Pyrrhic victory. The British could stand losses of that order. They were to stand them for the rest of the war.

On the very next day the British won perhaps their least expensive victory, when 3,000 men with 12 guns cornered a Boer commando a quarter of their size, with two guns, at Elandslaagte. The Boers were overwhelmed by the British artillery; continuous rushes of the British infantry held the Boers down, front and flank; and the cavalry charged home as the enemy began to withdraw. It was the same scenario as Talana Hill, and it netted the British 62 Boers dead, 104 wounded and 184 prisoners, against a total loss of 260 dead and wounded of their own. It was probably the only engagement in the war in which more Boers died than Englishmen.

From then on Joubert contented himself with investing White's forces in Ladysmith, in one of the more extraordinary of siege operations, in which 8,000 Boers with at first only 6 guns contained a British army of 10,000 with 44 guns.[15] Meanwhile the odds against the Boers were multiplying. Reinforcements were pouring into South Africa from all quarters of the Empire. The New South Wales Lancers were there already. The first Victorian contingent sailed on 20 October. The New Zealanders left on the following day, having been assembled in the incredibly brief time of a fortnight, completely from scratch. The first New South Wales contingent left Sydney on 28 October, amid scenes of delirious enthusiasm. On 30 October a Canadian contingent of 1,039 men, almost as large as all the Australian and New Zealand contributions put together, sailed from Quebec. Of more practical importance, 27,000 British regulars, horse and foot, left Southampton on the following day. By the end of November the imperial forces in South Africa amounted to 52,000 men, with 173 guns and 65 machine guns. The Boers had already lost their initial advantage in manpower, and were outnumbered more than four to one in artillery. The British had in fact already gone over to the offensive: on 22 November General Lord Methuen crossed the frontier of the Orange Free State from Cape Colony, driving a considerably inferior Boer force from their position at Belmont, for a loss of 366 against about 100 Boer casualties. It was back to the Talana Hill ratio, but one could perhaps accept losses of such an order as the price of victory. In a couple of weeks the British would learn to accept them as the price of defeat.

Chamberlain was confident. However, the British strategy might have seemed incredibly pusillanimous: of the total army of 52,000 in South Africa, 10,000 with 44 guns were penned up in Ladysmith; 1,000 with 6 guns in Mafeking; and a further 2,400 with 12 guns were sitting the war out in considerable comfort in Kimberley, along with Cecil Rhodes himself.

On 10 December General Sir William Gatacre led 3,000 men against a Boer contingent of some 1,700, who had occupied the railway junction of Stormberg in Cape Colony, about 25 miles south of the Orange Free State border. Gatacre knew how many Boers were laagered about Stormberg. He unfortunately did not know exactly where they were, nor did he think it important to find out. The British troops stumbled forward in column through the blazing heat of a South African summer sun at midday until they came under the fire of fresh, well-concealed Boer marksmen. The massacre continued until the British, unable to attack and too exhausted to retreat, surrendered. Gatacre lost in all 723 men, including 634 prisoners; Boer casualties were 8 dead and 26 wounded.

But it was the commander-in-chief himself, Sir Redvers Buller, who first achieved unmitigated disaster. On 15 December he moved across the Tugela near Colenso to the relief of Ladysmith, with 16,000 men and 44 guns. Louis Botha awaited the attack with barely 6,000 men and 8 guns. This time the ingredient for disaster was provided by the British commander simply losing his nerve. Having discovered from the volume of fire with which his advance was greeted that there must have been far more Boers barring the way than he had imagined, Buller concluded that there must have been far more Boers than there actually were. He thereupon devoted his efforts to securing the withdrawal of some of his guns, for which transport had broken down, in disregard of the simple military principle that to withdraw under fire is likely to be an enormously more costly business than simply staying put. The guns were in fact lost, and 145 English soldiers killed and 918 wounded, against Boer casualties of 6 dead and 21 wounded. Having just lost a battle in which he had employed 27 guns against a commander who had only 8, Buller now suggested that another British general with another 44 guns should surrender to a commander who had about 20: he heliographed to White in Ladysmith, advising him to burn his cyphers, fire off all his ammunition, destroy his guns and make the best terms possible with the besiegers. White disobeyed the order.

Soon afterwards, Lord Roberts landed in Cape Town to command the British forces in the war in South Africa. He would not perhaps have been competent to cope with a moderately able opponent, but he was competent to cope with a thoroughly inept one like General Piet Cronje, which was more than Methuen or Buller would have been able to do. Roberts's strategy was to march from Cape Colony on Bloemfontein, the capital of the Orange Free State, outflanking the Boer defences on the Modder river and thereby forcing Cronje to abandon the siege of Kimberley. He had available for this purpose by far the largest army that any British general had commanded in the field, nearly 40,000 men including 6,000 cavalry. Roberts had also been at pains to develop the imperial component of the army by making full use of the colonial contingents. Unfortunately the very first action of the Australians helped to confirm British fears about disciplinary problems, when a squadron of Victorian mounted infantry raided into the Orange Free State, terrorizing Boer civilians and burning their farmhouses. President Paul Kruger protested against this wanton destruction of private property, which he considered to be outside the proper conduct of war.[16] The incident was moderate compared with what was to follow, but the enduring South African distaste for Australian larrikinism had been engendered, just at the moment when the concept of imperial solidarity was beginning to acquire some meaning.

Roberts could hardly have failed to relieve Kimberley. He could hardly have succeeded in entrapping the Boer army at the same time had not Cronje possessed all the least rewarding characteristics of his race. Too ignorant to understand what Roberts might be trying to do, too arrogant to believe that the British could actually be capable of manoeuvre, and too torpid to leave his own laager and escape towards Bloemfontein, he allowed himself to be outflanked and encircled at Paardeberg, 55 miles from Bloemfontein. The record of British disaster was not yet closed, however. As Roberts marched into the Orange Free State, Buller hurled himself at the Boer lines outside Ladysmith again. His intention was strategically sound and tactically enterprising. The Boer lines were to be split in two by seizing the hill of Spion Kop in a surprise attack, launched by men attacking under cover of darkness with fixed bayonets and unloaded rifles. A characteristic British style of combat was undoubtedly apparent: the conception was daring and imaginative, the execution heroic and determined, the preliminary staff-work criminally negligent and irresponsible and the reactions of the High Command utterly torpid and hidebound. The initial assault was triumphantly successful. It was however then discovered that the area occupied was not the true crest of the hill, but a narrow salient in which the occupants could be raked by Boer fire from both sides. Buller might have resolved either to widen the salient at any cost, or to withdraw. He instead elected to fight a defensive battle in an impossible position, packing reinforcements into an area in which too many troops were huddled already. The end was another miserable British defeat, with 1,742 casualties against a Boer loss of 379. This time White signalled from Ladysmith, advising Buller strongly against 'another definite attack', and urging him to stick to steady bombardment.[17] Buller however was strangely resolved to try his luck once more.

He now attempted to outflank the Spion Kop position, by assailing another hill on the extreme left of the Boer flank, at Vaal Krantz. Once again the preliminaries were impressive: feint attacks kept the Boers confused, a heavy bombardment over the whole front concealed the actual British intention, and the final assault on Vaal Krantz was covered by a massive barrage by seventy guns, which may possibly have delivered the heaviest weight of shellfire ever before landed on a single position. The attack was successful. The Boers however continued to maintain a heavy and accurate fire on the position. Buller, who had started the action late in the day, decided to finish it early. Understandably reluctant perhaps to add too many more British casualties to his butcher's bill, he was prepared to abandon the whole plan in the interests of which those lives already expended had been sacrificed. The British hung on to Vaal Krantz for another day, then withdrew on 7 February. They had lost a further 374 men; Boer casualties totalled 60.

The Times History described Vaal Krantz as 'one of the feeblest performances in the history of war', adding that 'Vaal Krantz was Buller, and Buller alone'.[18] It was certainly true that no modern army had ever been whipped so repeatedly and decisively in the open field by a band of guerrillas. In one sense of course the Boer victories were irrelevant: within three weeks the army of the Orange Free State would be lost, Ladysmith and Kimberley would be relieved, and organized Boer resistance would be at an end. But it was hardly fair to single out the Vaal Krantz fiasco as being all Buller, as if the absence of Buller would necessarily have made a significant difference to British fortunes of war. Lombard's Kop had been all White; Stormberg had been all Gatacre; and on 18 February the great army invading the Orange Free State achieved a disaster that was all Kitchener. The British were feeling optimistic again. They had relieved Kimberley on 15 February, after the most spectacular cavalry action of recent times, when 6,000 British horsemen with lance and sabre rode down a Boer patrol of perhaps 200, thereby proving that there was a clear role for the cavalry charge and the *arme blanche* in modern warfare, at least against disordered and over-extended infantry, caught in the open field and outnumbered thirty to one.

Kitchener then resolved to confirm the superiority of the British soldier over the Boer by a frontal attack on the laager in which Cronje had slothfully allowed himself to be immured. It would have been possible to have written the script in advance. The British artillery preparation was undirected and ineffective; no attempt was made to brief the units taking part so that the operation could be adquately coordinated; and the British infantry attack, advancing without clear objectives and on a front too widely extended, simply ran out of steam. The usual ratio of casualties was achieved: 1,200 British as against 200 Boers. The end of course was only deferred: Cronje surrendered himself with 4,048 burghers on 27 February, and the way to Bloemfontein was clear, if not exactly open. He had probably been the worst of the Boer commandants, as Roberts and Kitchener were certainly the best of the British generals in the field. Despite this Cronje's losses in combat amounted to only 269, while Roberts and Kitchener had lost 1,867. Buller had not done much worse in Natal. Cronje had indeed lost his army as well, but it was not too inappropriate for the British to send him and his burghers off to St Helena for safe keeping. He was admittedly no Napoleon, but his opponents were not exactly Wellingtons, either.

Roberts showed his deficiencies again over the next few days. The Boer front was collapsing; Ladysmith had been relieved; Joubert was in full retreat; and Kruger had desperately prevailed on General Delarey to make a stand outside his capital. Roberts attempted to envelop the Boer forces again by repeated turning and outflanking movements, which held up the advance and exhausted men and horses. At length the British General French ran up against the combined forces of commandants de Wet and de la Rey at Driefontein, on the Kaal Spruit. This was perhaps the most clear-cut victory won by the forces of the British Empire in the whole course of the war. Generalship was of the usual level: no serious attempts were made to reconnoitre the Boer position, gain intelligence, co-ordinate the attacks, or harmonize the whole operation with the overall planning of the High Command, which was of course not working either. However the attack itself was as near perfect as might well be. For the first time the artillery stopped trying to neutralize undiscoverable Boer guns and concentrated on protecting the attacking infantry with a barrage of shrapnel; the troops went in with the usual determination, but with wholly unusual use of cover, attention to mastering the fire of their opponents, and with a depth of attack that allowed constant reinforcement of the firing line. British casualties amounted this time to only 402 against Boer losses of at least 300.

Driefontein showed how it could be done. It was how it would have to be done if the British were to have any hope of success against a competently-led army, with numbers and equipment roughly comparable with their own. It was in fact how it was almost never to be done again. The war was about to enter an enormously prolonged and tedious phase, which was to bring little military glory and deepening disenchantment to the British Empire. The extraordinary hysteria that followed the relief of Mafeking after an irrelevant siege indicated desperate self-doubt at the heart of the Empire. Little progress had indeed been made towards any kind of imperial unity in defence or foreign policy.

However, a further practical demonstration of the willingness of some colonial forces at least to serve in wars of peripheral interest was provided by the outbreak of the Boxer uprising in China, in June 1900. In genuine extremity the British government requested that the Auxiliary Squadron should be despatched from Australian waters to the scene of hostilities. The action, which might have been expected to have fulfilled the gravest Australian forebodings, instead provoked a new display of patriotism in Victoria. A Victorian naval contingent was organized, numbering about 200 all ranks, and accompanied by a similar detachment of 260 from New South Wales.[19] They sailed in the transport *Salamis* from Sydney on 8 August, supported by South Australia's mighty atom, *Protector*.

The expedition was in fact even less perilous than New South Wales's previous venture to the Sudan. The contingent advanced from Tientsin to Chengting-Fu, where they captured a number of mules and rescued some European missionaries. The Boxers kept well out of the way. There was eventually some shooting near Kalgan, but no Australians were injured.[20] They had none the less done what they had been sent to do. General Gaselee, commander of the British forces in China, acknowledged gratefully that the Australians had

rendered great assistance by furnishing guards and other ratings for railway service ... it only remains for me to say how excellent a political effect has been produced by the appearance on so remote a stage as North China by these fine Contingents from the Australian Commonwealth. They have been an object lesson not only to foreigners, but also to our Indian fellow subjects, of the patriotism which inspired all parts of the British Empire.[21]

Inspiration of this kind was needed more than ever before the end of 1900. The British tide of conquest rolled into Pretoria, the capital of the

Transvaal Republic, on 5 June 1900. The last of the pitched battles, nearly all of which had been won by the Boers, was over. But peace was more remote than ever. All that happened was that the Boers abandoned any attempt to fight a more or less conventional war, on relatively stationary lines. They reverted to their natural mode of combat, with small mobile commandos fighting a campaign of interception and ambush. It was not self-evidently a hopeless task. They might not be able to win a decisive military victory, but they could well hope to erode the will of the British to continue a wearisome and inglorious war over an area the size of France.

Nor was it convenient for London totally to ignore opinion in the Dominions: the endless sweeps in search of Boer commandos across the length and breadth of South Africa needed enormous numbers of mounted riflemen, which the colonies could provide far more readily than Britain. However the early enthusiasm to volunteer for service on the veldt had not entirely been sustained. Australia had sent 1,591 men in all in 1899, Canada 1,039 and New Zealand 215. In 1900 Australia had despatched a further 4,945, Canada 1,990 more and New Zealand another 2,136; 3,980 more Australians had arrived by March 1901, and 1,179 New Zealanders by April of that year. No more Canadians had arrived since April 1900. On 21 December 1901 the British government appealed to the Empire for reinforcements, just before Christian de Wet's burghers overwhelmed yet another British force at Tweefontein in a perfectly executed night attack, facilitated by totally incompetent patrolling on the part of the defenders. This time the casualty rate was the worst since Colenso: de Wet lost 44 men and the British 348.

It was no doubt true that in this kind of warfare the Boers had the enormous advantage of being able to choose the time and place for combat. There was none the less food for thought in the fact that, attacking or defending, their losses were usually out of all proportion lower than those of the British. One could not argue simply from the experience of the Boer War that modern technology had given the defence an overwhelming tactical advantage. The lesson seemed rather to be that the Boers, without the benefits of formal military training or a General Staff, had managed far better than the British to devise new tactics to suit the new technology.

The agony could not be prolonged much more. The Empire was rallying again to renewed appeals by the British government: 986

Canadians arrived in February. They were followed in March by the first contingent from the newly formed Commonwealth of Australia, 2,260 strong, and by 1,196 New Zealanders. The Boers had one more moment of glory, even at the eleventh hour: at Tweebosch in the Western Transvaal, Delarey won on 7 March perhaps the most brilliantly executed action of the entire war, inflicting about 790 casualties on a British column, suffering negligible losses himself, and taking prisoner the truly luckless General Lord Methuen.

Tweebosch was the last dazzling flare of Boer resistance. Peace was eventually agreed at Vereeniging. The terms were unquestionably generous, especially considering the appallingly total nature of the conflict. One of the more extraordinary features of a war suffused with anomalies was the apparent contradiction between the unreserved regard and admiration that the conquerors seem in general to have retained for the Boers, and the ruthlessness of the measures employed to achieve their suppression. While the Boers almost invariably regarded British prisoners as white men whose lives had to be preserved in a black continent, Kitchener shot Boer prisoners, not only for murdering natives, which the Boers would regard as the most venial of failings, but also for breaches of the Hague Convention, which the Boers had never heard of. The mortality of Boer civilians in the concentration camps actually reached 43 per cent in mid-1901, before declining to 2 per cent after control of the camps had been transferred at the end of the year from military to civilian authorities. Total deaths in the camps were admitted by the British to number 18,000 and claimed by the Boers to number as many as 26,000. Moreover, despite Chamberlain's assurances that this was to be a white man's war, Kitchener armed 10,053 non-whites serving as messengers, drivers, convoy guards and watchmen.[22] A harvest of enduring racial hatred had been planted in soil as fertile as any in the world.

The military image of the British Empire had fared no better than its moral prestige. Statistics can indeed be interpreted in different ways. There seemed however little ambiguity about the casualty figures. The forces of the British Empire lost in combat 29,592 men, including 1,853 missing. The Boers lost in killed, wounded and missing 7,308. Nor could this disparity be shown to reflect simply the exceptional incompetence of certain British commanders, or the particular difficulties of a certain style of combat. The figures were remarkably evenly spread. In the opening as in the closing stages of the war, attacking or defending, in pitched battles or guerrilla skirmishes, under Buller or under Kitchener, the British could expect to lose at least four men of their own for every burgher they accounted for. It was hard to see the bright side of this kind of arithmetic.

But it was precisely the all-important matter of imperial solidarity on which the South African War provided the least certain indications. The willingness and ability of Dominion governments to make effective contributions in a major war were still in some measure open to question. Enthusiasm and performance had alike shown considerable variation. For example, New Zealand, with a population of 810,536 sent 7,995 men in all to South Africa; Australia, with 3,765,339 sent 16,124; and Canada, with 5,374,315 sent only 6,051, 2,036 of whom arrived after the peace. Proportionately, New Zealand despatched nearly twice as many volunteers as Australia, and seven times as many as Canada. Relative performance in the field is of course impossible to assess objectively. One could only surmise that the proportion of casualties to total number of troops serving presumably bears some relationship to their zeal, if not necessarily to their competence. On this count, 6 per cent of the New Zealanders became combat casualties, compared with a figure of 6.5 per cent for both Canada and Australia.[23]

What however is not open to any question at all is the proposition that the different colonial contingents inspired very different feelings in the British High Command. Their praise for the New Zealanders was unrestrained. *The Times* historian says that 'it would be hardly an exaggeration to say that after they had a little experience they were by general consent regarded as on the average the best mounted troops in South Africa'.[24]

French praised the 'excellent conduct and bearing' of the New Zealand Mounted Rifles. Kitchener spoke of their 'exceptional bravery'. The War Record of the 1st Battalion Derbyshire Regiment referred to the 5th New Zealand contingent as 'as fine-looking and as useful a body of men as any in the field'. Sir Ian Hamilton affirmed, 'never in my life have I met men I would sooner soldier with than the New Zealanders'.[25] Similar praise was accorded to the Canadians. Lord Roberts wrote to Governor-General Lord Minto on 22 January 1900: 'The Canadian Regiment has done admirable service.' Major-General Hutton spoke of their 'steadiness under fire, gallantry in the field, and uniform good conduct in camp'. General Smith-Dorrien said of the Royal Canadian Dragoons and the Canadian Mounted Rifles that 'he would choose no other mounted troops in the world if he had his choice'.

The Australians were something else again. There was indeed considerable commendation for the Dominion that had provided more men and taken part in more fighting than any other of the overseas contingents. Colonel Rimington praised the New South Wales Mounted Rifles for 'their dash in attack, steadiness in action and alert behaviour on outpost duties. . . . Their cheerful conduct under privations and exposure is beyond praise.' The unhappy Lord Methuen described the South Australian Bushmen in the words: 'I cannot conceive any body of men of whom a commander has greater reason to be proud.'

There was however no doubt that Australian attitudes towards discipline appalled imperial officers. 'Major-General Hutton, reviewing the departing third battalion, second federal contingent, was provoked into shouting: "Stand still; why the devil don't you stand still when you are told. . . . Damn you, why don't you stand still." His farewell message to the troops was somewhat strained: "Soldiers without discipline are only armed men," he told the twitching ranks, "individuality is worth nothing, nothing, without discipline. . . ." '[26] British Brigadier-General Beatson abused the Victorian Mounted Infantry under his command as 'white-livered curs', and in somewhat improbable terms as 'a fat damned lot of wasters'.[27] Indignant Victorian members of the Australian House of Representatives asked for the pleasure of five minutes of the General's company, so they could punch his head on the floor of the House.

But worse was to come. A Victorian trooper named Steele was sentenced to ten years' imprisonment for abusing a British officer, who in Steele's opinion had besmirched the honour of his state. Then on 27 February 1902 Kitchener ordered the execution of two Australian lieutenants, Harry 'Breaker' Morant and Peter Handcock, on charges of having murdered eight Boer prisoners. Federal Prime Minister Barton explained to an anxious Australian Parliament that Morant, the son of an English admiral, was understood to have ordered the Boers to be killed in revenge for the apparent murder of his superior officer, Captain Hunt.[28] Morant and Handcock were not in any way under Australian authority at the time, as they were serving with the imperial forces in South Africa and therefore subject to King's Regulations. The horror was not without its effect, however: the Federal Government hastily legislated that no Australian serviceman should be liable to execution in future, except by the decision of the Australian government. This would necessarily increase any disciplinary problem that might already be apparent. The procedure was established by which Australians serving under British command would be able to appeal to their own politicians against orders or conditions that they chose to find objectionable.

It was a situation that fittingly symbolized the anomalous relationship that had long been implicit between Britain and the most imperial-minded of the Dominions. No part of the Empire could be counted on as much as Australia to hurl itself into any possible conflict involving an imperial interest. No part was more likely to disagree tirelessly and publicly with British police on any and every aspect of imperial defence. It was conceivable that the future of the Empire might well depend on the ability of the political brains in London and Melbourne to resolve this contradiction. The attempt was never made. The questions raised by the South African War were still wholly unresolved twelve years later, when a war of immensely greater magnitude raised the British Empire momentarily to a level of military power that it had never known before and would certainly never know again.

4   The recall of the galleys (1902–13)

The colonial governments were in an unusually co-operative mood at the Imperial Conference of 1902. Even the painful discords between Australian volunteers and British officers had left no obvious scars. The Australians were quite content to leave the peace settlement in South Africa in the hands of the imperial authorities, just as they had been prepared to leave the general control of the war itself. Barbara Penney suggests that this was partly 'because they agreed with Joseph Chamberlain's policy, partly because they felt the aims of naval supremacy and imperial solidarity for which they had fought were fulfilled, and partly because they trusted the British to act generously towards the vanquished . . .'.[1] But naval supremacy had not been at stake on the veldt, and generosity towards the vanquished was not an issue likely to raise strong feelings in Australia. What was important now was to establish a system that would develop the military co-operation displayed in South Africa into a genuine system of imperial defence. This was the more important in view of the dreadful display of British military ineptitude during the war, and the equally alarming evidence of British international unpopularity. The peoples of the Empire had clear and urgent reasons for constructing machinery for mutual support, since even their best efforts might be barely adequate in a war with another great power, and they could not be confident of getting help from outside.

Even in this truly critical situation London and Melbourne could never avoid treading on each other's coat-tails. On the very eve of the conference differing British and Australian views on good order and military discipline might have inflamed the embers of the Morant affair. The British officer-in-command of the troops taking part of the review in honour of the coronation of King Edward VII found it appropriate to confine the Australian Coronation Corps to barracks for disorderly behaviour. The British army could never agree to take the imperial contingents as it found them. But even this disagreement did not impair the co-operative mood of the conference. Nobody could fail to recognize the common problem of defence. Here the dawn of the new century had already seen two significant developments. The first and presumably ephemeral one was that British defence spending had greatly increased as a result of the South African War. Britain had spent £31.4 million on defence in 1890. This was admittedly £2 million more than any other European power except France, but it was £6 million less than France. In 1900 Britain had spent £116 million, or more than two and a half times as much as France. This could indeed be expected to readjust itself with the end of the war. But this was not all. German naval spending was forcing Britain to outlay twice as much on its navy as it had done before the Second Naval Law. For perhaps the first time in its history the world's greatest sea power was devoting more of its resources to its maritime strength than to the army that had performed so depressingly in South Africa.

The message simply was that in the new situation defence spending was likely to stay at levels of two or even three times what had been accepted before the South African War. It was an appropriate time to appeal to the Dominions, while some element of wartime patriotism still lingered. Expounding the situation, Chamberlain told the representatives dramatically that: 'The weary titan staggers under the vast orb of its fate.' Britain was spending 29s 3d per head annually on defence, New South Wales only 3s 5d, New Zealand 3s 4d, Victoria 3s 3d, South Africa 2s 6d, and Canada 2s. Canada indeed was not only apparently spending less on defence than anybody else in the world; it was spending nothing at all on naval defence; and naval defence was the essence of imperial defence.[2] By contrast the British were spending more per head than anybody else on defence, and three times as much as anybody else on naval defence. The solution proposed by the British Admiralty was still in no way for the Dominions to develop their own navies to supplement British strength. There could be 'no localization of naval forces in the strict sense of the word'. However, the Admiralty did want more colonial naval officers serving in His Majesty's Ships, and was even prepared to put up with a contribution of colonial seamen.

The Dominions were for once not in a mood to argue. New Zealand's Richard John Seddon agreed that there should not be a system of local navies, although he considered an imperial reserve of seamen absolutely

necessary.[3] Australia's representative John Forrest revived the traditional
Admiralty argument that: 'There is only one sea to be supreme over,
and we want one fleet to be mistress over that sea.' However the
Commonwealth government was not prepared to accept any greater
financial contribution towards the Royal Navy: Forrest apparently considered that Australia's main contribution to imperial defence should
consist of 'building up another Britain in the Southern hemisphere',
which it would presumably have done anyway. Similarly, Canada's
Prime Minister Laurier seemed to believe that his Dominion's major
effort for collective security would be the development of the Canadian
Pacific Railroad, which again was something that the Canadians might
have been expected to go ahead with, whether they had belonged to the
Empire or not. He did admittedly inform the conference that he was
'contemplating the establishment of a local naval force in the waters of
Canada'; but he also made it clear that contemplation was as far as he
was prepared to go at the moment: Canada could not make any financial
offer analogous to Australia and New Zealand. It would continue for the
time being to spend nothing.

Canada could perhaps afford to contemplate. Australia and New
Zealand did not feel themselves to be so agreeably situated. The Commonwealth government actually took a step without precedent in British
history, introducing in peacetime a Defence Act making all males
between the ages of eighteen and sixty liable to service for home defence.
Meanwhile the governments of Great Britain, the Commonwealth of
Australia and New Zealand reached a draft agreement that the naval
force maintained on the Australia Station should consist of not less than
one armoured cruiser, two second-class cruisers, four third-class
cruisers and four sloops.[4] Such a force would however still be totally
inadequate to deal with the squadrons that other European powers were
despatching to the Pacific.

Moreover, potential if hardly actual bases for foreign aggression were
moving closer to Australian shores. Germany was in New Guinea and
Samoa; France was in Tahiti and New Caledonia; and France was
clearly moving into the New Hebrides. Here again Britain's diplomatic
entanglements in Europe were cutting clean across imperial interests as
viewed by His Majesty's governments in the southern hemisphere. The
Australians not only feared the potential threat to themselves provided
by a French base in the Hebrides; they also believed that opportunities

for Australian trade and settlement in the islands would be enhanced by the removal of apprehensions of possible French intervention.[5] However the British had a double reason for seeking to conciliate France. In the first place the emerging naval race with Germany seemed to indicate the desirability of a cordial understanding with France, although it was impossible to imagine France actually supporting Germany in any conflict with Britain. Again, the alliance with Japan necessarily involved the danger of Britain's becoming involved in a war between Russia and Japan in which France came to the help of its ally. It could therefore seem expedient to establish a relationship with the French that would dissuade them from risking such a confrontation. It might even be possible to persuade the French to put pressure on their Russian allies to avoid a showdown with Japan in the first place.

It would of course have seemed simpler to have settled for a German alliance in the beginning. However the British were prepared to make a certain concession to Australian anxieties: on 15 January Chamberlain proposed that a joint Anglo-French protectorate should be established over the New Hebrides. Australian Prime Minister Barton suggested instead that Britain buy the New Hebrides for £250,000, the price the French were understood to be prepared to accept as a *douceur* for British annexation. Chamberlain in turn asked if the Commonwealth were prepared to foot the bill.[6] Barton argued that the New Hebrides issue was an imperial one, not merely an Australian one. However, Australia would be prepared to pay the cost of administering the islands. What was important was to avoid partition, which would be only one degree less obnoxious than direct annexation by France, although Barton generously added that 'Australia did not ignore the vast and varied interests which complicate diplomatic relations of His Majesty's Government as trustees for all parts of the Empire.'[7]

British naval power seemed perhaps more surely established than ever: in March 1903 Britain had forty-nine battleships built or building, the United States twenty-four, Germany twenty, France eighteen and Russia eighteen. Panic signals were none the less flying in London: King Edward VII had set off on a goodwill tour of Lisbon, Rome and Paris to build stronger bridges with the Continent; the Admiralty had decided to abandon the Atlantic to the United States;[8] and the War Office had concluded that it had become impossible to defend Canada.[9] Ironically the Americans themselves were at least equally confused and alarmed about potential global threats to their security: the General Board of the United States Navy decided in June to concentrate their entire battle force in the Atlantic against Germany,[10] at the same time that General Arthur MacArthur was prophesying an eventual war with Japan in the Pacific.[11] Anglo-French talks on the New Hebrides were renewed in July and a Treaty of Arbitration concluded in October.[12] Arthur Deakin, now Prime Minister of the Commonwealth, produced a variation of Barton's idea of outright purchase, recommending that the British government buy up the shares of the New Hebrides Company, as it had done with the Suez Canal.[13] It was ignored. As Russo-Japanese relations deteriorated rapidly in Asia, the Colonial Office offensively noted that there was 'nothing more likely to embitter our relations with France than to let the Commonwealth [of Australia] put its finger into the New Hebrides pie'.[14] It appeared as if the British were going to find it very difficult indeed to be both a European and an imperial power at the same time.

The storm broke in the Pacific on 8 February, when Japanese Admiral Togo sent his torpedo boats in to attack the Russian battle force at Port Arthur by night, without waiting for a declaration of war. Japan certainly seemed to need all that enterprise and deceit could do to even the odds. Russia in 1904 had twenty-two battleships built or under construction, and Japan only eight. The Russian battle force was admittedly divided into three fleets, operating in the Baltic, the Black Sea and the China Sea. However any one of these should have been almost a match for the whole Japanese Combined Fleet. But gamblers' luck gave the Japanese two aces: the Russians were incompetent and they were unlucky. The Japanese torpedo attack did not actually sink any Russian ships in Port Arthur. However two battleships were hit, and ran aground while trying to reach the open sea. The Russian Pacific Fleet was virtually out of action before the publics of the two countries knew that war had begun between them. A week later the Japanese First Army landed at Inchon, on the Korean coast.

It now appeared more expedient than ever for the British to resolve any differences still existing between themselves and Russia's ally, France, in the hope of being able to avoid fulfilling their commitments to their own ally, Japan. On 1 March, Arthur Balfour outlined a new horror story to the House of Commons: Britain might become involved with two other great naval powers, while a fourth waited rejoicing to exploit the consequences. One could carry this kind of argument to any lengths. The reality was that it would be unlikely that Britain would have to fight a great combination of hostile navies, without allies of its own. A diplomacy that at the same time committed Britain to war with France and Russia, and also alienated Germany, would surely have plumbed unprecedented depths of incompetence. The British were not taking any chances, however. An agreement was reached with France on 21 March 1904, covering Egypt, Morocco, Madagascar, Siam and the Newfoundland fisheries. In April the decision was taken to establish a condominium or system of joint Anglo-French rule over the New Hebrides. Naturally the Australians were not consulted.

Meanwhile the Japanese Second Army cut off Port Arthur by land. The initiative was now completely lost to the Japanese. Failing a radical change in the quality of their leadership, the most the Russians could hope for now was to get out of the war without excessive humiliation. Roosevelt's attitude vacillated. He told British Ambassador Spring-Rice that he had 'never anticipated in the least such a rise as this of Japan . . . if they win out it may possibly mean a struggle between them and us . . .'.[15] His fears were temporarily removed when the Port Arthur squadron finally sortied for Vladivostok on 10 August. The Japanese, outnumbered in the battle line, although possessing a substantial superiority in gunpower, held off cautiously. This alone saved the Russians from total defeat.

Naval talks began with France in mid-1905. But every continental entanglement was liable to mean a concentration of British power in home waters, away from the Pacific and Indian oceans, where naval supremacy had now gone completely to the Japanese. This had admittedly raised less alarm in Australia and New Zealand than might have been expected. Yet Creswell took the opportunity again to argue the absolute necessity for a permanent Australian fleet in the Pacific:

In no way could concentration at the 'heart of the Empire' be more materially assisted than by measures of safety for the extremities. . . . Of what use it is asked would any Australian Naval Force be after the destruction of the British Fleet. . . . The confusion of thought here is due to failure to recognise our place as a portion of the British Empire, and to regard as separate and independent, forces that are supplementary . . . a watchman in charge of a great warehouse is not a substitute for the police force but additional to and supplementary to it. . . .[16]

The confusion of thought perhaps went still deeper. It would have been appropriate for example to have asked of what use the British navy would be after the destruction of the Empire. The fact was that there was no way in which the British fleet could be destroyed, unless British diplomacy contrived by superhuman ineptitude that the United Kingdom should have to fight the rest of the world without allies. But there was also no question that exaggerated concern for home defence was leaving the rest of the Empire perilously exposed, and that the measures being taken for collective security by the Imperial Government were not reassuring to His Majesty's governments overseas. British and French squadrons began making goodwill visits to each other's naval bases. In August the Anglo-Japanese alliance was renewed, extending the obligations for mutual assistance to include the defence of India against a Russian attack, which had never been less likely. Then in October the new battleship *Dreadnought* was laid down, setting off a new and far sharper spiral in the naval race.

Dreadnought did not exactly add a new dimension to naval warfare. However, with a displacement of 17,900 tons and a speed of twenty knots, it was the largest, fastest and most powerful battleship in the world. Its ten 12-inch guns gave it a broadside of 6,800 pounds, compared with 5,300 pounds for the most powerful pre-*Dreadnought* ship. There was little doubt that any battleship of the *Dreadnought* class should be able to sink any pre-*Dreadnought*. On the other hand it would not be likely to be able to avoid being sunk by the combined attentions of two or more pre-*Dreadnoughts*. *Dreadnought* was not unmatchable. Nor indeed was it a perfect conception, even within its limits of power and size: when under way in heavy waters, vision in the forward turrets was obscured, and the 6-inch batteries were liable to be flooded. Least of all was it to be regarded as a British monopoly: the United States had authorized two ships of its class before the end of the year, and Japan had a 19,000-ton monster actually under construction before *Dread-nought* was even laid down. More seriously, Germany followed in November with a Supplementary Naval Law, providing for substantially increased expenditure, involving a programme of four Dreadnoughts, at a time when Britain had only three on order. There was thus a certain temptation to adopt a line harder than ever with Germany, while the Germans were still scarcely in a position actively to resent it. British Foreign Secretary Edward Grey owned to the opinion that 'if France is let in for a war with Germany arising out of our agreement with her about Morocco, we cannot stand aside but must take part with France'.[17] But the Anglo-French relationship itself was already involving serious tensions within the Empire: the Australians were furious at not having been consulted at all in the formation of the Anglo-French condominium for the New Hebrides.

On 26 September Deakin decided to establish a system of harbour and coastal defences for Australia, with a local naval force of twelve destroyers, to provide a torpedo flotilla, which would probably be the most destructive and economical deterrent available. This provoked the usual complaint from the British that: 'The supremacy of the Empire at sea must depend in any war on the victory of the Battle Fleets . . . the size of the Squadron in Australian waters should be left for the Admiralty to decide as the conditions alter on strategic grounds only.'[18]

Meanwhile troubles were multiplying in Europe. An agreement had been reached with Russia on 31 August 1907, delimiting spheres of interest between the two empires along their enormous frontier, from the Mediterranean to the Himalayas. This was already falling apart: in August 1908 the British emphatically refused to allow Russia to compensate itself at the expense of Turkey for the Austrian annexation of Bosnia-Herzegovina. Then in October Wilhelm II explained to the foreign press that the German people as a whole disliked England and wanted war, although he was himself a friend of England, and had indeed told the British General Staff how to win the Boer War.[19] This incredible indiscretion only served to intensify the naval race. British Prime Minister Asquith now expanded the two-power standard, claiming that Britain 'needs a preponderance of 10 per cent over the combined strength in capital ships of the next two strongest powers, whatever those powers might be'.[20] But this margin was clearly unattainable: in 1908 Britain had forty-eight capital ships built or under construction, Germany thirty and the United States twenty-nine. Moreover, Germany had or was acquiring seven Dreadnoughts, and Britain only six. The implications of this arithmetic were not entirely clear. There was however one physical fact that did not need interpretation: the entire British battle force was now stationed within reach of the shores of the United Kingdom. The Recall of the Galleys was well-nigh complete.

It meant, as Creswell said, that

the time is fast approaching when the existence of Australia 'will depend upon the goodwill of America and the politeness of Japan . . .'. That the present political circumstances in Europe compel the concentration of all the British battleships in home waters is a fact we are all familiar with. Fifteen years ago, this, if prophesized, would have been laughed at . . . it will be absolutely impossible for us to maintain our supremacy both in home waters and in the Far East. . . . The possibility of an alliance between Germany and Japan represents one of the greatest dangers to the British Empire that could well be imagined. . . .[21]

The situation deteriorated rapidly: exaggerated reports of German naval building suggested that Germany might have seventeen Dreadnoughts available for action by 1912, and Britain only eighteen. The British government now appealed to the Empire to provide some active assistance, while new naval estimates introduced in the House of Commons on 16 March 1909 contemplated the laying down of two keels for every one of Germany's. As with the South African War, there appeared to be a contest between the Dominions as to which could make its contribution first. The New Zealand government on 22 March offered to pay the cost of 'a first class battleship of the latest type' for the Royal Navy, with a second warship of similar standard to follow if necessary.[22] On the same day the Commonwealth of Australia cheerfully placed its resources at the disposal of the mother country.[23] Even the Canadians seemed to feel that the time had come for action, after seven years' contemplation: the Canadian government cautiously proposed the 'speedy organisation of a Canadian Naval Reserve in cooperation with, and in close relation to, the Imperial Navy . . .'. The naval supremacy of Britain was, in the view of Ottawa, 'essential to the security of commerce, the safety of the Empire and the peace of the world. . . . Whenever the need arises the Canadian people will be found ready and willing to make any sacrifice that is required to give the Imperial authorities the most loyal and hearty cooperation in every movement for the maintenance of the integrity and honour of the Empire.'[24]

Words were cheap. So far only New Zealand had actually made a definite commitment. However, on 4 April, the governments of New South Wales and Victoria offered to contribute proportionately to any offer by the Commonwealth, or, in the absence of such an offer, to pay for a Dreadnought themselves on a *per capita* basis.[25] Meanwhile the panic deepened: Germany's ally, Austria-Hungary, was beginning to construct Dreadnoughts, adding by at least 10 per cent to the odds against England. In this situation even the Admiralty was prepared to compromise: when Deakin announced flatly that the Commonwealth had resolved to establish a naval force that would be under its sole control while serving about the coasts of Australia, the British government made no serious objection. Indeed, the Colonial Office in its reply commented on the intention of Canada similarly to create its own naval *service*, interestingly misquoting the actual Canadian proposal to form a naval *reserve*.[26] Everything now declined into insignificance compared with the race with Germany: there was to be no attempt to maintain the two-power standard *vis-à-vis* the United States, and Asquith now insisted that the standard was 'not to be understood as a transcendant dogma, but as a convenient rule-of-thumb to be applied with reference to political and strategical considerations'.[27]

The Imperial Conference of July 1909 came up with a compromise that met Deakin's demands while permitting the Admiralty to save face: a Pacific squadron was to be formed, to which the Dominions should contribute their own 'Fleet Units'. Originally it was suggested that it should consist of the Australian Fleet Unit, the East Indies and China stations of the Royal Navy, and New Zealand's gift battleship. The proposal was made that Canada might also contribute a unit, but this was hardly rejected by the Canadian government, which was prepared to contemplate building for one ocean only. In essence the scheme envisaged an expenditure by Australia of some £3,700,000, with an annual outlay of £750,000, for the acquisition and upkeep of one Dreadnought of the 'Indomitable' class, with eight 12-inch guns and a speed of 27 knots; three unarmoured 'Bristol'-class cruisers, and six destroyers. The Canadian government submitted for approximately £1,370,000 as an initial outlay, with an annual expenditure of perhaps £600,000, for three cruisers and four destroyers. New Zealand, which had abruptly decided that it now favoured 'one great Imperial Navy', settled for an annual subsidy of £250,000, £150,000 of which would go to pay off the cost of its gift Dreadnought.[28]

As usual the decisions left something to be desired as a demonstration of imperial solidarity. Canada was simply not prepared to make a contribution to collective defence comparable with that volunteered by the Australasian Dominions. New Zealand was apparently determined to identify with Britain rather than associate itself with Australian initiatives, either because it feared domination by its huge neighbour, or because it hoped to profit by developing a closer relationship with Britain than the Australians were concerned to have.

Certainly the gulf between British and Australian thinking was now to all appearances unbridgeable. Deakin in particular had emerged in the eyes of Whitehall as a demon-figure, as unpredictable and enormously more embarrassing than Wilhelm II. His next bombshell arrived hard on the heels of the naval controversy at the 1909 conference. He wrote out of a clear sky to Colonial Secretary Lord Crewe suggesting what he termed 'a proposition of the highest international importance', an agreement involving 'an extension of the Monroe Doctrine to all the countries around the Pacific Ocean supported by the guarantees of the British Empire, Holland, France and China added to that of the United States'.[29] It was of course unthinkable that any recommendation from a Dominion government would ever be considered seriously in London. Crewe passed 'this curious letter of Deakin's' on to Foreign Secretary Grey. His only comment was at least genuine: 'Personally I rather dread a concrete discussion between Australia and ourselves on these subjects.'[30] Grey duly responded with a brief list of reasons for doing nothing about the project, which Crewe relayed to Deakin, adding with monumental insincerity: 'I shall always welcome an informal letter on this or any other topic of Imperial concern.'[31]

Deakin meanwhile was enjoying perhaps his finest hour. The Bill providing for the establishment of the Royal Australian Navy was put before Federal Parliament in Melbourne on 24 November. As Defence Minister Joseph Cook told the cheering Members: 'Our tutelary stages are past, our time of maturity is here. . . . In passing the motion we shall enter what has been called the great "Sea League" of the Empire; and the wardenship of the Pacific will be allotted to us as the worthiest and most adequate contribution to the defence of the Empire that the highest Naval authorities can devise.'[32] On 9 December the Governor-General informed the Colonial Office that the government of Australia 'will be glad if Lords Commissioners of the Admiralty will arrange for construction without delay of the armoured cruiser of the "Indefatigable" type, to be followed by the three unarmoured cruisers of improved "Bristol" type . . .'.[33] The Pacific was about to know a new flag and a new fleet.

The Australian move could not have been more timely. London was moving into ever more ominous international entanglements. Ever since 15 January 1906 the British Admiralty, the War Office and the Foreign Office had been considering in complete secrecy the possibility of a British military commitment to the Continent in support of France against Germany.[34] One embarrassment was no sooner evaded than another was embraced: on 13 July 1911 the Anglo-Japanese alliance was renewed in a form that would 'not in any event impose either upon the United Kingdom or upon Japan the obligation of going to war with the United States'.[35] Then on 20 July General Sir Henry Wilson, British Director of Military Operations, met to discuss 'the conditions of the eventual participation of a British army in the operations of the French armies of the North-East, in a war against Germany'. It was agreed that 'Britain will commit to the operations against Germany the totality of the forces which it has available for overseas expeditions, to wit: six active divisions, a cavalry division, two mounted brigades . . .'. It was indeed agreed at the outset that these conversations, 'deprived of all official character, could not bind the British and French Governments in anything'.[36] But even the most official of treaties can never bind a sovereign government in everything. A simple vote of the House of Commons would be sufficient to annul any formal commitment. An informal commitment could be more difficult to detach oneself from. The fact of the matter was that the Admiralty and the War Office were preparing to base the redeployment of British forces on the expectation of war against Germany in support of France. They were not preparing for a war against France in support of Germany. It would therefore be reasonable to expect that the French would begin to make their dispositions in the corresponding expectation of British support, and that any British government would be less embarrassed to provide this assistance than to find explanations why help would not be available.

The secret commitment to France became more inextricable month by month. In May 1912 the French naval authorities expressed a wish to pursue talks with the Admiralty regarding the 'care of the Mediterranean' in the event of war. Their notion in essence was that the Royal Navy should 'look after the Channel and the northern coasts of France, if the latter . . . will undertake the "care of the whole of the Mediterranean"'.[37] This precipitated an agonizing new debate on British naval strategy, with a scenario for a new horror story, this time for a war in the

Mediterranean against the Triple Alliance of Germany, Italy and Austria.

The implications of such a conflict were truly frightful. Britain's sixty-three battleships, built or building, would have seemed to provide a reasonable margin of security against Germany's thirty-six, especially when the British total included twelve Dreadnoughts against Germany's seven. However, the safety margin deteriorated rapidly if one added to the German total Austria's thirteen capital ships, built or building, including four Dreadnoughts; and Italy's twelve, also including four Dreadnoughts. The Triple Alliance would then have close to parity all told, and superiority in Dreadnoughts.[38] This indeed could never be the whole story. In the first place the Triple Alliance was already under strains that would be likely to make it inoperative in almost any conceivable war. The Italian naval offensive in the war with Turkey was enraging every other European power. Italian relations with Austria in particular could scarcely be worse. In any event Italian participation in the Triple Alliance would be required only in the event of an offensive war by France against Germany. In such a situation, Britain would be able to count on the support of France's twenty capital ships, built or building, including six Dreadnoughts, which would cancel out the Italian contribution; and possibly Russia's projected battle force of fourteen vessels, including seven Dreadnoughts, which would considerably more than cancel out the Austrians'. A combination of Britain, France and Russia against Germany, Austria and Italy in 1914 would thus be likely to oppose ninety-seven capital ships against sixty-one, or twenty-five Dreadnoughts against fifteen. This would seem to be a sufficient margin. But in fact it was in the highest degree improbable that Italy would support the Triple Alliance in a war against Britain, even if France were to take the kind of initiative that would bring Italy's adherence to the alliance into question. Nor was it easy to envisage the circumstances under which Britain would be fighting even Austria and Germany unaided.

The situation was made the more bizarre by the fact that the powers with which Britain had a genuine conflict of interests, relations with which were deteriorating all the time, were its own ally, Japan, and France's ally, Russia. The British and Russians had been supporting rival factions in Persia for the past two years. Then in 1912 Britain and Japan clashed openly in China. The Japanese had supported the

Manchus and the Kuomintang nationalists, while the British favoured the successful and anti-Japanese Yuan Shih-k'ai.[39] The Admiralty warned urgently that in 'the event of trouble with Japan, we should have to despatch at least 50 armoured ships to the Far East and that, in the circumstances of British and German naval strength in 1911, is impossible, for we could not send them without leaving our shores at the mercy of our rivals across the North Sea'.[40] At a time when Japan had in all eighteen capital ships built or building, including seven Dreadnoughts, this would certainly have seemed excessive. The fact was in any case that Britain could count on having some 106 ships of the class of armoured cruiser and above by 1914, against Germany's fifty, so it would have seemed possible to send a sufficient number to deter Japan without exactly leaving the shores of Britain naked to an invader.

The decision was to send nothing. First Lord of the Admiralty Winston Churchill told the Committee of Imperial Defence on 4 July 1912 that 'the North Sea must be our first care'. Admiral of the Fleet Lord Fisher agreed: 'The first necessity was certainty of victory in the North Sea.'[41] This had indeed been the unadmitted and still secret basis of British naval strategy since the recall of the galleys had begun in 1902. Its pursuit was now to lead to a still more inescapable commitment to France. The French naval attaché in London approached Churchill on 17 July to bring arrangements for joint action up to date. Churchill repeated the formula that 'no discussion between naval or military experts could be held to affect in any way the full freedom of action possessed by both countries'; but went on to explain British naval dispositions and suggested that the French 'aim at a standard of strength in the Meditn equal to that of Austria and Italy combined . . .'. The French attaché replied happily that 'they had already decided to move their six remaining battleships from Brest into the Meditn to form a 3rd squadron there, leaving the Northern and Atlantic Coasts solely to the protection of their torpedo flotillas . . .'.[42] The great diplomatic and strategic revolution was virtually complete. The armed camps had formed in Europe, and the lines of battle were drawn.

The agreement was completed on 10 February 1913. Its effect was to complete the concentration of Anglo-French naval forces in European waters for a war against Germany and its allies. The transformation of the naval scene in the past decade was astonishing: as Churchill himself admitted, 'in 1902 there were 160 British vessels on the overseas stations against 76 today'.[43] The Pacific in particular had been swept clean: the British now retained on the China Station only the armoured cruisers *Minotaur* and *Hampshire*, with main armaments of four 9.2-inch and four 7.5-inch guns respectively, and a speed of 22.5 knots; and the light, 25-knot cruisers, *Yarmouth*, with eight 6-inch guns, and *Newcastle*, with two guns of the same calibre. French naval power was represented by the quaint old *Montcalm*, marinating peacefully in Noumea, with its two 7.6-inch guns. Against these forces Germany had ready the protected cruisers *Scharnhorst* and *Gneisnau*, each capable of 25 knots and armed with eight 8.2-inch guns; and the three lighter 24-knot cruisers, *Emden*, with twelve 4-inch guns, and *Nürnberg* and *Leipzig* with ten 4-inch guns. It was of course true, as Commander-in-Chief China Station Sir Thomas Jerram said, that 'if the Japanese Alliance can be safely counted on, we have an overwhelming superiority and there is no more to be said . . .'.[44] But the Japanese alliance like the Russian connection was becoming increasingly open to question. Jerram was in fact consoling himself in these terms just as Anglo-Japanese rivalry in China flared again, the Japanese once more supporting an attempted coup by the Kuomintang, and their efforts again being crushed by President Yuan Shih-k'ai with massive British support, culminating in a bitter exchange of notes. The Japanese then promptly concluded a secret accord with Russia, under the terms of which Outer Mongolia became virtually a Russian protectorate, in complete disregard of the Anglo-Russian accords. With friends such as these, the British did not need enemies.

Admiral Jerram had naturally overlooked one factor. On 4 October 1913 the Sydneysiders poured down from the silvertail harbourside suburbs, from the terraces of Balmain and North Sydney and the opulent heights of Bellevue Hill, to cheer the Royal Australian Navy as it sailed into the harbour in brilliant sunshine. In the words of the official Australian historian, 'The Fleet was the Commonwealth's own creation, conceived in Australian minds (albeit at Admiral Tryon's suggestion), born after long struggles against British reluctance, never – except, perhaps, in the halcyon days of 1909–11 – thoroughly approved of by high British authorities.'[45] Admittedly, as Mr Corelli Barnett remarks, it 'amounted to only the battle-cruiser *Australia*, four light cruisers and three destroyers'.[46] But it was enough to alter the balance of power in the Pacific. *Australia* with its eight 12-inch guns and speed of 25 knots was by itself more than a match for the whole German

Pacific Squadron; of the four light cruisers, *Melbourne*, *Sydney* and *Encounter* were of the 'Yarmouth' class, fully capable as *Sydney* proved of catching and sinking any of the German cruisers; and probably none of them, least of all the battleship, would have been stationed in the Pacific but for the unremitting efforts of various Australian governments.[47] Australia had, as Deakin had prophesied, seized the wardenship of the South Pacific for the British Empire. It was just in time.

5 To the last man and the last shilling (1914–18)

The first real test of imperial defence came almost casually in 1914. On 29 July a cable was despatched from London to the other capitals of the Empire, warning the colonial governments to 'see preface defence scheme. Adopt precautionary stage. Names of powers will be communicated later if necessary.'[1] It was hardly a rousing call to action, and in fact it roused little action. The Australian Prime Minister did not even bother to summon the Cabinet. The Governor-General, Sir Ronald Munro-Ferguson, asked tactfully two days later if it might not be 'as well, in view of the latest news from Europe, that Ministers should meet in order that the Imperial Government may know what to expect from Australia?'[2] However, Ferguson's suggestion was sent in code, and the Prime Minister, Cook, did not have his code-book with him at the time, so he did not know what the Governor-General was suggesting until he returned to Melbourne on 1 August. Cook had no doubt himself in any event about what the Imperial Government could expect from Australia: he had already assured his audience in the little Victorian town of Horsham[3] that 'when the Empire is at war, so is Australia at war . . . all our resources in Australia are in the Empire and for the Empire . . .'. His Labour opponent Andrew Fisher put the same point more effectively at the equally small town of Colac,[4] claiming that Australia would defend England to 'our last man and our last shilling'.

Meanwhile the other colonies were already making their offers: in Canada Prime Minister Laurier offered an expeditionary force of 20,000 men, subsequently raised to 33,000, with the hopeful boast that there was in Canada but one mind and one heart; and in New Zealand William Massey announced that his government would consider the situation, and if necessary ask the people and Parliament to do their duty by offering an expeditionary force to Britain.

The Australians began taking effective action on 2 August. It was agreed that the vessels of the Royal Australian Navy should be placed under Admiralty control, and that an expeditionary force of 20,000 men should be prepared 'of any suggested composition to any destination desired by the Home Government'.[5] The home government did not however seem certain at first if it wanted to take up the Australian offer: the Colonial Office cabled on 4 August, three days after fighting had actually begun in Europe, that there seemed 'no immediate necessity for any request on our part for an expeditionary force from Australia'.[6] This view was repeated by a government spokesman in the House of Lords on 5 August. However on 6 August London cabled: 'His Majesty's Government grateful accept offer of your Ministers to send force of 20,000 men to this country and would be glad if it could be despatched as soon as possible.'[7] Munro-Ferguson replied that there was 'indescribable enthusiasm and entire unanimity throughout Australia in support of all that tends to provide for the security of the Empire in war'.[8] Australia had indeed already fired the first shot delivered by any part of the Empire against Germany, when the commander at Fort Nepean at Port Philip Heads, at last supplied with live ammunition, ordered a warning shot to be fired across the bows of the German steamer *Pfalz*, attempting to leave Melbourne. The shot missed, but the *Pfalz* stopped anyway. The war of the world empires had begun.

The British had already thought of an imperial mission for the Southern Dominions. On 6 August they told the Australian and New Zealand governments that they 'should feel that this was a great and urgent imperial service' if they could seize the German wireless station at Samoa, in the case of New Zealand, and the German bases at Yap in the Marshall Islands, Nauru on Pleasant Island, and New Guinea, in the case of Australia. Unfortunately London did not know how great a force would be required for these operations: when the New Zealand government asked for information as to the exact number of German troops in Samoa, the Colonial Office referred them to *Whitaker's Almanack*. In fact there were no German troops in Samoa. Nor were there any in the Marshalls or the Carolines. The only German military strength in the Pacific was represented by 61 European and 240 native soldiers in Rabaul, equipped with one machine gun and two saluting guns in New Guinea, without ammunition.

There was however a German Pacific squadron, about which the British government seemed strangely concerned. They had already invited the Japanese to act in the spirit of the alliance, and neutralize the

German forces in the Far East, despite an offer by the Germans themselves to exclude China and the Far East from the combat zone. But
Japanese intervention obviously raised the question of the disposal of
the German colonial territories. The British warned the Australians and
New Zealanders at the outset that any territory occupied by their forces
would have to be 'at the disposal of the Imperial Government for purposes of an ultimate settlement at conclusion of the war', although they
hoped that the action of the Japanese would not extend to the Pacific
Ocean beyond the China Seas.[9]

The Dominion governments went ahead with preparations for their
first acts of military aggression. A New Zealand contingent was made
ready with remarkable speed by 11 August, and embarked on two
troopships the following day. They then sailed off to Noumea to wait for
the Australians. The latter, 1,023 infantrymen from New South Wales,
plus six companies of the Royal Australian Naval Reserve, were
embarked on the armed merchant cruiser *Berrima* on 19 August. The
plan was to rendezvous at Port Moresby with *Kanowna*, carrying 500
men from a citizen force raised in North Queensland, who should have
been used to tropical climates. The operation unfortunately followed the
now familiar Australian pattern of chaos and insubordination. The fire-
men aboard *Kanowna* mutinied when they found that they might be
sailing into some danger; the citizen force was found to be ill-equipped,
untrained and quite unfit; and *Kanowna* was ordered to put back to
Townsville.

Meanwhile the New Zealanders descended on Apia on 29 August,
carrying a strip of a tablecloth tacked to a broomstick as a flag of truce.
The Germans, having no means of resistance, surrendered; and the first
enemy territory had fallen into British hands. Rabaul and New Guinea
were seized by the Australians on 17 September after brisk and quite
one-sided fighting, in which the Australians showed an unexpected
aptitude for jungle warfare. This left the Carolines, Marshalls and
Pelews still in German hands. It had already been resolved that Yap
should be left to the Australians, and the Japanese had been informed
accordingly, although the British apparently did not know exactly
where Yap was. What they did do was invite the Japanese to 'cruise in
the Pacific around Marianne and Caroline Islands in order to hunt down
German squadron which is believed to be in these parts and which will
prey upon British and Japanese shipping in the Pacific unless it is

attacked'.[10] The New Zealand government was indeed intensely anxious about the possibility that the German Pacific squadron might be able to attack the convoys taking the Australian and New Zealand expeditionary forces to the major battle zone.[11] The paradox was however that the Australians had wanted to unleash their navy to destroy the Pacific squadron in the first place, but had been diverted from this by orders of the Admiralty to prepare the expeditions against the helpless German colonies.

The Japanese had already taken advantage of the situation to seize the Marianas, the Marshalls and the Carolines. The Australians prepared an expeditionary force to replace them, but were told by London that as the Japanese had already been in occupancy for more than a month, it would be 'discourteous and disadvantageous' to turn them out. Australian and New Zealand troops were needed elsewhere, in any case. The opening stages of the war had not gone according to anybody's plan. The British had expected the whole affair to be settled in an afternoon, in a great clash of battle forces in the North Sea; the Germans had hoped to outmanoeuvre the French and rush their forces back east in time to crush the Russians before they could complete mobilization; Conrad van Hotzendorf dreamed of a vast, Napoleonic battle of Austrian manoeuvre in the plains of Poland; the French General Staff dreamed of a straight thrust to Berlin, with the 75s forcing the cowardly Boche to keep their heads down until they could be perforated by the new 60cm bayonets. What had happened was bloody checks and indecisions everywhere, leaving general staffs and governments to face the problem of devising new strategies as the old ones had proved thoroughly unrewarding.

This problem was peculiarly acute for the British. Their military contribution so far had been to land a token expeditionary force of four divisions in France, which had encountered the Germans first at Mons on 23 August. The experience had in many ways been most encouraging: the British professional army of 1914 was the best-trained force of riflemen in the world, and had handled the Germans almost as roughly as their predecessors had been handled by the Boers in the South African War. But this could only be a short-term effect. The British professionals could cope with the Germans in a static, positional war; but nobody could handle the Germans in a war of manoeuvre; and the Germans could be held to a positional war only by forces at least equal in numbers. Britain would therefore have either to commit mass armies to a continental war, like the other belligerents, or else use its over-whelming naval power to open new fronts against the Germans, to prevent their making a new bid for victory in the west. One minor effort at amphibious war had already been made: on 28 September Winston Churchill rushed three naval brigades and two divisions to Antwerp, checking a German rush for the Channel ports, in what Liddell Hart terms 'the first and last effort in the West to make use of Britain's amphibious power . . .'.[12] Other prospects opened up: to break into the Baltic to land a Russian army in Pomerania; to land at Salonika to open a new front against Austria; and perhaps to force the Dardanelles, seizing Constantinople and drawing in the Balkan states in a grand outflanking move against Germany.[13]

The last prospect became particularly appealing with the entry of Turkey into the war on 31 October. A British naval squadron carried out an ineffectual bombardment of the forts of the Dardanelles for twenty minutes on 3 November, thereby impelling the Turks to strengthen their defences. Then on 2 January the Russian Grand Duke Nicholas appealed for an Anglo-French demonstration against the Turks. There was in fact no serious danger to Russia from that quarter, but at least a successful move against Turkey would help to guarantee that Russia would eventually receive the gift of Constantinople, which had been promised to it on 9 November.[14] The difficulty was that there were no troops available, and the French were insisting that any that might become available should be concentrated on their own front. Churchill proposed instead an attempt by the navy alone to force the Straits, with the purpose of arriving in the Straits of Mamora, to provoke a revolution in Constantinople.[15] Arguments at this stage began to become incoherent and inconclusive. There was for example no assurance at all that a revolution in favour of the Allies would necessarily result from the appearance of the fleet before Constantinople, nor did anybody have any suggestions as to what the fleet would actually do if the desired revolution did not take place.

The alternative dream of a Balkan front of Greece, Bulgaria and Rumania coming to the aid of Serbia was even less concrete, as the Bulgars were in fact negotiating a loan from the German government. The situation would no doubt have been altered if the Allies were able to land an army of invasion, but against that the whole purpose of the exercise initially had been to avoid the diversion of troops from the western front. Moreover it was unlikely that any army that the Allies could possibly have assembled would have been strong enough to defeat the Turks in battle. Churchill was in any case adamant that any landing force should merely 'reap the fruits' of naval successes.[16] The consequences of naval failure were not seriously considered.

Any operation so irresponsibly conceived deserved to fail. The naval bombardment of the outer ports of the Gallipoli Peninsula began on 19 February 1915. It had in the meantime come to Kitchener's notice that there were actually troops at hand for a military demonstration. The Canadian Expeditionary Force of 33,000 men had arrived in England on 3 October. Their government had complained to the Australians and New Zealanders about the horrors and inadequacies of training facilities at Aldershot. The Australian and New Zealand contingents, some 30,000 strong, had accordingly been diverted to Egypt to complete their training. Kitchener now proposed that these units should be used as the nucleus of a landing force.[17] The French also began to assemble a division, under the command of General Albert d'Amade, still presumably recovering from a total failure of nerve suffered after his first encounter with the Germans.[18] Further strength was provided by Kitchener's decision to withhold the British 29th Division from commitment to the new offensive at Neuve-Chapelle on 10 March. However even this augmented force would still have been inadequate to have coped with the garrison that the Turks were believed to have installed in the peninsula since the Allied thrust had first been contemplated. The enterprise thus still depended totally upon the ability of the navy to deliver success.

It was too much for the British naval commander, who collapsed with a nervous breakdown. His second-in-command, Admiral de Robeck, began the bombardment of the inner forts on 18 March. The auspices were not too discouraging: the British army had just completed its first and perhaps most successful offensive of the war at Neuve-Chapelle, achieving limited and irrelevant gains after a brief, hurricane bombardment, but at least inflicting on the Germans casualties almost as great as it suffered itself. However by 22 March de Robeck was convinced that the Dardanelles could not be forced by naval action. His decision was taken after three of his old battleships had been sunk by mines, and three others, including the Dreadnought *Inflexible*, had been disabled. De Robeck still had twelve battleships left. Moreover the Allies possessed a margin of battle force strength over the Central Powers more than sufficient to support losses of this kind: Britain, France, Russia and Japan could deploy at least ninety capital ships against the forty-four available to the Central Powers. But the navy had never been wholeheartedly enamoured of the Dardanelles venture anyway. The scenario was accordingly changed completely: the army would have to land on Gallipoli to subdue the Turkish guns, already almost out of ammunition, to enable the navy to sweep away the mines so that its ships could proceed on to Constantinople. Logically of course the ships would not have had to go to Constantinople if the landing were successful. The whole rationale of the expedition had been lost already.

It went ahead none the less, even as the British suffered their most shattering defeat yet at Ypres, where the Germans, advancing behind clouds of chlorine gas, inflicted 65,000 casualties for the loss of barely 30,000 of their own. The only redeeming feature of this terrible defeat was the birth of the first of the legends that developed around the British colonial forces, crediting the Canadians with the feat of defending the gap in the Allied line opened when French African troops fled before the approach of the gas clouds. No human beings could have held their positions under the shock of chlorine without respirators. The fact was that the Canadians held the fringes of the gap, which the Germans were too slow to exploit, partly because they had not expected the gas to be so effective, but mainly because their troops were no more anxious to advance into a chlorine-impregnated atmosphere than the French had been to remain in one.

Another colonial legend was born on 25 April, three days later, when the Allied Expeditionary Force descended on the Gallipoli Peninsula. Some 78,000 men had been assembled under the command of Sir Ian Hamilton: the Australian and New Zealand Army Corps of 30,000; a French division of 18,000; 2,000 Royal Marines; 8,000 men of the Royal Naval Division; and the 20,000 men of the British 29th Division. They were approaching almost completely unfamiliar territory, defended by a fully prepared and alerted Turkish force of 62,077 fighting men, admirably commanded by the German General Liman von Sanders. Hamilton could hardly have hoped for success with fewer than 150,000 men. He hoped to compensate for the inadequacy of his force by diversions: the

French were to land at Kum Kale, on the Asian coast; the British at the southern tip of the peninsula; and the Anzacs further north, at Gaba Tepe. In fact only the French landing was totally successful, due largely to the lack of adequate close-in naval support.

The resources that might have provided success at Gallipoli were meanwhile being squandered in another unsuccessful and quite un-economical attack in the west at Festubert. Then over 31 May–1 June the British and German battle fleets clashed off Jutland in an indecisive encounter that served to reinforce the impression of timidity and in-decisiveness already provided by de Robeck's handling of the naval operations in the Dardanelles campaign. The Germans sank fourteen British ships for a loss of eleven of their own, of little more than half the tonnage of their British victims. They had in fact destroyed three British battlecruisers and three armoured cruisers against two of their own capital ships.[19]

Admiral Jellicoe had indeed fought with a caution and restraint amply justified by the fact that the German ships were better protected, their guns were superior in hitting power, their marksmanship was far more accurate, and their tactics, especially for night-fighting, were much more effective and adventurous. He was also hampered by belated and in-appropriate instructions from the Admiralty, and by the extraordinary failure of his own captains to keep him informed of the actual course of the battle. There was however little point in trying to apportion blame for a battle that on any account could only be regarded as a highly rewarding experience for the Germans. The fundamental reality was that the Royal Navy, with generally inferior ships, inferior tactics and a completely unsatisfactory system of operational control, simply could not hope to meet the Germans on equal terms at sea. As neither the British nor the French armies had shown much capacity to meet them on equal terms on land, and as the Germans were winning a handsome margin of superiority in the air, it was really becoming difficult to see exactly how the Allies were going to win the war.

One obvious answer was: more manpower. London informed the Australian government on 18 June that 'every available man that can be recruited in Australia is wanted'.[20] A further disastrous offensive at Loos in September showed why they were wanted: Anglo-French casualties amounted to over 100,000 against 56,000 German. But there was still serious disagreement as to where the human resources of the British and

French empires could most usefully be deployed. Serbia, on the point of collapse, was appealing for help again. A heroic attempt to regain the initiative at Gallipoli was defeated over 6–9 August by superior Turkish force and almost standard incompetence on the part of the British commanders. Some of the fiercest fighting of the war placed the key to success in the centre of the peninsula in the hands of the Anzac forces, but sheer exhaustion and the total failure of the British General Stopford to provide adequate support snatched the only chance of victory away. Meanwhile Anglo-French forces had begun to land in Salonika, in probably the most useless operation of the war, and other Turkish armies had surrounded a rashly-commanded British force at Kut in Mesopotamia. The 'Eastern' alternative was virtually abandoned; Gallipoli was evacuated; and the Dominion Prime Ministers were invited to London for a briefing on the new strategy of massive concentration on the western front.

The failure of the Gallipoli venture released twenty Turkish divisions for action in the Middle East, against Russia and against the British in Mesopotamia. The extent of the calamity was obscured for the Australian and New Zealand governments by the legendary achievements of their soldiers. The British High Command did not of course have the same consolation. The Anzac legend was in any event a contribution to mythology rather than to history. Nothing could detract from the incredible heroism and soldierly valour of the Dominion contingents. On the other hand they provided neither the largest component of the expedition, nor suffered the most casualties. Total Anzac losses amounted to 32,765 killed, wounded and taken prisoner. The French by comparison lost 47,000 men and the British 184,000. Nor did the reputed fighting ability of the Australians in particular seem a sufficient compensation for their less endearing characteristics. Chief of the Imperial General Staff General Sir Archibald Murray deplored the 'extreme indiscipline and inordinate vanity' of the Australians in Egypt.[21] Inordinate vanity is of course one of the inherent traits of men who know themselves to be good fighters: nobody ever accused the United States Marines of being modest or even tolerant: an agreeable lack of conceit is more usually found among men accustomed to being beaten. Discipline is necessarily a variable concept: the men of the 8th and 10th regiments, Australian Light Horse, who lost 75 per cent casualties in four hopeless charges against Turkish positions at Baby 700 on 7 August 1915, obviously possessed either discipline or an adequate substitute for it.

In any event the British General Staff had to make do with what they could get. By mid-1916 Sir Douglas Haig had sixty divisions in France. Five of these were cavalry, three from the United Kingdom and two from India, kept permanently in waiting for the hour of breakthrough that never came; forty-seven were infantry, from the United Kingdom; and four more infantry divisions were supplied by Australia, three by Canada and one by New Zealand, with an infantry brigade from South Africa. With these numbers Haig felt that he could afford to lose in round numbers some 500,000 men. On 8 July he almost succeeded.

The Somme offensive was the first great military operation on the western front employing exclusively the resources of the British Empire, and it was dedicated to the strategic concept of killing Germans.[22] It failed because British resources were simply not adequate to the task of overcoming the Germans on any battlefront in France,[23] and because the Germans were understandably able to inflict casualties far higher than they suffered themselves. By the time Haig called off the battle on 16 November, the Allies had lost a further 623,000 casualties, 419,000 of whom were British, while the Germans had lost 465,000, and only half of these on the British sector of the front. As the Australian official historian pointed out, a general who wears down 180,000 of the enemy by sacrificing 400,000 of his own troops has something to answer for.[24]

Haig was of course totally unrepentant. The generals reflected confidently that the military achievements of the year had 'left the position in all theatres of war infinitely more satisfactory and hopeful than it had been twelve months before'.[25] The situation had in fact deteriorated appallingly everywhere. Russia was collapsing; the Italian front had subsided into bloody stalemate; the Dardanelles had been a total failure; the Turks were triumphant in Mesopotamia; the British navy had fallen back on to a defensive strategy from which in fact it never emerged; and the submarine campaign had demonstrated Germany's potential capacity to blockade Britain into surrender. Military operations on the western front had contributed a pattern of attrition that would mean that the last Allied soldier would die at about the same time as the last German soldier. The Germans would then be able to claim the victory, by simply moving some of their victorious troops from Russia back to the western front.

This was the nadir of military thinking. On the other hand it was inaccurate to assert, as Liddell Hart did later, that the stupid and callous butchery of 1916 had in any sense broken the will or capacity of the British Empire to continue the struggle. It was not the case that in 'the swamps of the Somme and Passchendale was squandered the faith which founded an Empire'.[26] New divisions came forward to replace the old, and even the survivors were ready to fight again after a rest, with more skill if understandably less nonchalance. But battles like the Somme were indeed ominous portents for the fate of the British Empire.

The Empire however would not be necessarily endangered by casualties or even retrievable military defeat. The threat to its existence lay in the kind of mean, narrow mediocrity of intelligence and vision that could regard the Somme complacently as a rewarding military venture. Haig was indeed concerned about the impact of the fighting on imperial defence co-operation. The Australians in particular had him worried. He had decided as early as August 1916 that the troops were ignorant, and their commanding officer, Lieutenant-General Legge, 'was not much good'.[27] In December 1916 he complained to the War Office that desertion 'was assuming alarming proportions among the Australian troops'.[28] He accordingly proposed that the Australian government should allow him to shoot a few.

It was admittedly remarkable that the rate of desertion was four times as high in the Australian divisions as in any other units of the British Empire.[29] Convictions for being absent without leave were proportionately nearly twelve times as frequent. Overall figures for offences against military law showed the same undeniable pattern: 'In March 1918, nearly 9 Australians per 1,000 were in field imprisonment as against 1 per 1,000 in the British force, and less than 2 in the Canadian, New Zealand and South African.'[30] On the other hand it had to be noted that the Australians had lost 22,826 men at the Somme, more than three times as many as the Canadians, and that they had obviously fought at least as hard as anybody else: the Australian Corps had lost on average 8,960 men per division; the United Kingdom divisions, 8,133; the New Zealanders, 7,408; and the Canadians, 6,329.[31] Moreover the British tradition of generously applying the death penalty to encourage the survivors was not followed by other armies whose military record was at least comparable: the Germans, according to Crown Prince Rupprecht, carried out the death penalty for desertion only once in the entire war, while only twenty-three executions were actually performed after the mutinies in the French army in 1917. By contrast 346 executions were carried out in the British army, 55 on British troops and 291 on 'imperial' personnel, mainly camp-followers and Indians. The New Zealanders, ever prompt to follow the British lead, also shot two of their own men for desertion.

The Australian government still refused to apply the death penalty to men who had volunteered for service in an appalling war 12,000 miles from their own country, which remained immune from enemy action of any kind. Moreover they also refused to introduce conscription, which had been adopted by the British at the beginning of 1916 and by the New Zealanders in May.[32] The Australian people narrowly rejected conscription in December, and nearly half the soldiers on active service actually voted against the proposal.[33]

Despite all these failings it was still difficult to dispense with the Australians, especially as the plans of the British General Staff for 1917 envisaged more offensives, presumably in the hope that something would eventually give. General Sir William Rawlinson, commander of 4th Corps on the western front and esteemed a humbug by Haig, overcame his repugnance and wrote to Australian Prime Minister William M. Hughes that 'a sixth Australian division, with or without artillery, would be invaluable addition to fighting strength . . .'.[34] The Australian government hastened to oblige. The sense of imperial co-operation quickened at least some enthusiasm at the first meeting of the Imperial War Cabinet in March: Leo Amery wrote to Lloyd George in an evocative phrase about 'that Southern British World which runs from Cape Town through Cairo, Baghdad and Calcutta to Sydney and Wellington . . .'.[35]

But Amery's polyglot vision and eccentric geography themselves revealed how far the British were from admitting the simple fact that their survival as a great power depended on the continued voluntary support of the British Dominions, far more than on anything that might be forthcoming from Cairo, Baghdad or Calcutta. Secretary of State for India Austen Chamberlain amazingly pressed the claim that India was entitled 'to greater recognition than she had had – she had bled herself white at the beginning of the War to supply the deficiencies of the Empire in troops, arms, and guns . . .'.[36] He did not suggest what kind of recognition should be accorded Canada or Australia, each of which had suffered almost twice as many casualties as India, out of a population less than one-fiftieth the size. The conference in fact voted for disunity. The members agreed that 'the readjustment of the constitutional relations of the component parts of the Empire is too important and intricate a subject to be dealt with during the War', but placed on record their view that 'any such readjustment . . . should be based upon a full recognition of the Dominions as autonomous nations of an Imperial Commonwealth, and of India as an important portion of the same . . .'.[37] Smuts of South Africa noted with satisfaction that any idea of a future imperial parliament or imperial executive was 'negatived by implication'.[38] Whatever the war was bringing to the Empire, it was not a new dimension of unity.

There was of course unity on the battlefield, under the command of British generals for whom artillery served as a substitute for thought. Under a colossal bombardment that concentrated one gun on every 8 yards of front, the British First and Third armies attacked at Arras, the Canadians on the left assaulting Vimy Ridge and the Australians on the right attempting to storm the Hindenburg Line at Bullecourt, assisted by tanks. The Canadian effort was one of the most impressive military operations of the war: for a loss of over 22,000 casualties, they drove a superior number of German divisions back 6 miles. The Australians by contrast ran into disaster. They were instructed to attack the German defences without artillery cover, relying on the tanks to break through the barbed wire. The tanks tended to arrive at the wrong place, or at the wrong time, and proved alarmingly vulnerable to German artillery fire; and the difficulty of knowing where they were at any stage inhibited the British artillery from providing support for the Australians who incredibly pierced the Hindenburg Line under conditions that most soldiers on the western front would have considered impossible. Their very success brought their own destruction when the Germans counterattacked with supreme confidence and ample artillery cover. The Australian 4th Division was shattered, although the relieving 1st Division successfully repelled an attack by four times their numbers of Germans. The offensive was renewed on 23 April, with the Canadians driving at Fresnoy, and the Australians trying their luck at Bullecourt again. The result was an infantry battle of ferocious intensity, in which the Germans unquestionably took the honours.[39]

Crown Prince Rupprecht indeed noted with satisfaction that 'the

English troops show themselves far less tough to repulse than formerly, with the exception of the Canadians and Australians, who are on all sides praised for their bravery and skill in making use of the ground', and who also supplied about a third of total British Empire casualties in the disaster.[40] The Australians for their part were confirmed in a distrust of British generalship and also of British tank tactics, which was to be revived with even greater bitterness in the Western Desert twenty-five years later: Major Jacka's famous last words at Bullecourt, 'Come on boys! Bugger the tanks!' were to be echoed at El Alamein by Australians and New Zealanders in 1942.[41]

What was immensely more serious at the time was that the calamity at Arras coincided with the greatest victories of the German U-Boats in either of the two world wars. Now that the United States was safely in the war, Jellicoe admitted to American Admiral Sims that 'it is impossible for us to go on with the war, if losses like this continue'. Still worse, when the horrified Sims asked him: 'Is there no solution for the problem?' Jellicoe replied: 'Absolutely none that we can see now.'[42] This was understood to mean that Britain could last until 1 November at the latest, unless indeed somebody else was more successful than the Admiralty in discovering a remedy. President Wilson wrote bitterly to Sims: 'From the beginning of the war I have been greatly surprised at the failure of the British Admiralty to use Great Britain's naval superiority in an effective way. In the presence of the present submarine emergency they are helpless to the point of panic.'[43] On 11 August he told the officers and crew of USS *Pennsylvania* in even more emphatic terms: 'Every time we have suggested anything to the British Admiralty, the reply has come back that virtually amounted to this, that it had never been done that way, and I felt like saying, "Well, nothing was ever done so systematically as nothing is being done now." '[44]

Haig was at least doing something. Having concluded that the experience of the Arras offensive demonstrated 'that action of a wearing down character must be continued' and that 'the German Army was in reduced circumstances', he opened a new offensive at Messines on 25 May. It began with unprecedented success: the German defences were saturated by a bombardment of 2,400 guns, one to every 7 yards of front, and were for good measure blown up by mines crammed with 500 tons of explosives. British casualties were 17,000; German, about 25,000. It was in fact 'the first considerable battle in which the British losses were less than those of the Germans'.[45] This deviation from the standard pattern was soon to be corrected. By the time the fighting had died down on 14 June the British casualties had risen to about 26,000, more than half of which were Anzac.

Haig in any event had far bigger plans in mind. The wearing down process started again on 15 July, before Ypres, with a bombardment from 3,091 guns, almost twice as many as had been unleashed before the Somme, and nearly three times as many as were available to the Germans. This colossal exercise of brute force was in fact substantially successful, even though the Germans had modified their tactics since 1916 and were relying largely on a system of depth, in which the main impact of the attack would be absorbed by a few heroic machine gunners in strongly fortified bunkers. The bunkers were in large measure knocked out or at least revealed by the bombardment and were assailed by the Australians in some of the most ferocious hand-to-hand fighting of the war, forcing the Germans to revert temporarily to a more conventional technique of defence in line. However the bombardment also had the effect of turning the battlefield into an almost impassable quagmire, under a rainfall twice as heavy as could normally have been expected. Haig pressed on dauntlessly. On 4 October eight British divisions, four of them Anzac, made a renewed thrust for the hamlet of Passchendaele. It was again a soldiers' battle, of storming parties against the defenders of the blockhouses, and it resulted in an overwhelming victory for the Anzacs. The German official history described the encounter as 'the black day of 4 October'.[46] But nemesis was waiting again. The weather broke once more, and the British attacks bogged down totally in the mud.

The chief British General Staff Officer, Colonel J. F. C. Fuller, now suggested that a great tank raid should be delivered on a suitable sector, in view of the impossibility of continuing to use the machines in the mud of Flanders. Three hundred and eighty-one tanks were assembled, but the decision was made to convert the proposed raid into yet another major offensive from Cambrai to Valenciennes. No reserves were provided however, in case the operation was actually successful. The initial break-in on 20 November was apparently totally successful. The church bells rang out for victory in England. But the chances of attaining the long-sought breakthrough were dissipated: the British cavalry, brought up for the pursuit, dithered remarkably, and were finally scattered by flanking fire; the tank crews were exhausted and their machines breaking down; and a supremely brilliant attack by fresh German troops from the Russian front recovered virtually all the ground initially lost.

With vastly greater resources of men and especially of matériel, Haig had probably fought a campaign in 1917 even less successful than his efforts of 1916. The casualty ratio was almost the same: between May and November the British lost 448,614 men and the Germans approximately 270,710. But the most ominous feature was that the British had not managed to improve their kill-ratio, despite a three to one margin in the air and in artillery, and despite the introduction of the tank. German imagination and enterprise had kept pace with British accumulation of force. German morale had also survived incredibly well the depressing experience of fighting an unchangeably defensive battle against an enemy ever increasing in strength: the German army may never have fought with greater zeal and initiative than in its counter-offensive at Cambrai. One could only anticipate what might happen if the Germans were ever given the opportunity to meet the Allies on the western front on terms of something like numerical equality.

They were likely to be able to do so for at least part of the New Year. Russia was already out of the war. The Americans were admittedly in, but their manpower contribution was still insignificant. France and the British Empire were reaching the end of their resource of manpower. The Australian people rejected conscription again on 20 December 1917 by a margin slightly larger than in the 1916 vote. The Canadians introduced compulsory military service on 3 August, although the provisions of the Bill were not actually applied until 13 October, after a vicious election during which riots occurred in Montreal and the home of a prominent supporter of conscription was dynamited. More riots broke out in Quebec in March and April 1918: the federal police station was burned down, and four people killed in bitter fighting between rioters and the military, unfortunately supplied by Ontario.[47]

These domestic troubles did not appear to have any effect at all on the morale or discipline of the Canadian troops on the western front. This may at least have been partly due to the absolute insistence of the Canadian government that their troops should fight as a single corps, despite repeated attempts by Haig to scatter them throughout his command. The fact that Haig was prepared to yield at all however can be explained by the fact that the Canadians acquired at the very outset a reputation for being simply the most formidable troops in France, which was never seriously challenged. Major-General Essame admittedly affirms that 'all who fought in it gave the palm for the best infantry of the war on either side to the Australians';[48] and Liddell Hart judged the Australian commander, Sir John Monash, to have 'probably the greatest capacity for command in modern war among all who held command in the last war'.[49] Monash himself had no doubts at all: in a letter to Senator George Pearce he claimed that 'this record of the performance of my five Divisions and Corps Troops has not been surpassed in the whole annals of war'.[50] It is only fair to remark that this was not a universally held view: the official Australian war historian for example described the New Zealand Division as being 'possibly the most formidable opponent met by German infantry during the war ... the solidest, calmest looking troops in France',[51] as well as quoting the expert opinion of General von Kuhl that the Canadians were the best troops the British ever had.[52] A final objective judgement is obviously impossible, and is in any case unimportant: it did not really matter whether the Australians were the best infantry in the world, or merely among the best. What did matter was that the British commander-in-chief normally spoke as if they were among the worst. Haig indeed amazed Birdwood after Passchendaele by telling him that the Australian troops were among the best disciplined in the whole British Expeditionary Force, because 'when they are ordered to attack they always do so'. But this was only a momentary lapse on Haig's part. He had reverted to his original view by February: the Canadians were 'really fine disciplined soldiers now, and so smart and clean', but 'I am sorry to say that the Australians are not nearly so efficient. I put this down to Birdwood, who, instead of facing the problem, has gone in for the easier way of saying everything is perfect and making himself as popular as possible. We have had to separate the Australians into Convalescent Camps of their own, because they were giving so much trouble when along with our men and put such revolutionary ideas into their heads.'[53]

It was as always difficult to reconcile this picture of indisciplined fomentors of revolution with the unquestionable fact that Haig consistently used Australian and other Dominion divisions as elite storm troops, allotting to them tasks more demanding and dangerous than those reserved for most of the divisions from the United Kingdom. In the dreadful campaign that began with Messines and ended with Cambrai, just as in the catastrophe of the Somme, it was the colonial divisions that had fought the hardest and suffered the most: five out of ten Dominion divisions had suffered more than 100 per cent casualties, compared with seventeen out of fifty-two British: on average the Canadians had lost 103 per cent of their original strength, the Australians 97 per cent, the New Zealanders 95 per cent and the British 88 per cent.

There was perhaps no real mystery why the young men of the white Dominions should be proving themselves to be among the very best fighting troops of the world: they were the best physical specimens of countries that possessed extremely high standards of living, but at the same time had substantial proportions of their population engaged in outdoor work in climates that could generally be termed challenging and in parts of Canada and Australia at least could reasonably be termed appalling. The Canadians in particular were among the best-fed and best-educated people on earth, and were blessed with a climate peculiarly fitted to separate the strong from the weak. But the reasons could not be more than interesting conjectures. What was important was the fact that the British overseas produced fighting men comparable with any in the world, and that these men were still after four years prepared to volunteer to fight in the most appalling conditions in a war thousands of miles away.

Haig did not seem to find anything unusual in all this. He certainly saw no reason to believe that any improvement could be hoped for from the Australians until he was allowed to shoot a few.[54] Nor did he see any cause for concern in the general war situation: his only fear was 'that the enemy would find our front so very strong that he will hesitate to commit his Army with the almost certainty of losing very heavily'.[55] Nineteen days later the greatest military operation of all time fell on the British front between the Sensee and the Oise. The four months' battle that followed cost both armies something like three-quarters of a million casualties. It was however a genuine war of attrition, which the Germans could not possibly win. They retained their numerical edge up to the end of June 1918, but they were already opposed by odds of 24,000 guns against 18,000; 6,100 aircraft in the combat zone against 3,000; and 5,385 tanks against 90.[56] Their efforts might still have succeeded, but for the fact that their troops were exhausted, the scrapings of the German manpower barrel, only half as well fed as their enemies; they lacked fresh or adequately fed horses for cavalry or even for transport; and Ludendorff repeatedly fumbled his own strategy. Successive German bids for a breakthrough were stopped at Arras by the British Third Army; at Amiens by a scratch force under United States General George G. Carey; at Armentières by the British Second Army; at Château-Thierry by the Americans; outside Soissons by the French; and at Epernay by a combination of all Allied forces.

The troops of the British Dominions had played little part in actually checking the German offensives of 1918. The Australians had naturally fancied that only they would be able to stop the Germans: as 5th Division AIF swaggered north, enjoying rather than depressed by the sight of British deserters on the way, one of them called out to a French civilian: 'Fini retreat, Madame, fini retreat – beaucoup Australiens ici.'[57] The retreat was finished before the Australians reached the battlefront. It was however their role to provide impetus to the Allied counter-offensive, and convince the Germans that they had lost the war, and not merely a campaign. Ludendorff had hoped to hold the line of the Somme at least until the Allies were prepared to settle for a compromise peace. But the Australians stormed Peronne–Mont Saint-Quentin on 2 September, while the British and Canadians broke through the Drocourt–Queant line. The Australian achievement at Peronne may well indeed have been the most remarkable infantry achievement of the war: exhausted troops, without substantial artillery support, overran long-prepared and wired positions held by superior numbers of Germans, certainly no more weary than their attackers. The victors themselves had no doubts as to the reason for their success: Fritz had given the game away: as one of the attackers wrote home afterwards, 'if the German had had the fighting spirit of a louse, one battalion on the whole brigade front would have made it impossible to go forward; but he never fought an inch so far as we were concerned.'[58] This was in itself the best index of the Australian achievement: the most formidable army in the world was no longer prepared to put forward the kind of effort required to resist an Australian offensive.

Visiting Australian newspapermen eagerly attended a conference called by Haig after the battle, expecting some belated recognition of what their countrymen had achieved. Haig instead lectured them on the grave need to extend the death penalty to Australia's national forces. He noted, as a matter apparently worth recording, that the editors seemed 'very much surprised' by his choice of subject.[59] They should not have been: the whole experience of the Empire in the war had served to underline one simple fact of life: the British leadership would never be prepared to admit that the systems that produced the most dedicated and most successful soldiers they had could possibly be regarded as anything but inferior to their own. Haig even went out of his way to disparage the Canadians, probably the most generally highly esteemed army corps in the world: he told the Canadian Ministers of Defence and Marine, naturally 'well-meaning but second-rate sort of people', that their insistence on trying to keep their divisions united as a corps had meant that 'the British Army alone and unaided by Canadian troops withstood the first terrific blow made by 80 German Divisions on March 21st . . .'.[60] What the Canadians had frequently done alone and unaided was of course never mentioned. But Haig did not despair of the Empire: he found some officers from the South African Defence Forces, 'who are spending a few months with the Army to learn our administrative system', to be 'most pleasant and full of enthusiasm for the British Army and our people. . . . The war has broken down the feelings of prejudice which existed between Colonials and Englishmen in the Old Country. This is all most satisfactory.'[61]

It was perhaps not to be wondered at if this enthusiasm was most apparent among those colonials who were least exposed to the impact of British military leadership in France. Australia and Canada could apparently expect nothing from Haig, but Haig was expecting more from them than was humanly possible. The Australian Corps in particular was falling apart from sheer physical exhaustion. Officers and men mutinied briefly on 14 September when denied a night's rest after a week's continuous fighting.[62] The realization that efforts that should have been proclaimed throughout the world as supreme examples of military prowess were literally going unrecorded was also having its effect: 'in the 4th Brigade, which had snatched a costly victory from the difficult situation left by the failure of English troops on its left, a discontented section was growling: "Whatever we do they'll say *they* won the battle; next time we'll let them win it." '[63]

The blame was not entirely due to Haig's reluctance to admit that anything could be commendable about the military efforts of colonials. There was also a real semantic problem deriving from the ambiguity of the term 'British', which was normally used by correspondents to refer to troops from the white Dominions, as well as to those from the United Kingdom itself. The confusion was aggravated by the fact that the term 'imperial', which would seem naturally to imply 'colonial', was in fact used in Britain and most other parts of the Empire to refer exclusively to units from the United Kingdom. The result was that readers of news-paper reports of the fighting could gain only the vaguest impression of the respective contributions being made by the colonial divisions, and readers of *The Times* would never have known that the Canadians and Australians were taking part in the fighting in France at all.

William Morris Hughes had tried to do something about this. He had sought to counterbalance this policy of concealing the colonial con-tribution by inviting a troupe of publicists and men of letters to watch the Australians break through the Hindenburg Line, like a prudent pro-ducer inviting a gaggle of tame critics to the opening night of a variety show.[64] More seriously, he intervened directly and in the most un-compromising way to save the AIF from destruction. His concern was not only to save Australian lives and avert mutiny. Allied military advisers were still planning for the campaigns of 1919 or even 1920. But Australia did not have the resources of manpower to maintain its five divisions in the field, at the present rate of wastage. A smaller AIF in the final victory campaign would presumably mean a reduced voice for Australia at the peace conference. Uncertain of how much support he could count on in Melbourne, Hughes simply bluffed: when advised to arrange matters with Haig, he replied: 'I shall not see Haig or any one else. If the Belgian Government wants its troops withdrawn from the line it does not ask anyone's leave. It simply says they are to be with-drawn.' When his own General Monash demurred, Hughes told him that he wanted the troops out of the line by 15 October, and Monash's own position would depend on their being out.[65]

The anomalies and contradictions of the imperial relationship were reaching flashpoint even as the forces of the Empire moved on towards their most complete victory over perhaps their most formidable opponent. From one point of view at least, the German bid for an armistice on 11 November 1918 could only be regarded as representing the pinnacle of British power. In numerical terms at any rate, the defeat of Germany and the collapse of Russia left the British Empire the greatest military power on earth. The fact was that no country in the world in November 1918 had as many men actually under arms and available for service as Great Britain and its various colonies and dependencies. The measure of its naval supremacy in particular had never been approached before. The Royal Navy numbered at the end of hostilities 70 capital ships, 120 cruisers, 466 destroyers, 147 submarines, and 4 aircraft carriers and seaplane tenders. The German Navy, still the second largest in the world, was to be interned at Scapa Flow under British supervision. The United States Navy was indeed growing rapidly, but still numbered only 39 battleships, 35 cruisers, 131 destroyers and 86 submarines. For the rest, the British could deploy 16 more battleships, 48 more cruisers and 256 more destroyers than France, Japan and Italy combined.[66] The British had also developed by far the largest aircraft industry in the world, employing 347,112 workers, almost twice as many as the French. British military aviation could deploy 22,171 serviceable aircraft, 50 per cent more than the French, again the second-ranking power.

At the same time the achievements of British industry were not wholly reassuring. Germany, for example, produced as much steel as Britain and France put together. Even France by itself had outproduced the United Kingdom in almost every category of military hardware. Including equipment made available to the Americans, French industry had supplied some 109,000 trucks, 16,000 guns and 8,000 first-line aircraft. Britain by contrast had produced only 31,770 trucks, 7,410 guns and 3,522 aircraft for service in the western battle zone, and a considerably smaller quantity for the other theatres of war. Even the tank, originally a British conception, was being constructed in greater numbers in France than in the land of its birth: 2,385 British tanks were available for service at the end of the war, and 2,756 French.[67] The French aircraft industry had produced in all 67,982 airframes and 85,317 engines during the war years, compared with a British output of 55,093 frames and 41,034 engines; and the United States had produced in twenty-one months as many engines as British factories in four and a quarter years.[68] The effect of these figures could only be to call in question Britain's capacity in industrial terms to wage war successfully unaided against another major power.

Its capacity in terms of manpower was something else again. Britain had been undoubtedly able to deploy enormous and highly effective numbers of fighting men, although here again it could only be noted that Germany, with a population about the same as that of the United

Kingdom and the white Dominions, had been able to field an army 50 per cent larger than the united forces of the British Empire, including India. The figures of the imperial contribution were revealing in other ways too. What they showed most strikingly was that the various parts of the Empire showed markedly differing degrees of enthusiasm when it came to enlisting for service in the first place, and also for actual combat when they arrived at the front. For example, 11 per cent of the total population of the United Kingdom was in uniform at some time or other during the war; 8.8 per cent of the population of New Zealand; 6.9 per cent of the Australian; 5 per cent of the Canadian; 2.2 per cent of the South African; and 0.3 per cent of the population of India. There were of course several factors operating to distort these statistics: for example, Quebec, with 30 per cent of the population of Canada, produced only 5 per cent of its volunteers; and a relatively high proportion of the Australian population had to be retained for essential agricultural production. What was perhaps more truly significant was that 47 per cent of troops from the United Kingdom were listed as battle casualties; 66 per cent of those from Australia; 58 per cent of those from New Zealand; 49 per cent of those from Canada; 14 per cent of those from South Africa; and 9 per cent of the Indians. Moreover 6.7 per cent of the British casualties were prisoners of war; as were 8.3 per cent of the South Africans, and 9.9 per cent of the Indians, but only 1.9 per cent of the Australians and Canadians, and a tiny 0.8 per cent of the New Zealanders.

But the most impressive index was that showing how the actual numbers of killed and wounded were divided. On this basis the United Kingdom provided 79.3 per cent of the actual combat casualties; Australia, 7.0 per cent; Canada, 6.9 per cent; India, 4.3 per cent; New Zealand, 1.9 per cent; and South Africa, 0.6 per cent; while all the rest of the colonial Empire supplied only 1,317 killed and wounded out of a total of 2,998,583.[69] Moreover most of the British, Australian and New Zealand casualties and all of the Canadian were suffered fighting against the Germans, the most formidable enemy the Empire had ever faced, in the decisive theatre of the war on the western front; most of the South African casualties were involved in peripheral engagements against tiny German forces in Africa, as well as against other South Africans, who had seized the opportunity to rebel against British rule; and most of the Indian losses occurred at the hands of other Asians, the Turks, in campaigns admittedly more extensive but little more relevant to the actual outcome of the war.

All this pointed to one conclusion: the military relevance of the British Empire in a conflict with another great power depended on the fighting capacity of the British people themselves, in the Home Islands, Canada and Australasia. The South African contribution could only be marginal, so long as the fate of the African possessions depended on the outcome of warfare outside the continent; the huge Indian army could effectively be employed only against opponents as ill-equipped and unwieldy as itself; and the other colonies could provide only token contributions. It was indeed conceivable that the huge mass of the colonial Empire might be regarded as a positive military liability, considering the extent to which British resources had to be diverted from areas of higher strategic priority for the training and even defence of the Asian and African possessions. By contrast the Canadians in particular had provided supplies of munitions far beyond the requirements of their own armed forces: Canadian exports to the United Kingdom increased forty-fold during the war years, and Canadian factories produced 3,000 aircraft and 30 per cent of the ammunition used on the western front in 1917 and 1918. More remarkable still, the Royal Canadian Naval Service had grown to more than three times the size of the Royal Australian Navy in number of ships and nearly twice its size in personnel by the end of the war.

The British peoples, beyond the seas as well as in the Home Islands, had indeed demonstrated qualities that entitled them to be regarded as the most formidable power left standing after the defeat of Germany. How long they could hold this position would depend entirely on how well the imperial unity of the war years could be carried over into times of peace.

6 One-power standard (1919–25)

Imperial unity as understood before 1914 would clearly never survive the end of the war. This was indicated sufficiently clearly by the statistics of military performance. But the divisions were far more serious than even these implied. It was only to be anticipated that Smuts of South Africa should be looking forward to the dissolution of imperial authority into a 'dynamic and evolving system of states which would better take for itself the new name of Commonwealth', and in which the Afrikaaners would be able to reverse the verdict of Vereeniging and extend their authority over British South Africa as well as the original Boer states.[1] Nor was it surprising that the Canadians, appalled at the bitterness of the division revealed between Quebec and British Canada, should be concerned to affirm control over their own foreign policy. What was singular however was the chasm opening between the Anzac Dominions and the United Kingdom.

The issue here was basically over Britain's almost invisible ally, Japan. Colonial Secretary Harcourt had assured Munro-Ferguson on 6 December 1914 that: 'our fleets were so fully engaged in the North Sea, Atlantic, Mediterranean and in convoy of troops across the Indian Ocean that we could not spare enough to deal with the Pacific. We had therefore to call in Japanese aid.'[2] But the fact was that the aid of the Japanese fleet could hardly be shown to be indispensable. It was in the first place not very extensive: the battlecruiser *Ibuki* provided a superfluous escort for the First Anzac Convoy in September–November 1914; two destroyers patrolled the waters north of Queensland in January 1915; a cruiser visited Rabaul in April; two more visited Australian ports in July 1916; three cruisers and eight destroyers escorted Indian convoys to Alexandria in March 1917; and three light cruisers guarded the coast of Western Australia when the entire destroyer force of the RAN was moved to the Mediterranean. Moreover the Japanese presence was never actually militarily necessary, as the

Japanese ships never actually came in contact with the enemy. Finally the Japanese ships were in any case only required to substitute for the RAN, which would have been far more than sufficient to perform all the functions allotted to the Japanese had it only been allowed to carry out the duties for which it was created in the first place.

All this was realized and resented by the Australians. Munro-Ferguson warned Harcourt early in 1915 that 'Australia regards the Pacific as her "duck-pond" ' to such an extent that even the occupation of Samoa by New Zealand rankled a little, as 'it is felt that she got there thanks to the protection of the Australian fleet . . .'.[3] Feeling about Japan was much more bitter: the United States naval attaché noted with satisfaction that 'the Japs are thought over here to be on the make, and they hope that the US will stop them going too far'.[4] The explanation for Britain's invitation to Japan to intervene was in fact quite simple: the real advantage to be gained from Japanese intervention on the side of the Allies was that it ensured that Japan would not be intervening on the other side. The Foreign Office did not doubt that Japan would have to be bribed to stand by its alliance commitments: Grey indeed accepted that if Britain had barred the expansion of Japanese interests in the Pacific, it would have been to Japan's advantage to have thrown its lot in with Germany.[5]

What was involved finally was a simple division of the spoils of conquest. The question was how to carve up the former German colonies in the Pacific. It was a quadrilateral confrontation: the Japanese expected an appropriate reward for supporting the winning side; the United States, as personified by President Wilson, was fundamentally unsympathetic to territorial aggrandisement by the victors for any reason; the Australians were determined to annex the German colonies as an island barrier against future Japanese aggression directed at themselves; and the British were anxious to disregard Australian interests to placate both the Americans and the Japanese, if this were possible. Personalities were distinctly relevant.

The issue of Japan at least was one on which the United States and the Southern Dominions could find common ground. This was obscured for a time by wrangles on other issues: for example, Hughes assured Deputy Prime Minister Watt that he would certainly decline to agree to Wilson's peace terms as long as they had the effect of hampering Australia's tariff-making powers in respect of the mandated territories.[6]

He also complained that the British had not given the slightest prefer-
ence to Australian meat exporters, 'although the Dominions supplied
meat during the war at prices far below America . . . so far from those in
charge of the Empire's economic interests trying to help the Empire
hold its own they seem and indeed are playing into America's hands'.[7]
But distrust of the United States was overshadowed easily by fear of
Japan. Australian officials noted firmly that a recent comment on im-
migration in the Japanese press was 'couched in a tone which bodes no
good for Australia'.[8] In point of fact the British themselves were no less
apprehensive about their ally: as early as 1919 their Far Eastern problem as
such had been identified as the problem of Japan's position in China.[9] The
head of the Far Eastern Department of the Foreign Office noted that the
Japanese dispensation in Korea 'has been brutal in the extreme'.[10] The
British Minister in Tokyo commented that 'were the Japanese nation
as a whole to have its way, there would not be a single trade-mart of
any importance on the China coast or inland, any strategical position
on the whole north border of the Pacific, or a single raw material
producing district within the Pacific zone available for any one else'.[11]

At the very least one could hardly feel that an ally possessing these
characteristics was one with which any other power would care to be
associated for long. But there was a still more serious side to the problem
of Japan. On 25 November 1918 the Admiralty approved the notion of
'Lord Jellicoe undertaking a Mission to report upon the naval defence
and arrangements of the Empire, visiting each Dominion in turn'.[12] By
3 March, having got as far as Port Said, Jellicoe had already decided on a
formula for British postwar naval requirements, based on the need to
safeguard the security of imperial sea communications, without necessarily identifying any specific enemy whom it was appropriate to guard
against. He began by admitting the great difficulty in the way of attempting to compete with the United States, if that country were determined
to possess the strongest fleet of capital ships in the world. He was
accordingly prepared to settle for a battle force 'of a strength of 70% that
of the United States'. Such a force would not actually involve great
additional expenditure: it would in fact be necessary for Britain to
acquire only twelve more capital ships, constructed at a rate of three
per year, to achieve a total battle force of thirty ships of not much more
than ten years in age on average, as against forty-one ships of this order
that the United States Navy was expected to have in service by the end

of 1925. The burden of rearming to this level would of course be made still easier if the British were to take the modern German Dreadnoughts, *Baden, Bayen, Hindenburg* and *Derfflinger*, and add them to the strength of the Royal Navy.[13]

The same downright rationality that led Jellicoe to accept United States naval primacy as the wave of the future also led him to identify without hesitation the prospective enemy against which British naval planning should be directed. He reported from HMS *New Zealand* that 'Japan is as much a bogey to India as it is to Australia'.[14] In an enormously detailed memorandum to the Governor-General of Australia, he affirmed that it was 'almost inevitable that the interests of Japan and of the British Empire will eventually clash, and the two parts of the Empire most affected are Australia and India'.[15] He accordingly considered that 'the naval interests of the Empire are likely to demand within the next five years a Far Eastern seagoing fleet of considerable strength . . . composed of – 8 Battleships of modern 'Dreadnought' type. 8 Battle-cruisers, also of modern type. 10 Light cruisers. 40 Modern destroyers. 3 Flotilla leaders . . . 4 Aircraft-carriers . . .'.[16] The cost of provision and maintenance of this huge force was to be borne 75 per cent by the United Kingdom, 20 per cent by Australia and 5 per cent by New Zealand. It was therefore a matter of 'very urgent necessity for the establishment of a dock at Singapore large enough to take any modern ship'.[17] Jellicoe also endorsed unhesitatingly the views of Prime Minister Hughes on the strategic importance to Australia of the South Pacific islands: 'any foothold of Japan in an island of the Dutch East Indies possessing a good harbour would constitute the most serious threat to Australian sea communications to the westward and to Singapore, and is not to be thought of.'[18]

Jellicoe's unreserved acceptance of Australian strategic and racial attitudes was the more convincing in view of his general lack of enthusiasm for Australians in general and their navy in particular. He was for example glad to say that the bearing of the officers and men of HMS *New Zealand* 'has made a great impression on the better-class Australians. They have compared it with the bearing of men from the Royal Australian Navy to the disadvantage of the latter. . . . The greatest difficulty with which Australia is at present faced with regard to naval affairs is without doubt the absence of discipline . . . the R.A.N. lacks something which the R.N. possesses. . . .'[19]

What the RAN was indeed going to lack very soon was ships, unless orders for new construction were placed promptly. But the Australian government could not frame a rational naval policy until it could be certain what British strategy in the Pacific was going to be.

The situation was not really altered when Jellicoe's plan for annexing the latest German capital ships to the Royal Navy foundered with Battle Force High Seas Fleet, when the Germans scuttled their ships in Scapa Flow in June 1919. However Britain could hardly have lost a naval race with Japan, even if it could not have won one with the United States. Jellicoe's original component of sixteen capital ships for a Far Eastern Fleet might not have been available, but a force of that size would not be necessary to deter the Japanese. But the Admiralty had already rejected all of Jellicoe's proposals on 31 October,[20] apart from his recommendation that 'there is a very urgent necessity for the establish-ment of a dock at Singapore large enough to take any modern ships'.[21] Moreover, although in favour of constructing a dock at Singapore, the Admiralty did not apparently believe that Britain could spare a fleet to use the dock: they replied to a suggestion from the Foreign Office about the 'desirability of basing a powerful squadron upon Singapore',[22] by claiming that: 'Without considerable increase in Naval expenditure . . . they do not see their way to maintain Forces sufficient to support a strong policy involving a possible coercion of Japan.'[23] The Admiralty none the less considered 'a continuation of the Alliance in its present form neither necessary nor desirable'.[24]

But in fact the Alliance would be both necessary and desirable if the British government were resolved not to maintain an adequate fleet in the Pacific. The choice was clear, under the welter of irreconcilable official opinions. Nobody trusted the Japanese. The only question was whether it was more expedient to constrain their aggressive tendencies with an alliance, or coerce them with a fleet. There was no doubt that the protagonists of the alliance solution tended to be a trifle subjective in their arguments: Eliot for example expressed the view from Tokyo that he had never met with 'more honourable and reasonable colleagues' than the Japanese higher officials; deplored the 'vulgarly abusive epithets' used by British military and naval officers of high rank to describe the Japanese; and was sure that the alliance 'cannot but be beneficial to our Dominions, for at least it must tend to moderate any ambitions of the Japanese in the Pacific . . .'.[25]

What was quite evident was that the intrusion of Dominion opinion was no more welcome in this situation than it had ever been in any other: when Edmund L. Piesse, formerly Director of Military Intelligence for the Australian government and thereafter Director of the Pacific Branch of the Prime Minister's Department, arrived in Tokyo, Alston hastened to warn Curzon that he was not convinced that 'the discretion of Major Piesse could absolutely be relied upon . . .'.[26] It was of course desirable from the viewpoint of imperial relations that the Australians should not be allowed to discover that the Foreign Office still pretended that: 'From the moment Japan entered the war on August 23rd, the safety of Australia, New Zealand, the Pacific Islands, the Pacific Coast of Canada, Hong Kong, Wei-Hai Wei and the British Merchant Marine in the Far East was assured, and the complete destruction of Germany's power in the Pacific was merely a matter of time.'[27] It would have been all too easy for an Australian to have pointed out, in unequivocal language, that the very exiguous power of Germany in the Pacific had been destroyed by Australia and New Zealand; that Canada had never been in any real danger from anything, and had in any case been under the limited umbrella of the Royal Australian Navy; and that the British Empire in the Far East had never been under threat from anybody at the time except from Japan itself.

The regrettable truth was that this was still the case. The Australian Department of Defence reported frankly that: 'While the Naval strength of the Empire is disposed as at present, and while the Naval bases in the Far East and the Pacific remain so insufficient, it must be conceded that Japan could have a temporary sea command in the Pacific. . . . The ultimate fate of Australia is dependent upon the security of the Empire's sea communications but it must be conceded that Australia is exposed to the danger of invasion.'[28] In this situation it was understandable that Rear Admiral Sir Percy Grant, First Member of the Australian Naval Board, should have spoken of the 'sigh of relief' that the country would breathe if only the United States were to go to war with Japan and thus 'remove from us a deadly menace'.[29] This view was not without support even in the Foreign Office: Sir Bruce Alston now argued for 'the maintenance of an adequate Anglo-Saxon fleet in the Pacific, based upon say Hawaii and Singapore. . . . Even the Japanese militarists, reckless though they have shown themselves in some respects, would shrink from such a gamble with the fates.'[30]

The issue could not be avoided much longer. Meanwhile in Australia Hughes complained furiously that he was 'groping in the dark' in his attempts to extract some clear notions on imperial defence from the British.[31] Even the trustful New Zealanders had become sufficiently concerned to ask the Australian government for details of merchant ships that could be used for patrol or defensive purposes.[32] The Australians replied eagerly, adding for their part that 'information as to how far Lord Jellicoe's recommendations will be attempted by your Government would be useful'.[33] The only answer would of course have been that the New Zealanders had no idea. The British had in any case given the Jellicoe Plan away: as a Cabinet memorandum expressed it, their objective in the Far East was now the totally opposite one of maintaining 'peace and fair play for all nations' and avoiding competition in armaments.[34] But this was only one aspect of imperial disarray.

Canadian spokesmen had continued to insist on the overriding importance of what Borden optimistically called the 'league of the two great English-speaking Commonwealths[35] . . . the assured goodwill and clear understanding between Great Britain and the United States[36] . . . a virtual alliance between the two great English-speaking nations . . .'.[37] Their anxiety to develop a relationship of special cordiality with the United States mounted with Harding's victory in November 1921, in circumstances that made it at least unlikely that he would be leading the United States into the League of Nations. Part of the opposition in the United States to the League unquestionably was inspired by fear of what appeared to be the excessive voting rights of the British Empire.[38] Nothing could presumably be done about that. But something could be done about the other element tending to exacerbate Anglo-American relations, the alliance with Japan. In February 1921 the Canadian government recommended directly to the British that every possible effort should be made to find an alternative to the renewal of the Japanese alliance. It was proposed instead that Britain should 'terminate the Alliance and endeavour at once to bring about a Conference of Pacific Powers – i.e. Japan, China, the United States and the British Empire represented by Great Britain, Canada, Australia and New Zealand – for the purpose of adjusting Pacific and Far East questions'.[39] The Colonial Office replied that it would be necessary to consult the other Dominions before such a proposal could be approved.[40] The Canadians therefore pressed harder, emphasizing 'the very special

Canadian position in this matter. Of the Canadian people more than of any other people whatever it is true that their welfare and their security are intimately involved in any question vitally affecting the relations between the British Empire and the United States. . . . From the Canadian point of view it might become necessary to consider an alternative solution by which only those parts of the Empire desiring to do so should join in the renewal.'[41]

It was only fair to say that the Canadian point of view was not the only one possible. The Australians were also concerned that 'nothing be done to create diversion between us and the USA', as Hughes stated on 7 April. But as he also made clear, there was a security issue as well: 'we have set up the banner of a White Australia. . . . We are as it were the advance guard of the white population of the world.'[42] None the less the alliance with Japan meant everything to Australia, in Hughes's opinion, even if only as a means of curbing Japanese intentions of aggression. But the essence of the Australian position was simply that it was the country that had the greatest right to have its views on the alliance respected, as the country whose interests were most directly affected, and the country whose concern with imperial defence was indicated by the fact that it spent more on naval preparedness than all the other Dominions put together, as Hughes claimed. This was indeed an actual understatement: on a *per capita* calculation, Australia was spending 8s 2d per unit of population on its navy, New Zealand 4s 7d, Canada 1s 4d and South Africa nothing.[43] Figures for total defence expenditure were less disproportionate admittedly. The fact however remained that Australia's total expenditure of 17s 3d was of a very different order from South Africa's 11s 8d, New Zealand's 10s 7d and particularly Canada's 7s 3d.

It would therefore have seemed at the least extraordinary if the British government had inclined to the view of the Dominion that made by far the smallest economic contribution to imperial defence, and the national security of which could be affected only in the most minimal degree by the renewal or the abandonment of the alliance. The British did not however identify themselves with the Australian case: they merely told the Canadians that the proposal for a conference of Pacific powers 'is one which may well be discussed by the Imperial Cabinet, but it is impossible for us to prejudge at this stage in view of the attitude adopted by Australia'.[44]

But the Australian attitude was perhaps not inflexible. On 5 May 1921 the Admiralty made a proposal that would have gone at least part of the way towards allaying Antipodean anxieties. A naval base should be developed at Singapore, 'secure and self-contained against the maximum scale of naval attack, without fleet support, for a period of six weeks'.[45] So long as there was a base, one might always hope that a fleet might come from somewhere to operate from it.

The Four Power Naval Limitation Treaty signed by the representatives of Britain, the United States, Japan and France on 6 February 1922 did indeed arrest the naval race in the Pacific. In essence it was agreed that the ratio of 5:5:3 should be adopted for the relative size of the battle forces of the first three countries; that no new capital ships should be laid down for the next ten years; and that ships in service or already under construction should be scrapped before 17 February 1925 until the agreed tonnages had been reached. The result effectively would be to leave the United States and Britain with fifteen capital ships each by 1925, and Japan with ten. The two-power standard had been abandoned forever. The British Empire could now defend itself only on one front at a time. However it appeared that the British government was at least seriously thinking of fighting on a front outside the North Sea: on 22 February 1922 a committee chaired by Winston Churchill recommended that a properly defended base be built at Singapore, because if Singapore were lost during the first two or three months of a war with Japan, the whole of the Pacific might fall under Japanese supremacy, and many years might elapse before Britain or the United States would be able to re-enter in effective strength.[46]

The report of the Churchill Committee helped to allay imperial anxieties aroused by the Four Power Treaty. Hughes and Pearce both claimed that the treaty might bring peace to Australia and the Pacific for the next ten years. On 28 June the Australian government decided to cut naval spending by £500,000, pay off their submarine force, and scrap HMAS *Australia*, despite a final warning by Creswell, which could count as his last salute to the navy and the nation he had served so well.

Singapore shone forth again as the unifying symbol of Imperial defence. The British government decided in May to begin to implement the recommendations of the Churchill Committee. Support for the Singapore Strategy was not indeed unanimous, even among the defence-conscious. Admiral Sir Reginald Henderson argued that the main base for a fleet for the defence of Australia and the Pacific had to be Australia itself. Colonel Repington warned in the correspondence columns of the *Daily Telegraph* that it was 'the tradition of Japan to seize the initiative'; and that it would therefore be necessary to 'expect the loss of Singapore and Hong Kong before our Grand Fleet trails out there'.[47] But this was a cause lost long since. Prime Minister Stanley Bruce summarized the necessary viewpoint of Australia in a speech that set forth the basic articles of faith of Australian foreign and defence policy:

> We are driven to the conclusion that if we are to have an adequate defence of this country we must have some naval force and that can only be provided by alliance with some other power . . . to every serious Australian there is only one natural ally for us and that is the rest of the British Empire. . . . It is for us the Imperial Conference to try and evolve an imperial defence scheme that will give reasonable protection to the whole of the Empire without casting an intolerable burden upon the different parts. . . . At one time there was a suggestion that we should have a Dominion unit operating in the Pacific, to which all the Dominions should contribute. I think that Australia would welcome that today. . . . During the whole period covered by the attempt to bring about an Empire Defence scheme Australia has done more in regard to naval defence than all the other Dominions put together. . . . We have to try to maintain the unity of the whole and complete autonomy of the different parts. . . . We have to realise that the basis of an Empire foreign policy involves the whole future of the Empire. . . . If such a basis cannot be found I believe that failure to find it will eventually lead to the disintegration of the Empire.[48]

Moving to the actual issue of the Singapore base, Bruce then claimed, in perhaps the most perceptive vision of reality ever achieved by any speaker on the concerns of the British Empire, that: 'The provision of this base is a condition precedent to a large fleet being stationed in Australian waters or the Pacific. . . . Great Britain has recognised that the heart of the Empire is not now in the North Sea but has moved to the Pacific.' It might have been more precise, if less felicitous, to have suggested that the Empire had two hearts, one in the North Sea and the other in the Pacific. But in terms of defence policy, Bruce's vision was exact. The whole problem of imperial defence was the problem of the defence of the Eastern Empire. It had to be presumed that means could be found to defend the Home Islands themselves against an invasion from the European continent; Canada would be defended by the United States, and could not be defended against the United States; Africa was scarcely accessible, and in any event it could be expected that any fleet that could safeguard the Home Islands could also safeguard the sea routes to Alexandria or Cape Town.

This analysis of imperial realities should have seemed axiomatic. It did not however evoke general enthusiasm at the Imperial Conference of October 1923. The Canadians had already identified themselves with the interests of the United States to such a degree as to appear an American rather than a British nation, in any sense of the word. Asked by J. S. Woodsworth in the House of Commons if he acquiesced in the British decision to spend £10 million on developing the naval base at Singapore, Mackenzie King had replied unhelpfully that it was for the British government to decide their own policy, and for the Canadians to express no opinions concerning it.[49] At the Imperial Conference itself the main concern of the Canadian representatives appeared to be to persuade their colleagues to waive the principle of the 3-mile limit on the right of search at sea, in order to assist the United States in regulating the liquor traffic. On the general issue of Commonwealth foreign policy King took the essentially non-committal position that Canada 'has some responsibility to other parts of the British Empire as well as to herself', but that 'that responsibility and the extent of it will be determined by this parliament and will be determined, I believe, in a manner which will accord with the hearts and the feelings of the people of this country . . .'.[50] This could literally mean anything. Nor was he the only dispiriting presence. General Smuts of South Africa hastened to undermine the Singapore Strategy in its essence: he warned that he was 'very doubtful whether Australia or New Zealand could safely rely on a division of the Fleet in a future contingency for their protection by a movement of the Fleet from here to those waters. I am very doubtful about the whole thing.' He did not unfortunately suggest an answer to the problem of what Australia and New Zealand were expected to do if they could not rely on a fleet arriving.

The only practical alternative might have seemed to be to push on with the implementation of the original Jellicoe Plan for a Far Eastern fleet, to which Bruce had alluded. This was not proposed at the conference. The representatives did indeed note the 'deep interest of the Commonwealth of Australia, the Dominion of New Zealand and India, in the provision of a Naval Base at Singapore, as essential for ensuring the mobility necessary to provide for the security of the territories and trade of the Empire in Eastern Waters'.[51] But the conference also noted the 'necessity for the maintenance by Great Britain of a Home Defence Air Force of sufficient strength to give adequate protection against air attacks by the strongest air force within striking distance of her shores'.[52] This was both reasonable and necessary: the Royal Air Force had declined in strength and quality from being the most formidable in the world at the end of 1918, to being probably the weakest among the great powers five years later. There was however an essential difference between the two propositions: expenditure on the Home Defence Air Force would automatically help to secure the protection of the Home Islands; expenditure on a naval base at Singapore would secure the protection of the Eastern Empire only if there was sure to be a fleet available to be serviced by the base.

It would at least have been better than nothing. But nothing was what the Eastern Empire was going to get. The new British Labour Prime Minister, Ramsay MacDonald, announced on 20 February 1924 that his government 'have decided for the time being to incur no further expenditure on the *Singapore Naval Base*'.[53]

The Australians were used to feeling abandoned. General Sir Harry Chauvel, Inspector-General of the Australian Military Forces, had no doubt that the new British policy meant nothing less than exposing the Empire to Japanese aggression: as he reported to Federal Parliament:

> The reduction of the British Navy to a one-power standard, taken in conjunction with its strategic location in peace, determines that it will be unable on the outbreak of war to intervene effectively in the Pacific. The postponement of the programme to construct a first class naval base at Singapore must inevitably add to (if it does not indefinitely prolong) the time which will elapse after the outbreak of war, before a superior British Fleet will be able effectively to operate in the defence of Australia . . . in the meantime, an enemy possessing temporary naval ascendancy might find the way clear for . . . action against Australia.[54]

There was only one thing to be done. On 27 June Stanley Bruce introduced to Federal Parliament a five-year programme of naval rearmament, involving primarily the building of two 10,000-ton cruisers and two oceangoing submarines for the Royal Australian Navy, to help defend 'the most wonderful unprotected white man's country in the world . . .'.[55] The effect in economic terms was to more than double Australian naval expenditure, from 8s 2d per head in 1922 to 17s 2d per head in 1925, at a time when British naval spending had fallen from 26s 8d to 25s 7d per head; and Canadian, from 1s 4d to 2d. Bruce could at least feel that he had his reward: on 26 November the new Conservative government decided to commence at last construction of a naval base at Singapore.

This was still not quite the same as an option for a dynamic defence policy. Urgency was the last characteristic that the new regime was to show. The British Cabinet indeed came almost immediately to the conclusion that 'in existing circumstances aggressive action against the British Empire on the part of Japan within the next ten years is not a contingency seriously to be apprehended'.[56] The Eastern Empire could wait. How long it would have to wait would in turn depend upon the operation of the new one-power standard of imperial defence, defined impressively by the Chiefs of Staff as meaning that:

> The requirements of a One-Power Standard are satisfied if our fleet, wherever situated, is equal to the fleet of any other nation, wherever situated, provided that arrangements are made from time to time, in different parts of the world, according as the International situation requires, to enable the local forces to maintain the situation against vital and irreparable damage pending the arrival of the Main Fleet, and to give the Main Fleet on arrival sufficient mobility. . . .[57]

It may not be true that a badly expressed policy is necessarily a bad policy. One can however entertain misgivings about a defence policy that is literally incomprehensible. Certain implications could admittedly be discerned in the almost total darkness of the Chiefs of Staff's syntax. The British fleet should be at least as formidable as that of any other country in the world; the local defences of the various parts of the Empire should be sufficiently strong to hold out until the main fleet came to the rescue; and the main fleet should have bases to operate from when it eventually arrived on the scene.

But even this could not be taken as certain: the British supplied Australia with a confidential report on demand, which admitted that the chaos in China might lead at any time to armed intervention, and approved the concept of 'a strong position at Singapore and power to defend it'; but argued that a deliberate build-up of British naval strength in the Pacific might have a deplorable effect on Anglo-Japanese relations.[58] Winston Churchill indeed ridiculed the practice of 'measuring our naval strength against this fancied danger from Japan';[59] although serious observers had forecast the danger for the past thirty years, and there was in any case no other meaningful yardstick to measure British naval strength against. Defence planning indeed seemed to be increasingly relegated to some world of the imagination: when the Australian Inspector-General reported that 'local defence can only be maintained behind the sheltering screen of the combined fleets of the British Commonwealth', and that this meant that 'requisite fuel and repair bases must be provided at strategic points . . . to permit these combined fleets to operate',[60] the Committee of Imperial Defence produced a strategic review that simply assumed that the Singapore naval base had been completed; that a squadron of battlecruisers had been added to the Far Eastern Fleet; and that the British main fleet would arrive at Singapore within forty-two days of the outbreak of war. The British also agreed to modify the principles of the 1923 Imperial Conference, 'to cover the following specific two-power [*sic*] standard':

(i)   To enable a Fleet to be placed in the Far East fully adequate to act on the defensive and to serve as a strong deterrent to any threat to our interests in that part of the globe;

(ii) To maintain in all circumstances in Home Waters a force able to meet the requirements of a war with Germany at the same time.[61]

But the fact was that the Royal Navy was even now barely a match for the Japanese Combined Fleet alone, without considering how much of its strength would have to be detained to face a threat from a rearmed Germany. The British had two battlecruisers, *Renown* and *Repulse*, which could catch any of the Japanese battle force, but which also could not have fought any of them in a ship-to-ship encounter; they had *Hood*, which could indeed catch and probably fight any of the four Kongos, although certainly not more than one at a time; they had the ten Royal Sovereigns and Queen Elizabeths, which would be a match ship for ship for the four Fusos and Ises; but the Japanese now had the two eight 16-inch gun Nagatos, which would clearly be too much individually for any ship the British had yet in service. The odds were alarmingly even.

There was similarly little margin either way in the category of naval air power. The British were far stronger in seaborne air capacity, with 108 aircraft embarked in six carriers, supported by a dozen assorted flying boats or landbased seaplanes. The Japanese by contrast had only thirty aircraft afloat on the carrier *Hosho*. However they had a further 130 operating from shore bases. Moreover Japanese naval aircraft were already clearly superior to their British counterparts: the main Japanese torpedo bomber, the Mitsubishi B1M, had a speed of 130 mph and a range of close on 300 miles, as against the British Blackburn Dart, which could fly at only 110 mph for a total distance of 256 miles; and the Mitsubishi 1MF1 navy fighter, another outcome of the British aviation mission of 1921, was marginally faster and rather more versatile than the Fairey Flycatcher, which was to remain the only British fleet fighter until 1932, when it was replaced by an aircraft hopelessly inferior to its Japanese opposite number. Measuring British naval strength against that of Japan would indeed have been a useful and thought-provoking exercise.

In the meantime the Australian and New Zealand governments could ponder on the facts that the British navy was still strong enough to fight in only one ocean at a time; that there was still no Far Eastern fleet; that there was still no naval base at Singapore – even if there had been a fleet to use it; that the situation in China had been given up as completely unpredictable; and that HMAS *Brisbane* was on duty with the China Squadron 4,000 miles away.

7 Singapore strategy (1926–39)

Chauvel made the obvious comment on the Committee of Imperial Defence's flight of fancy: in his next report to Federal Parliament he again drew 'attention to the fact that the dependence of Great Britain upon sea communications which is the primary factor determining the location of the Fleet in peace and its employment in war, may render it impossible for the Navy to operate effectively in the Pacific for some time after the outbreak of war'.[1] At the Imperial Conference of October 1926 Bruce reiterated that the Singapore base was 'of the very greatest possible importance to every part of the Empire', and that 'Australia believed that the Singapore Base is absolutely essential'.[2] British Prime Minister Baldwin apparently agreed that the base was 'most urgently needed at the present time from the point of view of Imperial Defence'. He assured the conference that his government had 'recently decided to adopt a reduced scheme' for construction of the base.[3] This involved an unhappy compromise between the proposals submitted by the Admiralty and the Royal Air Force. The Admiralty wanted Singapore defended by six 15-inch guns. The RAF was content to have no 15-inch guns, but a squadron of torpedo-bombers instead, with adequate support for India. Baldwin opted on Treasury advice for three 15-inch guns and no aircraft.

The most that could be said in favour of this option was that it would save money. Economy again had become a disruptive element in imperial defence. The British themselves had cut defence spending by £13 million, or almost 10 per cent, from 1925.[4] They were thus hardly in a strategic position to require other parts of the Empire to spend more enthusiastically. Even Australia could not offer to give more: Bruce circulated a memorandum at the conference, explaining that the Australian people were paying 17s 2d per head on naval defence, the British 25s 7d, the Canadians 8d and the South Africans 2d. The anomaly of the situation haunted Bruce as he travelled back across

North America with New Zealand Prime Minister Coates. His emotions exploded in Winnipeg in a burst of Australian plain speaking.

No British subject [he informed the surprised but unmoved Canadians] could have much patience with a state that called itself independent and self-governing in one breath and in the next admitted that in a case of trouble arising it would have to call on someone else for defence. I have heard Canadians say that Canada has no need of defence. If that is the case Canada occupies a unique position among the nations of the world. It means that were she threatened she would rely upon the British Navy or upon her powerful friendly neighbour to the South.[5]

Coates was typically more restrained, remarking only that the Dominion governments would have to accept a fair share of their responsibility in defence. But Bruce had not finished yet: in a final gesture he lashed out at Vancouver, asking: 'How can Canada today possibly maintain that it is the equal of Australia, my great country? We made great efforts during the war, but these efforts were nothing compared with efforts made by the people of Britain. . . . If we in Australia feel that we have got to assume some of this burden, then it seems to me that Canada also should do so. . . . In Australia we have never suffered from any inferiority complex, but unquestionably some of the Dominions have. . . .'[6] In an effective insult he offered to lend Canada a couple of cruisers, if required.

The Canadians naturally resented this. Quebecois Lapointe argued at a banquet in honour of Mackenzie King: 'I cannot see by what power of reasoning it could be argued that autonomy implies more military obligations. May I even suggest that distinguished visitors, perhaps, would be better advised if they refrained from offering so much advice to the people of Canada as to how they should deal with matters which are exclusively their own business.'[7] King himself rejected Bruce's sneer about inferiority complexes, claiming that 'other parts of the Empire, more recently organised as self-governing dominions than ourselves, may not have felt equally secure in the matter of their status'.[8] All this was irrelevant and had nothing to do with the real issue. If it could be argued that contributions to imperial defence were a matter for the exclusive concern of individual Dominion governments, then imperial defence was simply a myth and it was every man for himself. What was more to the point, although it was a point that no Dominion Prime Minister was prepared to make, was that even the most defence-conscious members of the British Empire were in a condition that was not far short of defencelessness. Australia had a permanent army of only 1,582 all ranks, an air force 860 strong and an impressive navy numbering in all 4 cruisers, 12 destroyers and 3 sloops. Canada had a permanent army of 3,600, an air force of 470, and a navy of 2 destroyers and 4 minesweepers, equally divided between the two oceans. New Zealand had only 524 in its permanent army, and 120 in its air force, while 2 cruisers and 2 sloops were allotted to the New Zealand Station.

The Royal Air Force itself ranked in numbers behind the air services of Russia, Italy, France and Japan. In terms of quality, it may well have ranked lower still: Italy's best fighter, the Fiat CR20, was for example nearly 50 mph faster than Britain's Hawker Hyderabad. At sea, Britain's cruiser strength had declined to fifty-six, thirty-four of which would become obsolete and have to be replaced within the next ten years, compared with the 114 that had been available in 1914, and the seventy that the Admiralty considered necessary for the minimum defence of British sea communications. The Royal Navy's air component had dwindled from a great Naval Air Service of 2,949 aircraft in April 1918, to a Fleet Air Arm of 141 aircraft, supported by the eleven planes of Coastal Command.[9] The United States Naval Air Service had also declined from a strength at the armistice of 1,865 flying-boats and seaplanes and 242 landplanes. However it was in 1928 four times the size of the Fleet Air Arm; its aircraft were superior in every respect, with bombers carrying missiles twice the weight of those carried by any British naval aircraft; and half the class of Annapolis in 1926 had received some flying instruction.[10]

Moreover it was clear that the United Kingdom itself was experiencing a most unfortunate economic decline. World production of pig-iron had increased by 25 per cent between 1914 and 1929; United States production by 37 per cent; German by 12.6 per cent; and French by 100 per cent. British production had meantime declined by 26 per cent. Comparable figures for coal were: world production, 17.5 per cent; United States, 15.6 per cent; German, 28 per cent; French, 30 per cent; and British production, down 20.7 per cent. It might have seemed reasonable to suggest that what the British most needed was a period of massive rearmament, if only to redirect investment into technologically advanced growth industries.

What they got was something else again. On 28 July 1927 the Committee of Imperial Defence resolved that the 'British Empire will not be engaged in a European war during the next ten years and that the immediate plans of the Army should be based upon preparedness for an extra-European war'.[11] This did not mean that the army was to be reorganized as an elite seagoing strike force for service in war against a major power outside Europe. It meant simply that the British army should revert to the level of a colonial police force, as had been its mode of existence before the catastrophes of the Boer Wars had imposed some measure of reform. This would naturally mean a substantial economy in research and development, as the army would need to maintain only a level of technology required to cope with assorted Afghans and Arab terrorists. It would in consequence be utterly incapable of taking the field against any army prepared to fight in the conditions of the twentieth century.

This concept of defence on the cheap also found its chief advocate in Winston Churchill, the executioner of the Singapore base and the Far Eastern Fleet. Churchill had however a further devastating blow to deliver to any rational theory of imperial defence: he proposed successfully that the assumption that the army would not be required to reach a European standard of conduct for the next ten years should be reaffirmed in each succeeding year. It would therefore be both unnecessary and impossible to prepare for any future major war again: war was to be always ten years away for the British Empire.[12] However even the Australians were prepared to live with the proposal that the British army should be useless for service inside the area of Europe, so long as the British navy remained available for action outside. Military disarmament could be regarded as a purely British matter. Naval disarmament was an imperial one. Australian expressions of concern were of course ignored in London. Then in June 1929 Ramsay MacDonald was back in office, and work on the Singapore naval base consequently halted again, this time without the formality of consultation with the Empire.

For once, extraordinarily enough, views on defence in London and the Antipodes were roughly in coincidence. A Labour government had come to office in Australia too, under the impact of the world depression, as anxious as the one in Britain to cut expenditure on defence in the general hope of ameliorating social conditions. Compulsory military training was abolished, for the first time in twenty-six years; Bruce's spectacular programme of naval rearmament was not renewed; and in

October 1930 an Australian Prime Minister assured an Imperial Conference that his government had 'active sympathy for the reduction and limitation of arms and for the preservation of world peace'.[13] It was a passing mood. Scullin was replaced in office by Joseph Lyons in March 1931; Stanley Baldwin followed MacDonald on 24 August of the same year; and just over three weeks later, on 18 September, the Japanese army began to occupy Manchuria by force, following an explosion on the Southern Manchuria Railway. This was followed up by another military incursion at Shanghai, which directly imperilled major British commercial interests in China. Hughes had apparently been a little premature in his forecast of July 1922 that the Four Power Pact would bring peace to the Pacific for ten years. But he was still not as discredited a prophet as the British ministers who in 1925 had seen no prospect of a threat from Japan for the next ten years, or as Churchill, who had launched the self-perpetuating ten-year rule in 1928.

The implications were quite clear. Lord Vansittart, Permanent Under-Secretary of State for Foreign Affairs, accepted as a fact that Britain could not hold the Far East in the event of war with Japan.[14] In military terms the Empire could in fact hardly be regarded as a power at all. British defence spending had fallen to its lowest postwar level of £103 million. Canada possessed literally one service aircraft, a Hawker Audax biplane on loan from the Royal Air Force.[15] Australia had seventy aircraft, all second-rate, even by the standards of the RAF.[16] The Royal New Zealand Air Force consisted of twenty-two all ranks, with twelve service aircraft, of which nine were obsolete, and the remainder incapable 'either of sustained cooperation with the Army and Navy, or of acting independently in defence against air attack or as a deterrent to sea-borne raid attack'.[17] This was of course the direct consequence of Britain's having economized on defence under the ten-year rule, to an extent far greater than any other major power. Russian defence spending had increased by 138 per cent since 1923; French by 98 per cent; German by 57 per cent; Italian by 22 per cent; and even American by 18 per cent. British defence spending had actually fallen in the same period by 7 per cent.[18] The Empire might be helpless, but it had saved money.

From the viewpoint of the British Treasury this was apparently a satisfactory line of development. Treasury Secretary Sir Warren Fisher ridiculed merrily the prospect of Britain's defeating Japan at a distance of 10,000 miles as 'a chimera compared with which Alice in Wonderland was a serious essay'.[19] Sir John Pratt urged that it was a major British interest not to antagonize Japan, in the hope of persuading Tokyo to enter into a new round of disarmament talks.[20] Despite the fact that the Empire was helpless in the face of Japanese aggression, the Treasury indeed pretended that France was 'the only nation in a military and economic position to threaten Great Britain'.[21] The fact that there was no suggestion that the French had any intention of doing anything of the kind only served to strengthen the position of the Treasury, and proved that there was no need to alter the ten-year rule. The reasoning was unintelligible, unless one accepted the unspoken assumption that the fact that Britain itself did not need to be defended against France meant that the Empire did not have to be defended against Japan or Germany.

The ten-year rule was none the less rescinded in a Cabinet decision of 22 March.[22] Work was recommenced on the Singapore base, at an accelerated level: the first stage of the defences was now to be completed in two and a half years, instead of the originally scheduled five. This did not however indicate any serious switch to a hard line in the Far East: the Lytton Report of February 1933 indeed branded Japan as the aggressor in Manchuria, which was virtually unavoidable, but did not propose that any penalties should be inflicted on Japan by way of punishment. Its effect however impelled the Japanese to leave the League of Nations, claiming to have been insulted. They then delivered a further expression of their dissatisfaction with the League by crossing the Great Wall of China in April and threatening Peking. London naturally refused to be concerned: Foreign Secretary Simon merely commented wittily that the Japanese did not seem to know how to stop.

This oriental peculiarity might certainly have seemed to have unpleasant implications for the British Empire in the Pacific. Gaiety such as Simon's could hardly have been expected from the Australians. Australian Defence Minister Sir George Pearce warned Federal Cabinet that: 'The recent happenings in Manchuria, the powerlessness of the League of Nations, the futility of the Nine Power Treaty and the Kellogg Pact must make all thinking Australians realise the danger of our empty North.' However the only suggestion for appropriate collective action that Pearce could think of was to increase the population of Australia and move it around more: 'To help Britain in Singapore there is nothing more valuable that we can do than to people the North and Northwest.'[23] The British themselves seemed unlikely to welcome any more positive or short-term action from Australia in the Pacific. Chief of Imperial General Staff Field Marshal Sir Archibald Montgomery-Massingberd considered Australia's last hope, the United States, as at least as probable an enemy as Japan, and claimed that he would just as soon fight the Americans as anyone else, next to the Germans.[24] Chamberlain for his part hoped to improve relations with Japan, so as to be relieved from the expense of military preparations against that country. With this kind of thinking predominating in London it was no wonder that the Empire was at its usual loss in trying to fathom the actual directions of British defence policy. Stanley Bruce, now Australian High Commissioner in London, wrote to Pearce on 8 December that he had had a long discussion with the Chiefs of Staff at which Sir Maurice Hankey, Secretary to the Committee on Imperial Defence, had been present, where he had 'pressed them very hard to try and put their view frankly as to the line we should follow in laying down a policy over a period of years. . . . [It was] very difficult to get anything concrete and definite from them . . . we are driven back to formulating our own ideas.'[25]

There was perhaps never a time when the British had more reason for concealing the workings of their minds from the Australians. The Admiralty had protested again and at length about the inadequacy of the one-power standard, insisting that they required as a minimum requirement for security that they should be able to

send to the Far East a fleet sufficient to provide 'cover' against the Japanese fleet; we should have sufficient additional forces behind this shield for the protection of our territories and mercantile marine against Japanese attack; at the same time we should be able to retain in European waters a force sufficient to act as a deterrent and to prevent the strongest European naval Power from obtaining control of our vital home terminal areas. . . .[26]

This might indeed seem to be an exact statement of what the minimum security requirements of the British Empire consisted of. Chamberlain had other ideas. The situation had indeed necessarily been modified by the unknown scale of German rearmament.[27] Chamberlain was accordingly able to claim that: 'The chief menace lay at Home and not in the

Far East.'[28] It was therefore all the more appropriate to seek a *rapproche-ment* with Japan in the Far East. Nor should this be too difficult. 'In his view, Japan would never consider attacking Australia and New Zealand. Britain would never think of attacking Japan over Manchuria.'[29] Chamberlain therefore urged that Britain should 'postpone the idea of sending out to [Singapore] a fleet of capital ships capable of containing the Japanese fleet or meeting it in battle. By the adoption of this course we can materially reduce the heavy and increasing shipbuilding programme. . . .'[30]

More to the point, this would leave more money available for the development of an air strike capacity, which Chamberlain hoped would act as a deterrent to the use of force by any possible European enemy. Chamberlain was quite literally prepared to go to all lengths in the achievement of this goal: the squadrons allotted to the Far East would be recalled home, and the Fleet Air Arm, the fragile shadow of a once mighty Naval Air Service, already outnumbered five to one by the Americans and inferior in all respects to the Japanese, would be denuded of its remaining squadrons. Air power, in the form of the bombing plane, could indeed easily be represented as an instrument of war too terrible to contemplate: pacifists and air fanatics alike could draw satisfaction from the latest horror story conceived by the Chiefs of Staff, who estimated that in a future war 200 tons of bombs would be dropped in the first twenty-four hours, and 150 tons in each succeeding twenty-four hours, each ton accounting for fifty casualties, in the proportion of seventeen killed to thirty-three wounded.[31] Moreover, aircraft were im-pressively cheaper than warships, although the price had altered from the days when an Australian Labour member had claimed that it would be possible to acquire an armada of 2,800 battleplanes for one battleship: the ratio now was more like forty-three to one.

But arithmetic of this kind was completely beside the point. Air power and sea power were not alternatives: they were complementary elements in the system of imperial defence, with essentially different roles to perform. Warships could not defend cities from air attack, although it could be remembered that the Royal Naval Air Service had performed precisely that function in 1914–18. Nor presumably could they destroy an enemy's industrial capacity and break the will of his people by bombarding his centres of production and population, although they could certainly assist the efforts of the air force to that end by applying the weapon of blockade. On the other hand aircraft could not range hundreds of miles out to sea to interrupt an enemy's sea communications, ward off an invading force, or escort one's own merchant ships safely to port; although again seaborne air power could do all three most effectively. But the message was clear enough: expenditure on aircraft was likely to be expenditure on home defence; expenditure on sea power was expenditure on imperial defence; and between 1934 and 1935 British defence spending on the air force increased by £10 million, and on the navy by £8 million. There was no doubt where Chamberlain was putting his money.

This new variation on the Recall of the Legions was the more ironic in that air power had suddenly emerged as a possible means of giving a new reality to the bonds of Empire. Imperial Airways had flown from London to Karachi and thence to Calcutta in July 1933. In December the air route reached Singapore. Then in 1934 the Melbourne Centennial Air Race demonstrated the inspiring fact that the great cities of Australia were only two days' flying time away from Europe, and the rather less inspiring one that they were only ten hours' away from Japan. Moreover it was still possible to feel that the distribution of British air power, exiguous though it was, was not unreasonably insular: out of a total of 1,008 more or less serviceable aircraft, 580 were in the Home Islands, 175 at sea with the Fleet Air Arm, 96 in India, 60 in Egypt, 51 in Iraq, 12 at Aden, 6 at Malta and 28 at Singapore. To this one could add the 12 Vickers Vildebeestes of the RNZAF, and the 18 Hawker Demons in Australia. Chamberlain had largely succeeded in correcting this, however: the Chiefs of Staff noted in April 1935 that since the conference of 1921 'the "One-Power Standard" of naval strength has been adopted as the basis of Imperial Defence. . . . The major preoccupation of the RAF is the defence of Great Britain against air attack . . .'.[32] To that end the allotment of the new squadrons to be equipped would be: thirty-one for home defence, four and a half for the Fleet Air Arm, three for Singapore and one for the Far East.

Meanwhile a major world crisis was clearly developing. Italian and Abyssinian forces had clashed in December 1934 at the oasis of Wal Wal, about 100 miles inside the south-eastern border of Abyssinia. Emperor Haile Selassie appealed to the League of Nations, while the Italians pressed ahead with a military build-up, obviously in preparation for a full-scale invasion. Another manifest case of great-power aggression was obviously in train. This was however not the only issue. A military alliance between France and Italy was also in preparation, to maintain a balance of power in Europe against a revived Germany. The two Italian initiatives were running concurrently, and to some extent inter-dependently. Haile Selassie appealed to the Council of the League of Nations on 14 December 1934. Mussolini issued a directive to his ministers on 20 December to prepare for war against Abyssinia. France extended some concessions to Italy in Africa on 7 January 1935. Dis-cussions between the General Staffs of the two great western powers began immediately, with the French agreeing to interpose an army corps between the Italian forces on the front against Austria, and France's own Yugoslav allies, to facilitate co-operation in a drive into Austria, where they would all link up with France's other allies, the Czechs.[33] Meanwhile the Italians discreetly attempted to sound out British opinion on their projected invasion of Abyssinia. The fact that they were unable to elicit any clear indication of British policy could seem positively encouraging, under the circumstances. The first Italian divisions left for East Africa via the Suez Canal on 5 February 1935. A new impetus to a western *rapprochement* was given when Hitler intro-duced conscription in Germany on 20 March. Mussolini promptly invited British and French representatives to attend a meeting at Stresa on 11 April. The old wartime alliance was apparently on the point of revival.

Such a development would have made German aggression in Europe impossible. Germany could never have risked a thrust to the East, leaving the western alliance intact in its rear. Nor could it conceivably have amassed the strength to have been able to challenge Britain, France and Italy simultaneously, even disregarding the smaller powers that the Big Three would undoubtedly have been able to rally around. On the other hand it could hardly be pretended that Germany would itself be seriously endangered by the alliance: an Italian crossing of the Austrian Alps, or a French lunge towards the Rhine were military operations sufficiently hazardous to be justified only by actual German aggression. The balance of power would have been achieved again, and the peace of Europe secured for as long as the balance continued to operate.

This would of course have meant a tacit agreement to let the League of Nations die from neglect, and return to what Vansittart had complacently and self-righteously termed 'the old – and vicious – "balance of power" '.[34] But Vansittart himself had been ready enough to warn against the dangers of applying the letter of the Covenant of the League of Nations against Japan over the annexation of Manchuria. The fact was that no other great power showed any sign of actually believing in the League of Nations as anything having more relevance than the Kingdom of Fairies. The United States had never joined the League; Japan had left it; Italy and France were seeking the balance of power, or rather a preponderance in their own favour; Russia strove for collective security, or at least the division of the capitalist West; even the British in practice saw the League as a means to the supreme end of peace, rather than as an end in itself. They were none the less – for the sake of an insincere gesture of belief in an irrelevant organization – about to destroy the balance of power, demoralize France, drive Italy into an alignment with Germany and create the only circumstances that would have war in Europe a practical possibility. They were also about to achieve the extinction of Abyssinia and the permanent discrediting of the League.

Part of the trouble was, as Corelli Barnett beautifully puts it, that any British government was dependent on the votes of a bourgeoisie ever ready to abandon itself to 'the fidgets of moral indignation'.[35] Moral fidgets have no doubt contributed even more than physical ill-health to the misery of the human race. But there were other factors present as well. Fear was of course the key. The extraordinary rate of German economic recovery was having its impact on British political and public opinion. Characteristically the British government chose neither to emulate the German technique of massive direction of investment through government contracts, nor to strengthen the Stresa Front to keep the German volcano under constraint. They sought instead the path of conciliation. In an attempt primarily to ensure that German naval rearmament would take place along clearly defined directions, the British agreed, without consulting France and Italy, that Germany should be allowed to construct capital ships up to a tonnage 35 per cent that of Battle Force Royal Navy, and submarines up to parity with Britain.[36] The agreement of June 1935 violated both the letter of the Versailles Treaty and the spirit of the Stresa Front. But the British had never believed in the moral validity of Versailles, and they had never seriously considered the practical implications of the Stresa Front. The

British were not interested in cementing alliances for a conjectural war against Germany: they were concerned to create a situation in which alliances would be irrelevant, and in which they would therefore not have to worry about meeting their obligations.

At least equally relevant was the domestic political situation. Unemployment in the United Kingdom still numbered about two million. The Labour Party had in consequence been making alarming gains in by-elections all through 1934. Then in November a public opinion sampling of more than half the total British electorate had recorded an incredible popular vote of sixteen to one in favour of applying economic sanctions against an aggressor, and three to one in favour of military sanctions. The implications of these tests were of course as unclear and unsatisfactory as such samplings normally are: there was also an eleven to one vote in favour of an all-round reduction of armaments by international agreement; and an eleven to two vote in favour of the abolition of military and naval aircraft. But clearly any country contemplating aggression would not disarm totally in the first place, and countries that had disarmed totally would not be able to risk applying sanctions against it.

The British government had decided on its policy by May 1935: it was therefore appropriate to summon the representatives of the other Commonwealth countries so that their views could be recorded. Simon had written to Ambassador Clerk in Paris that it was 'hadly necessary to say that His Majesty's Government in this matter is inspired by the friendliest feelings for Italy, nor that they have any reason to feel that Italian policy towards Abyssinia need have an adverse effect on British interests...'. The objective therefore was 'to recommend the Abyssinian Government to follow a policy more in accordance with modern conditions by recognising Italy's claims to take a fuller part in increasing trade between Abyssinia and the outside world...'.[37] But it was very clear that the Italians were not concerned with increasing trade, but with conquest; and Britain's friendly feelings towards Italy were scarcely demonstrated by the concentration of a huge armada of 144 ships in the eastern Mediterranean, poised across the Italian supply route to East Africa.

Meanwhile panic signals were understandably starting to fly from the capitals of the Commonwealth. Major-General McNaughton summed up comprehensively Canada's capacity for defence in any international crisis: there was not a single modern anti-aircraft gun of any sort in the country; there was not one service aircraft capable of actually flying on operational duties; there was not one bomb that such an aircraft could have dropped if it had been able to fly; and total stocks of field artillery ammunition would suffice for ninety minutes' normal rate of fire.[38] The prospects for Australia were utterly without even the relief of black comedy. Joseph Lyons desperately suggested that with British naval power concentrated in the Mediterranean, Japan should be placated by a formal recognition of the annexation of Manchuria: given a choice, Australia would rather see Japan move west against China than south against the British Empire.[39] This kind of thinking was however not appreciated in London: Lyons was informed coldly that such action would have been inconsistent with Britain's responsibilities towards the League of Nations.[40]

It was difficult to take seriously a policy that apparently placed a higher priority on the League of Nations than on the survival of the British Empire, and was prepared to alienate Italy in Europe without doing anything to conciliate Japan in the Pacific. The stage was set for the traditional confrontation between the two ends of the Empire. Foreign Minister Sir Samuel Hoare met the Dominion High Commissioners on 29 July 1935. The New Zealand representative had not arrived. Canadian Ferguson expressed misgivings about the application of sanctions, warning with perfect truth that there would be no effective support for such a move except in the Empire, and he was not even sure of that. It was however Bruce who stated flatly the objectionable reality that all concerned 'should refrain from bluffing ourselves any longer about the real strength of the League'.[41]

This of course was exactly what the British were determined to go on doing for as long as possible: the alternative to the League was alliances, and alliances meant rearmament. It was however alarmingly obvious that Dominion support was going to be hard to enlist, for such a programme of desperation: even faithful New Zealand was in the throes of a change of government and could not be relied upon to come to the party: in Wellington, Acting Prime Minister Sir Arthur Ransome spoke of New Zealand's love of peace and its tradition of support for the United Kingdom, deplored the dangers of too much talk about things best left alone, and considered that there was a difficulty in deciding how far the Covenant of the League of Nations should be honoured.[42] Sir George Mounsey expressed the misgivings of his colleagues in the Foreign Office that 'we will be faced with the situation that in our endeavours to uphold what is now rather a three-legged League, we find ourselves suddenly faced with the first step in the disruption of the British Empire'.[43]

This forecast of imperial disarray came at a time when British strategic planning was also in total confusion, with the Joint Planning Sub-Committee warning that at least two months' notice would be required before British forces could co-operate effectively on a war basis, and Cabinet refusing to order the mobilization of reserves because of 'the resounding effect that it would have on public opinion both at home and abroad'.[44] They still however could count on one ace in the hole: it was hoped that the presence of Field Marshal Smuts, the apostle of appeasement, the arch-enemy of the Singapore base, would 'probably help us a lot in educating Dominion opinion'.[45] There was no doubt that the Dominion whose opinion was considered to need educating was Australia.[46]

This was a melancholy if hardly unusual decision for the British to arrive at on the very day that the Australian government agreed to allow their new cruiser HMAS *Australia* to be retained in the Mediterranean, against hostile Italian reaction in the event of sanctions being applied. The British attitude was the more remarkable in that the Australians were not in fact told until 17 September that naval preparations were being taken in the Mediterranean at all.[47] They were then assured that it was hoped that these measures would have a 'tranquillising' effect on the Italians, despite the fact that Mussolini was clearly concentrating submarines in Sicilian waters and strengthening his air forces in Sicily.[48] Meanwhile the Dominions Office began to put pressure on New Zealand, as the most susceptible of the Dominions, insisting on the need to re-affirm loyalty to the League of Nations and 'keep in step with France', again despite the fact that there was clearly nothing that the French wanted more than to let the Italians have their way in Africa and preserve the Stresa Front.[49]

British hopes that Australia and New Zealand might prove to be the Dominions most active in support of British policy were abruptly upset by a vigorous speech by former Prime Minister Hughes, stressing the dangers to the British Empire of an intervention by Britain between Italy and Abyssinia.[50] Hughes's speech could have been read to imply that in such a situation Britain might well be acting alone. The Foreign Office promptly condemned Hughes's statements as extremely tactless.[51] It was even suggested that Hughes was giving 'a very wrong idea of the Australian attitude'.[52] But the fact was that the governments of both the Pacific Dominions were intensely anxious about the implications for their own security of British commitment to the League of Nations. The New Zealand Prime Minister refused to make any statement on the issue. However New Zealand High Commissioner Sir James Parr was instructed to support the British 'on the understanding that any action to be taken will be collective action as contemplated by the Covenant'; he was particularly not to vote for sanctions without further instructions.[53] Australian Prime Minister Lyons said that Australia was prepared to co-operate, but desired most of all the unity and safety of the Empire, and considered sanctions ineffective anyway.[54] The Canadians similarly doubted the feasibility of applying sanctions 'in the absence of important states from universal membership . . .'.[55] The New Zealanders had meanwhile hardened their position: on 5 September they opposed 'any attempt to apply economic sanctions without a general and effective application by all other members of the League', and suggested that the dispute was 'a quarrel in which the British Commonwealth was not directly concerned'.[56]

Even South Africa seemed to be temporarily at odds with the official London line: te Water, who had arrived instead of Smuts, spoke vaguely about the dangers of black barbarism, and asked if it was really too late to admit that a mistake had been made in letting Abyssinia into the League in the first place. But no united Commonwealth front could ever be achieved about anything: the Canadians now took up the original New Zealand line of joining with other League countries 'in considering how by unanimous action peace could be maintained'; while the New Zealanders now insisted that it would be the end of the influence and authority of the League if it were to remain inert, with the small states losing most. Only Bruce actually refused to state a position at all: he treated the representatives to 'a survey on nutrition and health, sanitation and agriculture', subjects dear to every Australian heart, but deliberately chosen to give no inkling of what the position of his government might be on the matter of sanctions.[57] He was a little more explicit on 17 September, when he stated flatly that Australia would be most reluctant to resort to sanctions, and that almost any alternative would be preferable. Asked by New Zealand's Sir James Parr if Australia would be prepared to let Mussolini attack Abyssinia with impunity, Bruce suggested that it might be better to state openly that the existing machinery had failed and let the League go.[58]

Bruce cabled to Prime Minister Lyons that he had deliberately refrained from clarifying Australia's position so far. Meanwhile the Australian government ordered the cruisers *Canberra* and *Sussex* to remain on watch off the west Australian coast on learning that the Italian cruiser *Quarto* was believed to be heading for Batavia.[59] The periodical *The Bulletin* on 25 September hailed this further demonstration of imperial naval co-operation by Australia as evidence that 'the Lion is gathering his cubs about him'.[60] Probably no more inappropriate image for the process actually under way could very well have been found. But the nostalgic rhetoric had a certain applicability. The Italian invasion of Abyssina on 2 October, without declaration of war, compelled the Dominion governments to consider what they would actually do if the British applied sanctions in pursuance of their League obligations, and the Italians responded by force of arms. Australian Attorney-General Robert Menzies indicated at least one of the internal anomalies of the Commonwealth relationship when he argued in the House of Representatives that for a Dominion 'to declare its neutrality in a war to which the British Crown was a party would be tantamount to secession'. Moreover, as Menzies pointed out, neutrality cut both ways: Australia could hardly expect Britain to accept responsibility for Australia's security if that Dominion were to shrug its shoulders at war problems that vitally affected Britain itself.[61] But these constitutional dilemmas were only chimeras to frighten lawyers with. R. G. Casey put the realities of the situation with traditional Australian explicitness: 'Whatever the outcome of this unfortunate dispute may be, one thing seems clear – the countries which comprise the British Empire must by all means at their disposal put their strength into the Empire . . . neither the policy of White Australia nor the physical defence of this country could be maintained in opposition to any one of a dozen hostile nations.'[62]

Casey overstated the case. But the fact of the matter was simple enough: any kind of forward policy in the Mediterranean was perilous to the interests of the Empire, if it meant leaving the Empire hopelessly vulnerable in the Pacific.[63] By the same token it would be impolitic to alienate Japan so long as there was any danger of a crisis developing in the Mediterranean. Britain had to be strong everywhere, or weak everywhere. Certainly a forward policy in Europe, which would break the Stresa Front against Germany, without any clear scheme to either conciliate or contain Japan, could not be justified in terms of imperial interests. The British went ahead, none the less. Sanctions were applied in November.

However the British had in mind a way out of the dilemma, which the Dominion governments were not consulted about either. Cabinet decided on 2 December to empower Foreign Minister Hoare to discuss with Pierre Laval the delaying of the imposition of oil sanctions.[64] Dominion views were sought on 8 December.[65] The result was chaos, once more. Having agreed to support the British in applying sanctions, however reluctantly, the Dominions did not immediately appreciate why there should now be delay in applying the only sanctions that could have any direct effect upon Italy's capacity to wage war. This applied even to the Australians, who, having been told two months after the event that the British were concentrating their naval forces in the Mediterranean, now made HMAS *Sydney* available for service, 12,000 miles away from their own shores. But the delay on oil was only part of the scheme that Hoare discussed in Paris with Laval, without any prior cognizance by the Dominions. Cabinet approved on 9 December the substance of a plan for a compromise partition of Abyssinia, preserving the independence of the state at the cost of two-thirds of its territory. The Dominions were informed on the following day.

The chaos on this occasion was far more serious. Once again Bruce remained true to himself: by saying practically nothing, he at least conveyed tacitly the impression that Australian public opinion would not be unduly concerned at any technique that extricated them from a peril they had not wanted to get into in the first place. Canadian Vincent Massey, on the other hand, did appear concerned about possible domestic repercussions in Canada. New Zealand was similarly apprehensive but inexplicit. The most vehement and moralistic objection came once more from South Africa. The country that had advocated wrecking the Singapore Strategy on the ethical ground of the need to appease Japan, now advocated wrecking the Hoare–Laval Plan on the ethical ground of the need not to appease Italy. Moral pretensions were in fact irrelevant in both cases. The South Africans had opposed the

Singapore Strategy because it would have meant that British fleet units that otherwise could have been available for their own defence would have been diverted to the defence of other parts of the Empire. The fact that these other parts needed defending while South Africa relatively speaking did not was of course not considered. Similarly, the South Africans were now prepared to set the interests of the Eastern Empire at risk again, because of their fear that an Italian-dominated Abyssinia might mean that a black people who had once been the most formidable military power on the continent might be formed into a huge native army with European officers and European technology to make them more formidable than ever.[66]

Te Water repeated his objections on 14 December, reinforced by a cable from his government conveying its 'profound dismay' and warning that 'the Union, and doubtless the lesser Member States of the League, will not be prepared to continue their support of a body which is ready to sacrifice their interests in time of need to the arbitrary dictates of more powerful nations'.[67] The New Zealanders, characteristically more conciliatory, regretted 'very much that they are quite unable to associate themselves with the proposals . . .'.[68] It would have been utterly improbable that the views of New Zealand and South Africa would have any effect in determining British views now, any more than those of Australia had ever had in the past. But the Hoare–Laval Plan was doomed anyway. Mussolini was set on a military solution, which had become all the more important from the viewpoint of prestige after the unpromising start of the campaign; and the moral fidgets of the British public did the rest. Hoare resigned on 18 December. The last pretence of collective security had failed; Haile Selassie was about to lose all of his country; Italy had been injured, humiliated and forced into a position of economic dependence on Germany; and the utter lack of mutual trust and coherence within the British Empire had been demonstrated again. There was no need to look for redeeming or consoling aspects in the Abyssinian affair. Total and immaculate disaster had been achieved.

It is sometimes possible to pretend that disaster may have a therapeutic effect, by teaching lessons that are too painful and unambiguous to ignore. This might indeed have seemed to be the case with the British government in the winter of 1935–6. The Defence Requirements Committee had reported alarmingly on 21 November that Japan meant 'to dominate the Far East, as Germany means to dominate Europe. We must, of course, employ all the resources of diplomacy to avoid ruptures anywhere . . . but the fact remains that we are living in a world more dangerous than it has ever been before, that we can count on no one but ourselves unless we are strong.'[69] This was certainly perceptive, although it failed to state the very relevant consideration that the reason why Britain could count on no one but itself was that it had thrown away two great alliances since the war, in the Far East with Japan and in Europe with Italy, without even attempting to put anything concrete in their place. With diplomacy like that, one would need to be a superpower to last very long. But the essential point was that Cabinet responded to the Committee's report by embarking on a rearmament programme including the construction of seven new battleships, four aircraft carriers and twenty cruisers, and particularly the provision of an air force of 3,800 planes by 1937 and 8,000 by 1941.[70] It was undoubtedly a turning-point in British history. It should have been above all the moment for a new departure in imperial co-operation, in which British plans were pooled with at least those Dominions that could be counted on for effective support, to co-ordinate policies in a genuine programme of imperial defence. What happened was the opposite.

The British Cabinet decided on rearmament on 25 February 1936,[71] despite the assurances of Foreign Secretary Anthony Eden that there was no undue need for panic, as there was no likelihood of a German–Italian *rapprochement* in Europe.[72] The New Zealanders were obviously anxious to repair relations with Britain, which might have been impaired by their opposition to the Hoare–Laval solution: their High Commissioner reported to Wellington that he and Stanley Bruce had agreed that 'our Dominions would be willing and desirous of discussing British proposals with British Ministers, having in mind the obvious advantages of each doing what was best not for itself only but for the common whole'.[73] In perhaps the most blatant indication of contempt for Dominion opinion in a long and consistent history of such indications, the British released an official statement on the wireless on 10 March that 'all the British Dominions had been consulted and had fully acquiesced in the Government's programme as contained in the White Paper'. As the New Zealand government pointed out furiously on the following day, 'As His Majesty's Government in the United Kingdom are aware, this statement, if it was made, is contrary to fact. His Majesty's

Government in New Zealand, who have not yet considered the defence programme set out in the British White Paper, have neither formed nor expressed any opinion on the subject. . . .'[74]

Far worse was to come. There was a conspicuous reason why the Dominion governments would not have been consulted in the preparation of any British programme for rearmament: its provisions necessarily tended to cut across their own defence planning. The Australians discovered to their intense concern later that month that they might be unable to obtain modern aircraft from Britain for the Royal Australian Air Force, as new orders for the RAF were apparently absorbing all available British productive capacity.[75] This situation hardly reflected thinking on an imperial scale in London, but it was at least understandable. What was less easy to appreciate was the unwillingness of the British to assist the Australians in finding the obvious alternative, for reasons that could hardly be related to strategic considerations. The obvious alternative was of course for Australia to build its own aircraft, utilizing initially the resources of its major industrial plant, General Motors-Holden. The British government vehemently opposed this. 'The argument which Britain continually advocated was that the Air Ministry could not divulge defence secrets to an undertaking which contained a foreign element. However this was simply a screen to cover its real fear, the loss of the Australian market'[76] for automobile engines. Nor did the British have any more time for other prospective allies outside Europe. The Dutch government cautiously approached London in July for informal talks on the mutual defence of their colonial empires. The Committee of Imperial Defence did in fact consider the Dutch aspect seriously enough to conclude that 'faced by a formidable scale of attack, and with a vast area to protect, the position of the Dutch is most difficult'.[77] They accordingly suggested that the Dutch should improve their own defences.[78]

Insularity was hardly an unusual manifestation of British defence planning. There was even less than usual operating to mitigate it during the later months of 1936. A military rising had developed in Spain on 16 July; and the prospect of a new confrontation with Italy emerged after Mussolini agreed on 25 July to supply Francisco Franco with aircraft to transport his rebel African army to the Spanish mainland. Eden's hopeful dismissal of the possibility of a German–Italian *rapprochement* seemed more wide of the mark than ever when Hitler announced on the following day that Germany would be following Italy's lead in supplying air support to the Spanish rebels. Any chance of an Anglo–Italian *détente* was indeed made incredibly remote when Eden himself criticized Mussolini in September for intervening in Spain. By contrast, Hitler hastened in the following month to recognize the annexation of Abyssinia to the Italian Empire. The Australians, desperate at the delay, finally resolved in October to build their own aircraft, and formed the Commonwealth Aircraft Corporation for the purpose, although they yielded to British pressure to the extent of agreeing that a representative of General Motors-Holden should not be allowed to become managing director.[79] The British were not yet beaten, however: they offered to sell Australia production rights of the Fairey Battle, a single-engined bomber of considerable range but low speed, difficult to compare with any other combat aircraft; and the Westland Lysander, an army-co-operation aircraft uniquely unsuitable for almost every conceivable combat function in the South Pacific.[80]

Meanwhile the Empire was gradually shifting gears on defence policy. The British increased their arms expenditure from £188 million in 1936 to £280 in 1937; Australia, from £6.5 to £8.8 million in the same period; and the Canadians actually doubled their defence spending, from £2.5 to £5.2 million. This was still of course scarcely ruinous: Canadian defence spending per head was only a third of Australian in 1936. Even so, Mackenzie King felt it necessary to assure the House of Commons that Canada was under no obligation to come to anybody's assistance in any circumstances: 'There are no commitments and no undertakings in the nature of commitments between this Government and the Government of Great Britain or any other Government.'[81] Whatever relationship the countries of the Commonwealth might stand in in relation to one another, they were certainly not allies. Nor perhaps did there seem any apparent need for alliances: Neville Chamberlain actually spoke on 29 January 1937 about the need to pursue a policy of 'political appeasement and economic collaboration' to relieve international hostilities,[82] and Hitler immediately responded with his most resounding peace offensive, proclaiming that there was no humanly conceivable object of dispute whatever between the German people and the French, and that he wished for sincere and hearty co-operation with the British government and its people.[83]

The British Chiefs of Staff did not find the prospects reassuring, however. Reviewing the problems of Empire defence in preparation for the impending Imperial Conference, they reported that it was now necessary to regard Japan as the second most important enemy of the British Empire after Germany, and affirmed that the security of the United Kingdom and the security of the naval base at Singapore were the two keystones on which the survival of the British Commonwealth of Nations depended.[84] They were also appalled at the condition of British air defence: it was estimated that Germany would have 800 modern bombers available for service by May 1937, while the RAF would have only forty-eight.[85] Their concern was shared by the Air Ministry, which was demanding a force of 1,589 bombers, supported by only 474 fighters, 85 per cent of which were to be stationed in the United Kingdom. It was perhaps an unpromising time for the Australian government to attempt to purchase fifty of the new Bristol Blenheim bombers, which would at least have been superior to the Battle in every imaginable respect. Certainly the Air Ministry simply failed ever to supply the aircraft to Australia. They did however provide the Turkish air force with two complete squadrons instead, on the grounds that it 'was of particular importance that everything possible be done to keep countries like Turkey within our sphere of influence by providing them with aircraft'.[86] As Dr McCarthy comments: 'Finland obviously came into this category. By 1938 it too had been supplied with Blenheims. This principle of political supply could be extended: by June 1939, 126 Hurricanes had been promised to Rumania; 24 Spitfires to Greece, and a further sixty Blenheims and Spitfires to Turkey.'[87] None of these modern aircraft had been made available or even promised to any of the Dominions.

It was not surprising that the representatives of the Commonwealth should have assembled for their conference in mid-1937 in even more than their customary state of apprehension and uncertainty. The Australian delegation were particularly concerned about the implications of growing Japanese influence and apparent aggressiveness in the Far East: they had been specifically briefed to ask the British 'if the present policy of accommodation to Japan was a temporary one pending the strengthening of British defences?'[88] Not that Stanley Bruce at least was particularly averse to conciliating Japan: he was becoming increasingly irritated over the question of recognition of the Italian conquest of Abyssinia, for fear that it might reopen the problem of Japanese annexation of Manchuria, and evoke more Japanese resentment.[89] Defence Minister Parkhill stated the problems of the Eastern Empire flatly:

The basis of Australian Foreign Policy may be summarised as participation in Empire Naval Defence for the defence of seaborne trade, as a deterrent to invasion and as a general defence against raids . . . if Japan is in a position to carry out a military operation against any of these members (Australia, New Zealand, India) the British Commonwealth will have lost either its military strength or its cohesion of common interest to any extent which makes *any* part of it an easy prey to any aggressive power.[90]

The Admiralty did not really dispute this: First Sea Lord Chatfield agreed with the Australians that 'the security of Singapore was absolutely vital to our position in the Far East . . .'. However he assured them that they could regard the fleet 'even when inferior in numbers by one heavy ship, as at least equivalent in fighting value to the Japanese Fleet . . .'.[91] These assurances apparently moved Lyons, not the most formidable of Australian Prime Ministers, to an expression of loyalty as unqualified as anything ever said by a New Zealand Prime Minister: he considered that it was

the duty of those assembled at the Imperial Conference . . . to accept wholeheartedly and loyally the general principles in regard to national affairs which had been laid down and followed with so much courage, generosity and wisdom by the United Kingdom, to support without qualifications the declarations on the subject which that Government had made, to stand solidly behind that Government and to cooperate in the fullest possible measure with the efforts of that Government to secure world appeasement and peace.[92]

But first it was desirable to find out exactly what those principles were. Parkhill urged Federal Treasurer R. G. Casey to remind the conference that Australian security depended on 'an impregnable Singapore and the despatch of the Main Fleet thereto in war'.[93] For once Australia was actually supported by New Zealand in an expression of concern. New Zealand Prime Minister Savage settled his nation's problems by remarking that 'New Zealand with her own resources could do nothing. She must sink or swim with the United Kingdom. This was the keystone of New Zealand Defence Policy.'[94] Statistic-minded New Zealand Finance Minister Walter Nash added that it appeared that Singapore might not be able to hold out for more than

sixty days if it were besieged. Chatfield did not exactly agree, but
admitted that the powers of resistance of the garrison would deteriorate
rapidly in the third month. The problem of the endurance of the
Singapore base was indeed far from merely a scientific one: the situation
in China had been deteriorating for months, and on 7 July a clash
occurred on the Marco Polo Bridge, 30 miles from Peking, between
Japanese troops and soldiers of the Chinese 29th Army.[95] The Japanese
Cabinet of Prince Konoye reluctantly agreed to authorize partial mobilization on 14 July, while still denying any intention of 'an all-out attack
on Peking'.[96]

Lyons now proposed that 'a survey be made of the problems of
Australia as a source of maintenance and supply . . . in a war in the Far
East', in the event of Singapore proving insufficient. He also asked again
that as 'the establishment of peace on a permanent footing is declared
to be the aim of members of the British Commonwealth of Nations, it is
appropriate for a common understanding to exist between the Members
of the British Commonwealth as to the manner in which such measures
should be concerted to . . . the achievement of the common ideal'.[97]
Neither of his proposals was taken up. He did however elicit the first
serious suggestion that the Eastern Empire might not be able to count
on the assurances of naval support that Parkhill had been determined to
secure, and that Chatfield appeared to have given just a few weeks
before: the Admiralty now said that it might be necessary to rely on
economic pressure primarily to defeat Japan, as a successful fleet action
was the only apparent means of forcing an early decision, and, as the
British now admitted for the first time, 'the strength of the fleet that
could be sent to the Far East must be governed by consideration of our
home requirements'.[98] This presumably implied that in certain circumstances home requirements might be sufficiently demanding to make it
impossible to send a fleet to the Far East capable of providing cover
against the Japanese. However Chatfield hastened to add that Australia
did not have to regard the danger of invasion as real, as the Japanese
would have to rely on shipborne aircraft for their air support.

This would have been no comfort at all, if anybody had been prepared
to check the figures out. The fact was that the Japanese Naval Air
Service had a more than sufficient margin in numbers, and an overwhelming margin in quality of aircraft, to be able to overwhelm any
possible combination of landbased or seabased British air power in the

Far East. At the time of Chatfield's statement the British Fleet Air Arm consisted of some 214 shipborne aircraft, supported by about 180 land-based planes of the Royal Air Force Coastal Command. The Japanese Navy had at least 300 carrier-based aircraft, with an equal number operating from shore. The discrepancy in quality was horrifying. The major British naval strike weapon was the Blackburn Shark torpedo-bomber, with a top speed of 152 mph and a maximum range of 546 miles, which was about to be replaced by the slower and shorter-ranged, but immensely more reliable, Fairey Swordfish. By contrast, the Japanese Nakajima B5N1 was far and away the best torpedo-bomber in the world, with a speed of 217 mph and a range of 684 miles. The main British fleet fighter, the Hawker Nimrod, had a top speed of 195 mph and a range of 300 miles. The Japanese Mitsubishi A5M2a flew at 265 mph faster than any fleet fighter the British were to have for another three years, with a range of 460 miles. And the Japanese navy's shorebased bomber, the Mitsubishi G3M2, with a speed of 236 mph and a range of 3,000 miles, was 48 mph faster and had four and a half times the endurance of Coastal Command's Avro Anson.

Nor did either the British or the Australians have any landbased capacity that could seriously challenge Japan in the air. The RAAF was still flying Hawker Demons, good-looking seven-year-old two-seater biplanes, 30 mph slower than the Nakajimas. They were just beginning to receive the first of a thousand Ansons, which were indeed astonishingly rugged reconnaissance aircraft, but carried too light a bomb-load to be effective against big enemy warships. The New Zealanders were still stuck with the hideous Vickers Vildebeeste, a slightly inferior equivalent of the Shark. There were absolutely no single-seater interceptors suitable for modern warfare in any part of the Eastern Empire at the time. The only British aircraft in the Far East or Australia in 1937 that would have had any chance at all against the Japanese navy planes would have been the twenty-four Bristol Blenheims sent out to Malaya later in the year.

The implications of this balance of arms were clear. The British Empire needed most urgently a massive expansion in naval air power to safeguard its lines of communication, coupled with the development of a Fighter Command of sufficient strength to overcome any possible aerial attack upon the United Kingdom itself. What was done was very nearly the opposite. British aircraft production was geared to the

creation of a huge bomber force, on the theory that this would either
deter a potential aggressor from starting a war, or at least enable Britain
to make a contribution to a European war more economical in terms of
lives and money than the commitment of a large army. Home defence
was to be secured essentially by giving priority to the production of
anti-aircraft weapons.[99] But the fact was that nobody actually knew
whether bombers could contribute significantly to victory or not. What
could be assumed was that whether a sufficient number of bombers
could prevent or win a war or not, an insufficient number of fighters
could most certainly lose it. In any case, bombers and anti-aircraft guns
would have relevance essentially in a European war: what would be
needed against Japan was something that could protect ships and bases
against the Mitsubishis and the Nakajimas. However the dreadful inadequacies of the Fleet Air Arm were concealed rather than corrected:
in a supreme example of parliamentary weaseling, Geoffrey H. Shakespeare, Parliamentary and Financial Secretary to the Admiralty, when
asked to supply the figures for the naval air capacities of Britain, Japan,
the United States, France, Italy and Germany, provided data for everybody except Japan, thereby leaving out the only information that really
counted.[100]

But the fact was that tangible British interests were likely to come
under threat only in the Far East: there was no reason at all to doubt
that the last thing that Hitler desired was a second war between Britain
and Germany. Germany's interests lay manifestly to the East, against
Poland and Russia. It was probably true that victory in this direction
would make Germany the preponderant and unchallengeable power in
Europe; but this did not necessarily imply that Britain's own position
would suffer in any sense except that of relative power status. In any
event if the British were really concerned about the balance of power in
Europe, they would presumably have made certain of Italy. It could
scarcely be imagined that the British, having abandoned a front with
Italy against Germany for the sake of a gesture towards collective
security, would then be considering going to war with Germany to
preserve the balance of power.

Decisive, pragmatic, co-ordinated strategic planning in the capitals
of the Empire was probably more urgently needed at the beginning of
1938 than at any other time in the history of the world. European and
Asian crises were becoming increasingly entangled. In July 1937 Japan,

fearful of Russian intervention, had made cautious approaches to Germany for an anti-Comintern front. Meanwhile Anthony Eden had decided with uncharacteristic perceptiveness that 'joint action with the United States' might be helpful in the Far East.[101] United States President Franklin D. Roosevelt was thinking along similar lines: early in November he expressed the fear that 'Japan, if not tackled soon, would mop up first the British possessions in the Far East, then the Dutch'.[102] On 12 December Japanese aircraft sank the United States gunboat *Panay* in the Yangtse. Roosevelt then instructed his Chief of Naval Operations, Admiral William D. Leahy, to send the head of the Navy War Plans Division, Captain Royal E. Ingersoll, to London for consultations with British naval planners.[103]

In one sense Roosevelt's anxieties were premature. The Japanese government, as distinct from the more belligerent young officers in the Services, were concerned almost exclusively with Russia, not with Britain or the United States. The Foreign Ministry was convinced that Japan should 'through diplomatic manoeuvres . . . draw Great Britain and the United States to her side. . . . The important issue in Japan's diplomatic policy is to effectuate the alienation of Great Britain and the Soviet Union.'[104] This naturally was not fully appreciated by the Australians: a Cabinet meeting of 24 February was informed by Chief of Staff General Blamey that there were only 320 field guns and 13 tanks with which to defend the Continent. Blamey himself did not think that even these would be essential, because Japan would never dare to send an invasion fleet as far as Australia while the British fleet was still in being.[105] This was however exactly the problem. Prime Minister Lyons had assured Federal Parliament in August 1937, after the Imperial Conference, that he had no fears for Singapore: 'as it is the keystone of Empire defence in the Eastern Hemisphere, its capacity to fulfil its functions should be undoubted'.[106] He was not so sure now. On 10 March he cabled to Chamberlain, telling him that he had received information that in the event of war Great Britain might not be able to defend its overseas possessions, and expressing concern, as all his predecessors had done, about the absence of official advice on imperial strategy from the British government.[107] Chamberlain's answer was understandably less than comprehensive: it was the policy of the British government to preserve trade routes, to protect the United Kingdom, and to defend Singapore, which provided the whole point of the naval

defence of the Empire east of Suez.[108] What Chamberlain did not say
was whether it would actually be possible for Britain to do all three at
once.

Attention in both London and Canberra was in any case immediately
wrenched from the Far East when the union of Germany with Austria
was accomplished on 11 March. Here at least Lyons had good advice to
offer: he told Chamberlain on 20 March that 'an understanding with
Italy would be the most valuable contribution to appeasement at the
present time and in the best interests of the Empire', and hoped that 'no
effort will be spared to come to terms with Italy'.[109] No effort was made.
Instead Chamberlain delivered a speech in the House of Commons on
24 March, indicating that in certain circumstances it might be necessary
for Britain to go to war to defend a country such as Czechoslovakia,
necessarily the next item on any possible programme of German expansion.[110] This was defending the balance of power with a vengeance.
It was unfortunate if purely fortuitous that on the same day Canada
should have actually cut back its defence spending by $2 million,
thereby becoming the only country in the world actually to reduce its
scale of military preparedness in 1938, while Defence Minister
Mackenzie explained that by far the largest group of Canadian opinion
would join with Great Britain or the League of Nations in a war for a
principle or for the safety of the liberty of the world, but they would also
refuse to imperil Canadian liberty by accepting in advance that Canada
must automatically agree to support either Great Britain or the League.[111]

This was an example of the moral fidgets indeed. As such, it was not
likely to be reflected in Australia. Lyons hastened to assure Chamberlain
that Australia was prepared to co-operate in pushing ahead with defence
plans for peace and the integrity of the Empire, although he added that
Australia was also fully prepared to support Britain if it in fact after all
decided not to go to war in the event of aggression against the Czechs.[112]
New Zealand also had a helpful suggestion to make: His Majesty's government in New Zealand admitted politely that 'they fully realise that
His Majesty's Government in the United Kingdom are much nearer the
problem, and more intimately affected by possible results than are His
Majesty's Government in New Zealand, but they would regard it as
deplorable if Russian assistance in the prevention of aggression was not
secured'.[113]

Russian assistance was overwhelming, and apparently available.[114] It had however already been rejected: an offer from Litvinov for a Grand Alliance against aggression had been dismissed by Halifax on the grounds that there was no useful purpose to be served by concerted action or military agreements that would divide the powers.[115] None the less something approximating to a British–French–Russian front came momentarily into being to deter Hitler from intervening in Czechoslovakia on 21 May. But the mood passed almost at once. Britain and France began immediately to apply pressure on Czechoslovakia to agree to a negotiated settlement with Germany. In Australia Foreign Minister Hughes expressed his hopes for a peaceful solution to the European problem;[116] and in Ottawa Mackenzie King explained why it was impossible for anybody to count on Canada: 'At the present time there are no commitments, so far as Canada is concerned, to participate in any war. Equally there are no commitments . . . whereby we agree to remain neutral under all circumstances . . . Parliament will decide upon our course when and if the emergency arises, in the light of all the circumstances at the time.' King concluded regretfully: 'It must be recognized that this policy is not wholly satisfactory. . . . It is not an ideal solution . . . we have worked out a satisfactory and enduring solution of the relations between the several members of the British Commonwealth in peacetime; we have not yet worked out a completely logical solution of the position in war time.'[117]

It might have been truer to say that nothing had been worked out, and nothing was working. London was co-ordinating with nobody. Nor was there any disposition to admit that while there could be no common bond of interest uniting the whole Empire, there were certain situations in which certain parts of the Empire could be expected to co-operate for mutual support. The nations blundered on in darkness. Attorney-General Robert Menzies came back to Canberra after a visit to Germany 'convinced that it would be wrong had Europe drifted into a war in which the merits were distributed'.[118] Mackenzie King announced in terms of outrage that he could not allow the British to establish a Royal Air Force training establishment in Canada: 'Long ago the Canadian Government finally settled the constitutional principle that in Canadian territory there could be no military establishments unless they were owned, maintained and controlled by the Canadian Government. . . . A reversal of that principle and that historical process at this stage is something the Canadian people would not for a moment entertain. . . .'[119]

He was however fully prepared to allow British airmen to train in Canadian air force establishments, and also to establish a Canadian factory to build heavy bombers for the Royal Air Force.

Subterfuges and evasions of this kind were enough in themselves to suggest that the Commonwealth relationship did not provide an ideal basis for exchanges between sovereign states. But it was not only the British who had their problems. The Japanese found themselves confronted by a military clash with Russia on the Manchurian border at Changkufeng, arousing the old fear that they might 'be conquered without the least resistance if the Soviet attacks suddenly'.[120] In this situation the Germans offered an alliance providing for immediate mutual support in the event of war. Japanese Foreign Minister Ugaki stalled however, insisting that any such alliance would have to be directed against a communistic nation, of which there happened to be only one in the world at that time, and that it would have to omit Britain and the United States.[121]

Britain thus had still almost unlimited opportunity for a diplomacy of *realpolitik* when the Czech crisis flared again in the first week of September 1938. Indeed the British position could only be described as uniquely favourable. The British Empire was under no direct threat anywhere. Germany wanted peace and commercial partnership; Japan wanted British mediation and co-operation in China; the United States was exploring the possibility of British naval co-operation in the containment of Japan;[122] the Russians were indefatigably approaching London to confirm an alliance with the West to contain Germany; and France was about to abdicate to London its independent discretion in foreign affairs for the sake of ensuring that it would always be on the side of Britain, since it was not possible to be sure when Britain would ever be on the side of France. Italy was indeed still bitter and alienated; but Italy dreaded an expansion of German power in Europe almost as much as France or Russia did. The possibilities of playing the balance of power game were dazzling, with enduring peace or at least easy victory the prize for statesmen of vision.

There did not seem to be any in London with quite that sort of vision. On the other hand there was no lack of politicians with all too much vision to discern danger. Britain's military position was admittedly appalling. It was also evident that some parts at least of the Empire would opt for either neutrality or minimal participation in a European war: the Irish would certainly give no assistance, and Hertzog of South Africa drafted what amounted to a declaration of neutral intent on 1 September. The Americans were told on 7 September that 'it was becoming clear that the Dominions were isolationist and there was no sense in fighting a war which would break the British Empire while trying to secure the safety of the United Kingdom'.[123] But this misrepresented the situation absurdly. No one could really doubt that the parts of the Empire that had made a relevant contribution in 1914–18 would fail to do so again. Ireland, Quebec, the Transvaal and the Orange Free State might indeed decline to come to the party; but their assistance had been in large measure counterproductive before. Australia would be there, as would New Zealand, Ontario, British Columbia, Natal and Cape Colony. India would have no choice. Nor could anything but the most deliberately partial view discern any end to a European war except a quick and easy defeat for Germany. The Germans had at most forty-eight divisions available, inadequately equipped and hopelessly unprepared for combat.[124] France at the lowest estimate could deploy forty-seven divisions, with a similar number in reserve. The Czechs had thirty-five divisions, in a defensive position from which it would have taken the entire strength of the *Wehrmacht* to displace them. The Russians had mobilized their fleet, moved forty divisions up to the Polish and Rumanian frontiers, and had a further forty in support. The mass of the Red Army could supply on mobilization at least another 140 divisions. The two and possibly three divisions that the British Empire would be able to provide in the first few weeks of war would hardly be necessary.

The situation was different in the air. The *Luftwaffe* possessed in all 3,307 front-line aircraft, of which probably 2,200 were combat planes.[125] The British possessed 816 bombers and 322 fighters of which admittedly only 116 bombers could be regarded as anything like front-line planes, while of the fighters only the 60 Hurricanes could be regarded as anything like a match for Germany's Messerschmitts. However the Czechs had a reasonably modern air force of 1,360 aircraft,[126] and the French cannot have possessed fewer than 650 bombers and 220 fighters, while the Russian air force was probably numerically stronger than the *Luftwaffe*.

There could be no doubt that the Germans would succeed in doing an immense amount of damage before they were defeated on land. There was also no reasonable doubt that they would be defeated on land very quickly indeed, unless Italy were to come in on their side and Russia were to stay out. But the Italians were far too involved in Spain to contemplate intervening on behalf of a nation they had good cause to wish to see defeated, and there was every possible indication that the Russians fully intended to participate in a western war against Germany.[127] In any case the confrontation might have seemed to offer a tantalizing choice to the British: they could either rally France, Czechoslovakia and Russia together for an easy war against Germany, which would preserve some kind of balance of power in Europe and would force Japan into dependence on British goodwill in the Far East for fear of being overwhelmed by a victorious Russia; or alternatively they could force the French to abandon Czechoslovakia and reach a compact with Germany, which again would leave Japan isolated and with no alternative but to cooperate with Britain and the United States in the Far East. In this situation it would have required a diplomacy quite out of normal experience to have abandoned Czechoslovakia, rebuffed Russia, allowed Germany, Italy and Japan to become allies, and finally to have gone to war on behalf of Poland in 1939.

The Dominions were as usual employed to provide an excuse for weakness, rather than a basis for strength. Ireland and South Africa could not be counted upon, but Ireland and South Africa were virtually irrelevant in a military sense. Australia had already given assurances of support. Canada was saying nothing, because Mackenzie King had collapsed with sciatica, and was keeping all copies of foreign cables by his bedside without showing them to his ministers. However even King had implied what everybody knew, that Canada would have to assist Britain if the latter became involved in war as a result of German aggression. On 12 September ex-New Zealand policeman – now High Commissioner – William Jordan expressed his country's position perfectly at Geneva: 'The New Zealand Government would be ready to support Czechoslovakia on the merits of the case if there was a prospect of a peaceful settlement and [if] in spite of this Czechoslovakia was attacked by Germany. But with this proviso we could say that if the United Kingdom was involved in war rightly or wrongly, New Zealand would support her, right or wrong.'[128] On the same day however Halifax pretended to French Foreign Minister Bonnet that he was unable to make precise statements of the character of any future British action in support of France, because he 'could not commit the Dominions in advance of circumstances'.[129]

This in fact was exactly what the British were about to do again. Chamberlain flew to Berchtesgaden to meet Hitler on 15 September. Mackenzie King raised himself from his bed of pain and inertia to assure the British Prime Minister that 'the whole Canadian people will warmly approve this farseeing and truly noble action'.[130] New Zealand's Prime Minister Savage similarly described Chamberlain's action as 'a historic gesture in the cause of peace', but added, as Mackenzie King was highly unlikely to add, that his country's attitude could be summed up in the one sentence: 'Wherever Britain is, we must be.'[131] King did at least cable Chamberlain again on 27 September, while Europe waited for news of the expected German assault, affirming his complete accord with Chamberlain's policies and promising to summon the Canadian Parliament if war broke out. As a further contribution to international harmony he also cabled Hitler, suggesting that he get out of Berlin for the time being as an aid to clearer thinking.[132]

There was no doubt that all the Dominion governments shared in the common relief when the latest European crisis was averted by the Munich partition. Mackenzie King was truly euphoric: he assured Chamberlain on 30 September that the

heart of Canada is rejoicing tonight at the success that has crowned your unremitting efforts for peace. . . . My colleagues in the Government join with me in unbounded admiration at the service you have rendered mankind. Your achievements in the past month alone will ensure you an abiding and illustrious place among the great conciliators whom the United Kingdom, the British Commonwealth of Nations, and the whole world will continue to honour.[133]

The Australians were equally relieved, if less fulsome: Sir Earle Page told the House of Representatives on 5 October that the whole world 'welcomed with relief the outcome of the Munich negotiations, and owed a deep debt of gratitude to those who had made their success possible . . .'.[134] But at least there was no pretence of uncertainty in Canberra as to what would have happened if the negotiations had failed: when Labour spokesman John Curtin asked directly whether the government would have committed Australia to war if a struggle had broken out in Europe, he got a direct answer: William Morris Hughes, now Minister for External Affairs, replied that no formal committal would have been necessary: 'We should have been committed to war and no power could have saved us from it. . . . No power in the world could keep open the highways of our overseas trade except Great Britain. . . . In this fateful hour we believe that there is no other way in which we can be true and loyal citizens of Australia.'[135]

If the Eastern Empire was thus automatically committed to assist Britain in a European war, it was more important than ever for the Eastern Empire to know what was going to happen to it in the event of Japanese aggression while the Australian and New Zealand divisions were absent on the other side of the planet. According to Dr Johnson, the certainty that he is going to be hanged in a fortnight tends to concentrate a man's mind wonderfully. The minds of the New Zealand Chiefs of Staff had not yet been brought to the point of concentration at which they could contemplate the implications of Japanese supremacy in the Pacific. But they had finally nerved themselves to recognize that this was on the cards, and to bring notice of the possibility to the New Zealand government. They reminded their ministers that in October 1937 they had submitted a review on the defence of New Zealand to the Committee of Imperial Defence. They had then taken as their basic assumption 'that the United Kingdom had available an adequate naval reserve to enable a fleet to proceed to the Far East in sufficient strength to serve as a strong deterrent against any threat to the Empire's interests in that part of the globe . . . the c.i.d. commented as follows:— "To take note that the standard of naval strength referred to in the report of the NZCofS had not yet been approved by His Majesty's Government in the United Kingdom. . . ." '[136]

So in effect a naval reserve was not available, and the Singapore Strategy did not exist. British promises or assurances over the past eighteen years were meaningless. The Dominions would be leaving themselves defenceless if they were to send troops overseas to assist Britain in a war against Germany. By the same token the British would have to be prepared to leave Europe to Germany unless they wanted to lose their Empire. This should hardly have come as a surprise to anybody who could count up to twenty, or even fifteen. The strength of the British battle force was insufficient for its global responsibilities, and had been ever since the one-power standard had been accepted. The New Zealand Chiefs of Staff were not yet prepared to go this far. But they warned the government that it had to be assumed 'that for a period which may amount to one of months, the Japanese fleet will be un-challenged in the Pacific. . . . The key to the situation is Singapore. . . . Should Singapore be captured or rendered unusable, a totally different situation would arise, which we regard as beyond the scope of this appreciation.'[137] The British Chiefs of Staff could of course find some comforting words for the New Zealanders: they argued that the 'value of small forces, resolutely handled, particularly when operating in un-developed territory, should not be underestimated. . . . It may suffice to recall the drain on our own resources in the last War caused by the gallant resistance of the small and entirely unsupported German forces in East Africa. . . . In certain circumstances, the air arm provided a means of rapidly and powerfully reinforcing small centres of re-sistance.'[138]

This was pure dreamland. Nothing could have been less relevant to the particular problems facing the Australians and New Zealanders than the experiences of quasi-guerrilla warfare in German East Africa. Jungle fighters hiding behind trees were not what was wanted to stop the battleships and aircraft carriers of the Japanese Combined Fleet. Talk of the value of the air arm in this context was even more misleading, as the Japanese were hopelessly superior in both quality and quantity. In the circumstances the Chiefs of Staff could really make no more helpful suggestion than to 'reaffirm the need for close co-operation with Australia'.[139] Meanwhile the Australians were wondering whom they could co-operate with. An External Affairs report on the disposition of the Americans was baffling and not altogether encouraging. The depart-ment's officers had discerned a mood of increasing friendliness in the United States towards the United Kingdom, but this was still modified 'by a great deal of suspicion and combined with a very firm determina-tion not to become embroiled outside the shores of America'. Further there was apparent 'a certain jealousy of the United Kingdom's position, nourished by a constant suspicion that the United Kingdom was intent on entangling the United States'. The general attitude in America was one of looking to the United Kingdom to deal with the European crisis, but without any great tendency to blame the British for the actual crisis, although the United Kingdom was denounced in some quarters 'for the betrayal of the democracies'. It might have been a little difficult to make anything very positive out of all this, but the report concluded with at least one concrete observation, the implications of which were quite unmistakable: there was not a single anti-tank gun in the United States that actually worked.[140]

There was only one thing to be done. No previous experience of adversity had induced Australians to lay aside their vociferous party differences; but on 12 December the House of Representatives grimly united to authorize an increase in defence spending to £21 million per annum, from £8.8 million in 1937. Part of this additional expenditure was to provide for the increase of the first-line strength of the RAAF by a further 116 aircraft, from its present total of 96.[141] In an attempt to ensure that at least some of these aircraft would be worth having, a surprise request was sent to Lockheed Aircraft Corporation for fifty of their new and untried A-28s, renamed the Hudson by the RAF and the RAAF. The superiority of the Hudson over the Anson for all forms of Coastal Command duties was at least impressive: it had twice the armament, four times the bomb-carrying capacity, three times the range and about another 80 mph of speed. As such, it was not surprising that the British should have decided that it was too valuable an aircraft to be diverted to the Pacific, even though the Australians intended the Hudson specifically 'for defence against Japan as the British would be pre-occupied in Europe and unable to protect Australia':[142] Air Marshal Sir Cyril Newall proposed that the RAF should absorb 'the entire output of the Lockheed factory in an attempt to head them [the Australians] off from buying Hudsons even though it may mean giving up some of the earlier deliveries of the Beaufort',[143] a British aircraft superior in many ways to the Hudson, but unavailable for service until 1941.

No better indication of the nature of British priorities could be given than the fact that having refused to sell Australia their own latest aircraft, and having attempted to impede the production of aircraft in Australia itself, the Air Staff should now attempt to prevent Australia from obtaining alternative aircraft from the United States. Once again the two extremities of the Empire were viewing international developments from totally different viewpoints. Australian Defence Minister Street attempted to tie the British down on 6 December with the flat statement in Federal Parliament that: 'The Australian Commonwealth looked to Great Britain to station at Singapore in an emergency a fleet strong enough to safeguard the Empire's interests.'[144] But Shakespeare was not going to be caught as easily as that. Queried again in the House of

Commons, he replied that Street's statement was indeed a true statement of the position of the Australian government.[145] He did not however suggest what a true statement of the position of the British government might be. Nor did he inform the Australian government of the decision of the British Chiefs of Staff in February 1939 that the strength of any fleet that might be sent to Singapore in the event of Japanese aggression 'must depend on our resources and the state of war in the European theatre'.[146]

The trouble was that the situation was deteriorating rapidly in both Europe and Asia at the same time. The Japanese had continued to hope for a *rapprochement* with the British until March 1939. Ambassador Hotta had reported back to Tokyo from Berlin in October that he was convinced that 'German-Italian relations are bad because of colonial problems', and that 'Germany is endeavouring to be intimate with England in diplomatic affairs . . .'.[147] Japan had therefore no alternative but to try to do the same. Finance Minister Ikeda was similarly assured that it would be 'impossible for the finances and economy of Japan to exist if we are to compete with the United States and England'.[148] Foreign Minister Arita was prepared to accept the portfolio in December only on condition that the Anti-Comintern Pact should not be strengthened to the extent of waging war against Britain and France.[149] Even the comparatively 'gung-ho' Japanese navy viewed the anti-Comintern coalition as essentially a basis from which to make 'a reasonable approach to the United States, England and France'.[150] Even as late as 22 January 1939 Arita was still advising the Emperor that Soviet Russia was to be assumed as the main objective of the Anti-Comintern Pact and that England and France, 'by themselves, will not be assumed hostile. . . . Should Germany and Italy declare a war with nations other than the Soviet, for reasons other than to eliminate the Comintern, we do not intend to give any military aid at present or in the future.'[151] However this mood had shifted by 3 March to a conviction that Japan must 'always be a supporter of Germany and Italy'.[152]

Meanwhile the Germans and Hungarians had completed plans for the annihilation of Czechoslovakia.[153] Bohemia and Moravia became German protectorates on 15 March. Two days later Chamberlain proposed a conference to meet threats of German aggression against Poland and Rumania. The British were once again in a position of total commitment to the European continent, as in 1914.

The situation was alarming enough to impel even the ailing and amiable Lyons to ask Chamberlain urgently if 'Australia is entitled to assume that in the event of war with Japan the United Kingdom Government would send a fleet to Singapore within appropriate time capable of containing Japanese fleet to a degree sufficient to prevent a major act of aggression against Australia.'[154] Chamberlain again replied that it would 'still be His Majesty's Government's full intention to despatch a fleet to Singapore', in the circumstances indicated, although 'the size of the fleet would necessarily be dependent on (a) the moment when Japan entered the war, and (b) what losses, if any, our opponents or ourselves had previously sustained'.[155] Lyons apparently regarded this as sufficient assurance. Meanwhile the Dominions hastened to support a new departure in British policy, which appeared virtually certain to involve the Empire in a European war. Mackenzie King actually came out from under the cloak of non-commitment to warn the House of Commons that if 'there was a prospect of an aggressor launching an attack on Britain with bombers raining death on London, I have no doubt what the decision of the Canadian people and Parliament would be'.[156] On the same day Australian Attorney-General Robert Menzies announced unambiguously that: 'If Great Britain is at war, we are at war, even though that war finds us not in Europe but defending our own shores. . . .'[157]

Menzies at least bore in mind the possibility that the contribution of the Eastern Empire to a British war might well consist in defending its own territories against Japanese aggression. The Australian and New Zealand governments had already decided in March to hold a conference with the British in Wellington on 14 April on the defence of the Pacific.[158] The time was certainly urgent. It was also most unpropitious. The British were in no mood to spare time for thinking about anything other than European security problems. As late as 23 April the British High Commissioner in Wellington was still imploring the British government to grant New Zealand a loan of £5 million for defence, on the interesting grounds that 'it would be deplorable if New Zealand had to turn to America'.[159] Chatfield replied curtly that he could not 'place very high priority on the New Zealand defences . . .'.[160] Reports prepared for the conference highlighted causes for alarm. Both the Dominion governments agreed as a first principle that the course of a war in the Pacific would 'in the long run presumably depend upon two factors: the availability of Singapore as a Fleet base, and the arrival of British reinforcements'.[161] But this was precisely what the British were being more evasive about than ever: the Chiefs of Staff would agree only that a fleet 'would have to be sent to the Far East to give cover to New Zealand, Australia, our Eastern possessions ... while sufficient strength would be maintained in home water to contain the German Fleet'.[162] But in this event 'we should have to depend on the French Fleet to restrict Italian naval action in the Mediterranean'.[163]

Menzies was becoming increasingly uneasy: on 24 April he made his first radio broadcast as Prime Minister, after the death of Lyons, telling his countrymen that little as he was given

> to encourage the exaggerated ideas of Dominion independence and separation which exist in some minds, I have become convinced that in the Pacific Australia must regard herself as a principal, providing herself with her own information and maintaining her own diplomatic contacts with foreign powers; I do not mean by this that we are to act in the Pacific as if we were a completely separate power; we must of course act as an integral part of the British Empire. We must have the fullest consultation with and co-operation with Great Britain, South Africa, New Zealand and Canada. But all these consultations must be on the basis that the prime risk in the Pacific is borne by New Zealand and ourselves.[164]

It was true that Menzies did not know just how much at risk Australia and New Zealand were. The British Admiralty had in fact just sent an officer of their own Plans Staff to Washington, to try to persuade the United States to 'send a strong naval detachment to the Far East to operate from Manila and Singapore, in restraining and opposing any Japanese advance into the Southwest Pacific'.[165] The reason for this startling request was that the British had now decided to create a new naval force, 'Force H', for operation in the Mediterranean against Italy. Force H would in effect consist of those units that would otherwise have been available for despatch to the Far East. As the Admiralty explained to Admiral Leahy and his Head of Plans Staff, Rear-Admiral Robert L. Ghormley, 'if Great Britain were at war with Germany and Italy in the Atlantic and the Mediterranean, it might be impossible for the British Navy to reinforce Singapore. In this event, command of the west and south Atlantic, as well as of the Pacific, would have to be assured by the United States Fleet.'[166]

The Dominion governments were of course not aware of these exchanges. Menzies still found it simple enough to appreciate that any ships that the British might decide to retain in the Mediterranean would have to be deducted from what otherwise might have been available for the defence of the Eastern Empire. The situation could obviously be improved only if it were possible for the Anglo-French front in Europe to be strengthened. It was also obvious where such added strength was likely to be found most readily. Russia might be repugnant, but it was on any paper calculation by far the most formidable military and air power in the world, and on all the evidence Russia was desperate for an accommodation with the West against Germany. Litvinov had presented at least his fourth proposal for a defensive arrangement between Russia and the West on 17 April. In the circumstances, Menzies was prepared to put the security of the Empire before his most intense ideological predilections: he told High Commissioner Stanley Bruce on 22 May to tell Chamberlain that while Australia attached 'much importance to preserving friendship with Japan and would therefore be unhappy about any Russian agreement which applied to the Far East, we agree that opportunity should not be lost to make an effective agreement'.[167]

Menzies's urging might have seemed to have been particularly timely: the Pact of Steel was concluded between Germany and Italy on the same day, leaving Russia the only unattached great power in Europe. A Russian alliance might therefore have seemed literally priceless to the British. Litvinov's proposal was in fact deliberately ignored for two weeks, until his replacement by the equally determined but infinitely less congenial Molotov.

Meanwhile the Australians and New Zealanders desperately considered what they could do with what they had. It was agreed that Australia should have responsibility for air reconnaissance and defensive action for the area New Guinea–Solomon Islands–New Hebrides. New Zealand would similarly look after the New Hebrides–Fiji–Tonga zone. This arrangement was perfectly rational: New Guinea was on Australia's doorstep, and the New Zealanders had long been convinced that Fiji and Tonga were the keys to New Zealand's defence. The problem was how to carry out the responsibilities that had thus been assumed. The New Zealanders urged that the Fiji Defence Force should be expanded to a total of 1,300 all ranks; that landing grounds should be prepared in both Fiji and in Tonga; and that New Zealand aircraft should be allowed to operate from these grounds in time of war. To assist in these preparations the New Zealanders undertook to meet any expenditure necessary for the defence of Fiji, above the figure of £500,000 per annum agreed to by the British government. For the first time in history a British Dominion was actually assuming responsibility for the defence of a Crown Colony. More than that, the New Zealand government decided to establish a garrison on the cable station of Fanning Island, due north of the Cook Group and three degrees above the Equator. Fanning had been attacked by a German raiding party in 1914, and New Zealand was determined that its communications with the world outside should not be endangered in this way again. A garrison of two unfortunate officers and thirty other ranks was duly despatched with two machine guns, to hold Fanning Island against the Japanese Combined Fleet.[168]

Understandably the New Zealand government was unwilling to undertake any further overseas military commitments at the time. The Australians for their part faced a prospect that could only be termed appalling. Having failed to encourage the British to respond positively to the Russian approaches, Menzies made a further desperate appeal for 'a generous approach by France' to Italy, in the hope of detaching Italy at the last moment.[169] This was no more successful. On 5 July he and his Cabinet contemplated the latest horror story prepared for them by External Affairs. If the guesswork of the officials had been accurate, there would indeed have been nothing to do except surrender the Empire on the spot to anybody willing to take it. The Germans, according to Hughes, had 'an amazing array of efficient machines: 10,000 aircraft, 5,000 tanks, efficient to the highest degree'.[170] In fact total German strength in the air amounted to 4,161 first-line aircraft, of which some 1,929 were actually available for combat. Tank strength was approximately 2,000. These numbers did not in fact give the Germans a satisfactory margin of strength even against the combination of Britain–France–Poland: taking even the lowest estimate of French and Polish capacity, the three powers would have been able to deploy a three to two superiority in armour, and something like parity in the air.[171] It was of course true that such a calculation would have left Italy and Japan out of the picture as potential allies of Germany. But it would also have omitted Russia as a potential enemy of Germany, which would have far more than redressed the imbalance.

Menzies and his Cabinet could not know any of this. All they had to base their plans on were estimates of German strength, which over-stated the reality by two and a half times, and the horrifying and un-deniable evidence of the debility of the British Empire. There were for example no heavy anti-aircraft guns outside the United Kingdom. Nor were there any single-seat fighters. Canada, South Africa and Burma had no combat aircraft at all. India had seven squadrons, with a total strength of about 60 aircraft in all, composed mainly of Audax light bombers, Wapiti army co-operation planes and Valentia troop trans-ports, all utterly obsolete biplanes; useful against the Afghans, useless against any modern aircraft, unless covered by fighter escorts, of which there were none. Malaya had its twenty-four Blenheims. New Zealand still had its twelve awful Vildebeestes, which in the absence of fighter cover have been flown only on suicide missions. The RAAF could rally some 246 aircraft, of which 164 were operational. These comprised eighty-two Ansons, fifty-four Demons, seven Wirraways, and twenty-one Seagull floatplanes. It could therefore be said to be reasonably well equipped for reconnaissance and anti-submarine duties, and perhaps for army co-operation, preferably against the Afghans. The tragic truth was that the RAAF lacked both a strike capacity and an interceptor force. It could neither attack nor defend.

The only comforting reflection that imperially minded Australians might have drawn from their military position was that at least Britain's own security was hardly weakened by its responsibilities towards the Empire: the Malayan Blenheims were almost the only British weapons to be found outside the European zone which would have been of any utility in a European war. The excellent 3.7s were all in the Home Islands; so were all but thirteen of the tanks; so were all the aircraft built since 1938, apart from the Spitfires and Hurricanes on order to Rumania, Greece and Turkey. The situation might have seemed super-ficially different at sea: the British China and East Indies squadrons still deployed a combined strength of seven light cruisers, five destroyers, thirteen escort vessels and sixteen submarines. But the main British Empire naval presence in 1939 as in 1914 was the Royal Australian Navy, now developed to a force of two 8-inch gun cruisers, four 6-inch gun cruisers, five destroyers and two sloops, with the capacity for a rapid increase in its number of escort vessels by the conversion of big merchant ships and trawlers. Interestingly the RAN was in fact the only armed force of the British Empire actually to have increased in strength relatively and actually between the wars: in 1919 it provided 3 per cent of the cruiser strength and less than 1 per cent of the destroyer strength of the combined naval forces of the Empire. In 1939 the respective ratios were 11 per cent and 5 per cent.[172]

What was obviously lacking was a successor to HMAS *Australia*. Sir Harry Chauvel accordingly suggested that Australia acquire two battleships as quickly as possible, explaining that God had made Australia an island, so it behooved its people to make the most of this providential fact. Menzies for his part could find comfort only in the thought that the Japanese could be no more sure that the Americans would not come to Australia's help, than he could be that they would. The only person unperturbed was Blamey, who was not convinced that ships were vulnerable to attack from the air after all, and was accordingly still reasonably confident that the British would be able to spare a sufficient fleet to cover Australia.[173]

Unquestioning faith of this kind was all that the Commonwealth could have for comfort as Europe rapidly moved towards war. There was indeed no time for rational calculations of chances of survival, although regrets and last-minute urgings were fully appropriate. The British government sent a warning to Germany on 22 August. The news reached Menzies two days later. He was still prepared to say that he did not despair of a peace settlement, but that no preparations for war could be neglected. On 25 August he warned the Australian people that the world might be at war at any moment, and that 'we in Australia are involved because in plain English the destruction or defeat of Great Britain would be the destruction or defeat of the British Empire and would leave us with a precarious tenure of our own independence . . .'. It was therefore necessary to make all preparations that would 'enable us to co-operate in the most effective way with other British countries in the honouring of a great British guarantee [to Poland] and contributing to the security and well-being of the Mother Country of all British countries'.[174] This might not have been pitching the argument at a high level of intellectual enquiry, but intellectual enquiry and constitutional pettifogging were alike irrelevant. The situation might or might not be exactly as Menzies had described it, but it was simply not practicable for Australia or New Zealand to act as if it might possibly be otherwise. A British decision for war would leave them defenceless, but a British defeat would leave them helpless. They could not stop the British from going to war. They could only do what they could to avert a British defeat and hope for the best.

What they could not hope to do was to act in accordance with other Commonwealth countries, as Menzies had hoped. The apparatus for such co-operation simply did not exist. The practical consequence of the myth of the Commonwealth relationship was that no Commonwealth government could be committed in advance to the support of any other, simply because not all of the Commonwealth governments were prepared to undertake such a commitment. Total unity was apparently impossible, so partial unity was unacceptable. Britain, France and Poland were allies, but Britain, Canada and Australia were not.[175] The anomaly of the situation was the more apparent in that the Dominion governments proceeded to adopt war measures precisely as if they had in fact been committed to an unbreakable alliance. The Canadian government had already dispersed the mobile force across the country, in readiness for rapid mobilization. On the night of 25 August the Canadian Department of National Defense advised military districts: 'Adopt Precautionary Stage against Germany.'[176] The British government was told that the Royal Navy would be permitted to use Canadian facilities on the Atlantic seaboard.

Menzies meanwhile continued his last-minute efforts for peace in Europe, reminding the British government that 'it would be strange if we should fight, each believing his cause to be just', and suggesting that he had 'been much struck by what appears to be a real advance in Hitler's last statement'.[177] On 28 August he proposed that Chamberlain should suggest to Hitler that the Polish Corridor was open to negotiation after all.[178] It was in a sense far more negotiable than the Sudetenland had ever been. However this Australian advice went the way of all previous recommendations from the Antipodes. The British government asked on 29 August that the ships of the Royal Australian Navy should be held in immediate readiness for war. The Australian Navy Board reminded the government that this would mean that the imperial war telegram would have to be obeyed as soon as received, but despite this recommended that a second Australian cruiser should be sent to European waters. Here indeed the Australians could hardly be too generous: the Federal Government agreed that the ships of the RAN and their personnel should be placed at the disposal of the British government, but that no ships other than HMAS *Perth* should be taken from Australian waters without prior Australian consent.

Meanwhile Poland had mobilized, on publication of the German demands. As fighting began on the Polish–German frontier, Mackenzie King placed all Canadian armed forces on a war footing and announced in a press release that his Cabinet had unanimously decided 'in the event of the United Kingdom becoming engaged in war in the effort to resist aggression ... as soon as Parliament meets, to seek its auhority for effective co-operation by Canada at the side of Britain'.[179] Parliament was in fact not due to meet until 7 September. The Australian parliament was due to meet the day before.

Menzies in the meantime continued his efforts to avert disaster, even after the shooting had actually started: he warned Chamberlain on 2 September that there had been 'more reasonableness than might have been expected by Hitler, and any pointblank refusal on the part of Poland might very well affect public opinion even here'.[180] But his task was hopeless. The British government after some preliminary hesitations declared war on Germany at 8 pm Australian time. An hour and a quarter later Prime Minister Menzies told his people that 'in consequence of a persistence by Germany in her invasion of Poland, Great Britain has declared war upon her and that, as a result, Australia is also at war'.[181] It might not have been a precise lawyer's definition of the constitutional position, but it expressed the reality exactly. There was no practical choice open to the Eastern Empire. It was a matter of simple cause and effect. Australia was at war because Britain was at war, just as Menzies's predecessor, Joseph Cook, had said in August 1914.

8 Their finest hour (1939-41)

Menzies's other assertion, that there was 'unity in the Empire ranks – one King, one flag, one cause',[1] was perhaps less appropriate than it would have been in 1914. There was indeed solidarity where one might have expected it, in the English-speaking Dominions of the Old Empire. Canada had not yet declared war, but King cabled Chamberlain on 3 September, asking 'to receive your appreciation of the probable theatre and character of main British and allied military operations, in order that we may consider the policy to be adopted by Canada. We should also like to have your Government's present appreciation of the nature and extent of British and allied requirements as regards supplies and particularly the relative urgency of the needs for various commodities which Canadian producers could furnish.'[2] This was thoroughly practical, as could be expected from Ottawa. The emotions were coming from elsewhere.

At 1.55 am on 4 September the New Zealand Parliament authorized their government to tell London that: 'His Majesty's Government in New Zealand desire immediately to associate themselves with His Majesty's Government in the United Kingdom in honouring their pledged word. They entirely concur with the action taken, which they regard as inevitably forced upon the British Commonwealth if the cause of justice, freedom and democracy is to endure in this world . . .'.[3] They concluded the business of the day by singing 'God Save the King'. By contrast, Ireland opted for neutrality, and South Africa declared war on 6 September, only after a change of government. Canada seemed as usual to have no statement to make.

These mixed responses naturally occasioned some uncertainty in Washington, ever unsure as to how the mechanism of the British Commonwealth actually worked, if indeed there was any mechanism to work. Secretary of State Cordell Hull telephoned King on 5 September, asking if Canada was at war because Britain was at war, as was apparently the case with Australia. Somewhat disingenuously, King assured Hull that Canada could be committed to war only by the decision of its Parliament, which was not due to meet until 7 September. In a revealing display of New Deal informality, Roosevelt, who had been listening to the conversation on another line, then cut in to tell King that he would accordingly exclude Canada from the Neutrality Proclamation until a formal declaration of war had been made by Ottawa. The significance of this was that it meant that war supplies ordered in the United States by Britain and France could still be moved across the border for as long as Canada stayed neutral. Roosevelt concluded by gaily assuring King that he would keep in touch with him.[4]

It was one thing to declare war on Germany. It was something else to know how to go about fighting her. The Australian government simply did not know what kind of contribution would be most appropriate for it to make.[5] The Labour Opposition assured the government on 6 September that: 'We stand for the maintenance of Australia as an integral part of the British Commonwealth'; but could only promise that it would 'do all that is possible to safeguard Australia and at the same time, having regard to its platform, will do its utmost to maintain the integrity of the British Commonwealth'.[6] This was hardly a clear direction. Meanwhile the British had replied to Mackenzie King's cable of 3 September, promising to send an appreciation of the military situation later, and in the meantime advising the Canadians that 'provision of naval vessels and facilities and of air force personnel would be of most assistance . . .'.[7] A further memorandum of the same day suggested that Canada consider as an immediate programme 'the despatch of a small Canadian unit which would take its place alongside the United Kingdom troops'.[8] It was appreciated that no early statement was likely on the despatch of an expeditionary force from Canada. None had yet been asked for from Australia. But the New Zealand government had already decided unilaterally to mobilize an expeditionary force of 6,600 men for service in or out of the country. The pattern of imperial action in wartime was already becoming a trifle confusing.

One confusion could at least be got rid of promptly. The Canadian Parliament met as prearranged on 7 September. The situation was at least singular. Canada had already mobilized for war. The Governor-General's Speech from the Throne said that Parliament had been summoned so that the government might seek authority for the measures necessary for the defence of Canada, and to provide for expenditure 'which has or may be caused by the state of war which now exists'.[9] But the Conservative Opposition would support to a man participation in the war on the side of Britain. So would the Social Crediters. Any opposition to the policy of the government (already arresting Nazi sympathizers throughout Canada and conferring on war plans with the British) would have to come presumably from within the ranks of its own supporters. In the ensuing debate it was in fact the Opposition that clamoured for an expeditionary force, while King promised that his government would never introduce any measures providing for conscription for overseas service.

King had argued in defence of this position by saying that not even Australia had considered sending an expeditionary force to Europe.[10] But New Zealand had. So indeed had the Royal Australian Air Force, which proposed sending a six-squadron force overseas. But Australian thinking was completely confused by an appreciation from the Dominions Office which arrived on 8 September, suggesting two possible courses of action for the country to adopt. On the one hand, if Japan were friendly, it would be appropriate for Australia to send troops overseas, possibly to relieve British units in Singapore, Burma or India. If however Japan remained neutral, then Australia should hold formations ready for the defence of Singapore, New Zealand and the Pacific Islands. But the British did not want the proposed Expeditionary Force of the RAAF, preferring instead that the RAAF should replace RAF squadrons overseas when the Australian squadrons had been re-equipped with modern aircraft.[11] It was all very confusing and not a little discouraging. In the first place the Australians could all too easily imagine a third alternative posture from Japan: one of hostility, in which case they considered that their forces should be sent overseas only in defence of Australia itself. Nor were they gratified by the idea that the most useful function that Australian servicemen could fulfil was to take up garrison and police duties to relieve British servicemen for the actual battlefront.[12] The rejection of the RAAF expeditionary force was also unaccountable, since it would not have been difficult for the British to have re-equipped the Australian squadrons as they arrived. The net result seemed to be that 'on advice from London, squadrons that might promptly have gone overseas remained in Australia and – an important consideration for the RAAF – a Force headquarters and three wing headquarters commanded by senior offices of the RAAF were not established in the theatre of war'.[13]

But the fact was that neither London nor Paris knew what kind of a war they should be fighting at the time. French Commander-in-Chief Gamelin had proposed on 6 September that his forces should start 'leaning against the Siegfried Line' to test its strength after 17 September.[14] But the Polish air force had largely been destroyed already in combat or on the ground, the initial Polish defensive strategy was in ruins, the Germans were racing for Warsaw, and the Polish government was appealing for aid. The French actually began an infinitely cautious movement of skirmishers across the frontier on 8 September. The British began dropping leaflets, allegedly in an attempt to keep the air war humane in the west, regardless of what was happening to Poland in the east.

The British had another reason for preferring a non-provocative air bombardment of Germany: seven bombers had been lost out of the twenty-nine unleashed in a strike against Wilhelmshaven on 4 September, to Chamberlain's great distress.[15] This was however not going to be the final answer. On 22 September Stanley Bruce intervened directly, suggesting to Under-Secretary for Air Balfour that Australia, New Zealand and Canada should pool their resources for the training of air personnel, to serve in Britain as members of their own Dominion air forces. Meanwhile Polish resistance had collapsed, and the Dominion governments wrestled with an appreciation of the world situation from London, which suggested that Russia was the key to the future; that Turkey's insistence on staying neutral would make it impossible to defend Rumania if the Germans were to move in that direction; that a stalemate in the west was now likely until a possible Allied offensive in the spring of 1940; but that even so time was on the side of the Allies.[16] More seriously, the appreciation noted that there was little evidence of any genuine desire on the part of Japan for an understanding with Britain. This naturally helped to convince the Australians that it would be hazardous to send an expeditionary force of any size overseas until the position of Japan had been clarified.[17] Menzies suggested hopefully that Britain would not in fact be asking for large military forces, and that the most vital assistance of the Dominions would be in providing trained airmen.

It was also possible that the dilemma might be solved by calling the war off altogether. The elimination of Poland might well have appeared

to have removed the basic reason for fighting in the first place. The
German peace offer was made on 6 October. The British Cabinet had
however already considered a telegram from General Smuts, the assassin
of the Singapore naval base, the opponent of conciliation with Italy, the
leader of the Dominion that could be counted on to make the least
relevant contribution to the general war effort. Smuts advised that 'any
German peace offer now will not be sincere but will simply be meant as a
peace offensive to weaken us'.[18] This assessment was almost certainly at
fault; the whole thrust of German diplomatic activity was towards the
East, and there was every reason to believe that Hitler would have
welcomed any settlement with Britain and France which would have
enabled him to enjoy the fruits of his victory over Poland. It was
however congenial to Chamberlain, who had already concluded that
Hitler was a madman with whom fair dealing was impossible. After
further exchanges with Smuts, Chamberlain replied on 12 October that
no reliance could be put on the promises of the existing German
government.[19] No heed was taken of an urgent message from New
Zealand that it was 'essential that, without the slightest degree weakening our determination to bring an end to aggression once and for all,
no door should even at the present juncture be closed that might lead to
a peaceful solution whether by international conference or other possible
means'.[20] Menzies for his part hoped that victory would be followed by
'a great display of generosity and justice', and that Germany would be
expected 'to play her part as a great nation on a footing free and equal.
Those who advocate not mere defeat but the destruction of Germany
pay too little attention to the problems which are and will be presented
by Russia, Italy and Japan.' The New Zealanders repeated their anxiety
'to seize the earliest possible moment for sincere and constructive peace
discussions'.[21]

   This was no mere display of appeasement or defeatism: the Australian
government in fact decided on 21 October to allow all the ships of the
RAN to be sent out of Australian waters on British directions, provided
that they were sent back as soon as complications arose in the Far East.
Meanwhile the British continued to assure Canberra and Wellington
that the danger of Japanese aggression was in fact remote and that in any
event 'long before Japanese action threatened Australia or New Zealand,
America would be at war'.[22] They did not however tell the Dominion
governments that they had given the Americans to understand that

their position in the Far East was critical, and that they were 'counting on full American co-operation and support'.[23] On the contrary, War Minister Hore-Belisha told New Zealand Acting Prime Minister Fraser that it 'would be safe to take a chance on the continued neutrality of Japan'. Moreover he had been assured by the French General Staff 'that the Maginot Line was virtually impregnable . . .'. Accordingly it was suggested that New Zealand's expeditionary force should be sent to the Middle East, which 'was a very central position, and training facilities were excellent', presumably to release British troops stationed there for service on the actual battlefront.[24]

Fraser expressed regrets on sentimental grounds that his troops were apparently not to be allowed to complete their training in the United Kingdom itself. However New Zealand would be guided by British direction as usual. In any case the New Zealand government was anxious to get its First Echelon overseas anywhere, because 'the retention of our voluntary system of recruiting is to some extent dependent on the knowledge and the fact that the men will serve overseas'.[25] This was not so evidently the case in Australia. The Australian government was still reluctant to send any number of troops overseas before the defence position in the Far East had been clarified. Moreover Supply Minister Casey, who had been visiting the front in France at the invitation of the British government, considered the defences on the British front to be dangerously inadequate, and was prepared to advise against allowing Australian troops to be placed in a hopeless position there.[26] A further complication was provided by the Dutch, who after assuring the Australians that the Netherlands East Indies were well able to defend themselves even if Holland was at war in Europe, tentatively suggested that exchanges on defence problems might be held between Dutch and Australian officials in Batavia.[27]

The Australians were however being given no time to consider their problems rationally. Stanley Bruce warned Menzies on 17 November that the New Zealanders had apparently decided to send the First Echelon of their expeditionary force overseas as soon as possible after 20 January and that 'owing to the shortage of shipping the War Office wish to arrange the dates of despatch of both forces so that the same ships can be used on alternative trips'.[28] Australia had of course not yet decided to send an expeditionary force at all. But Bruce's cable was accompanied by a rather condescending one from Churchill, which assured Menzies without the least justification that: 'A Japanese attack upon Singapore would require at least 50,000 troops to undertake siege operations for some four to five months. . . . The Admiralty would make such dispositions as would enable them to offer timely resistance either to a serious attack upon Singapore or to the invasion of Australia or New Zealand. . . . The Admiralty can be trusted to make appropriate dispositions to meet events as they emerge from imagination into reality.'[29] It was of course by no means evident that the Admiralty could be trusted to do anything of the kind. Menzies hastily warned the New Zealanders that it would be important to 'watch developments of the next three-four weeks before committing ourselves to despatch of our Division overseas'.[30] He also protested to Casey that Cabinet was not yet satisfied

having regard to the figures you give relating to the number of British Divisions in France, that presence of Australian Division is sufficiently urgent to justify us in incurring risk with our own defence position. One thing in particular is puzzling us [he added]: it seems to be assumed that approximately 40 vessels and relevant naval convoy could be obtained at short notice to transport special Division to Egypt, yet the Commerce Department has for weeks been endeavouring to get some sort of satisfaction in relation to shipping urgently needed to transport our export commodities. . . . We cannot reconcile these two things. It would appear that, having regard to the shipping position, we must determine the relative priority of such things as wool and wheat and the special Division.[31]

But Menzies was not going to get the time to determine such priorities. The New Zealand government had already told the British on 20 November, without telling Canberra and before receiving Menzies's warning cable, that they would in fact be sending the First Echelon overseas in January.[32] On 21 November Menzies received a cable from Fraser that the Second New Zealand Expeditionary Force was about to depart; that there was no time to discuss the matter; and that New Zealand Prime Minister Savage would be making a broadcast to this effect on 23 November.[33] Trans-Tasman co-operation was working no more smoothly than it had in August 1914.

Menzies might feel that he had little choice. He now told Fraser that Australia too would be sending 6th Division overseas as soon as it had reached a suitable stage of training, but regretted that it had not been possible for the New Zealand government to consult with him before making their own decision, especially as the two governments had already agreed to exchange views on defence policy.[34] On 29 November he announced that an Australian division would be leaving as well as the NZEF. This immediately precipitated a new British appreciation of the war situation, calculated to allay Australian resentment: it was considered unlikely that the United States 'would impassively watch the acquisition by Japan of naval bases in the west and southwest of the Philippines . . .'. In any event 'should Japanese encroachment begin, or should Great Britain pass into a state of war with Japan, the Admiralty would make such dispositions as would enable them to offer timely resistance, either to a serious attack upon Singapore or the invasion of Australia and New Zealand'. However these dispositions apparently 'need not take the form of stationing a fleet at Singapore, but would be of a character to enable the necessary concentrations to be made eastward in ample time to prevent a disaster'. The appreciation was accompanied by a suggestion that Australia establish an army corps in the Middle East by sending another division.[35] Menzies angrily replied that the Australian government had not considered creating a second division for overseas service. Resentfully developing the theme to Casey, he remarked that

having regard to the importance of coordination with New Zealand and to the points you make about the value of releasing British troops from the Middle East, we are prepared to agree [to the despatch of 6th Division overseas. However, he said that he was] bound to tell you . . . that we do so under protest as we feel that in this matter we have been in effect forced into a course of action which we would not otherwise have adopted. For example, we resent being told that shipping is already on its way for the purpose of collecting our troops on January 2nd when we were not consulted before the departure of the vessels. It is the general feeling of Cabinet that there has been in this matter a quite perceptible disposition to treat Australia as a colony. . . .[36]

In this mood Menzies could only have regarded as positively offensive a strangely euphoric cable from Churchill, in which he proclaimed that the Admiralty

were most grateful to Australian War Department for loyal and clairvoyant strategy which has to the uninstructed eye denuded Australia of naval forces. . . . The Admiralty regard the defence of Australia, and of Singapore as a stepping stone to Australia, as ranking next to the mastering of the principal fleet to which we are opposed, and the duty of defending Australia against serious attack would take precedence over British interests in the Mediterranean . . . the Admiralty were prepared to close the Mediterranean at Gibraltar and the Suez Canal and sacrificing important interests in that area proceeding to relief of Singapore or aid of Australia in event of serious attack.[37]

Menzies could however reflect that it was not only Australian wishes that Churchill did not seem to think it important to regard: the Canadian 1st Division of 7,449 officers and men arrived in England on 17 December. It had been clearly understood between London and Ottawa that news of their arrival would be withheld for two days for security reasons, and then released first in Canada. Churchill broadcast the news of the division's arrival on 18 December, without reference to the Canadian government.[38] Imperial co-operation in wartime was off to a distinctly ominous start.

It did not of course halt the progress. On 5 January the 6,529 all ranks of the First Echelon of the Second NZEF left Lyttleton Harbour. Australia's 6th Division, 6,571 strong, sailed from Sydney on 10 January. Twenty-five years of history seemed to have vanished as irrelevant: the furies in slouch hats were crossing the seas again to support the British in a European war, leaving their own huge dominions utterly defenceless against possible aggressors far nearer home: the most dreaded fighting men in the world were sailing to take up their duties in the scruffy peacefulness of the Middle East, releasing British soldiers for the serious business of combat. It might have seemed an odd way to fight a war.

The prevailing mood in London and Paris might indeed conservatively have been described as odd. Both the British and French governments were concerned at the apparent superiority in manpower and matériel that they expected the Germans to be able to deploy against them in the spring. But their concern expressed itself in unexpected ways. Roosevelt had written to Chamberlain on 11 September assuring him that it was 'definitely a part of the Administration policy' to secure the repeal of the arms embargo, allowing Britain and France access to the war production of the United States.[39] Chamberlain had however explained to Roosevelt that this war was not going to be won by vast clashes of men and armour

1 LEFT TO RIGHT: General Louis Botha, J. X. Merriman, General Jan C. Smuts.

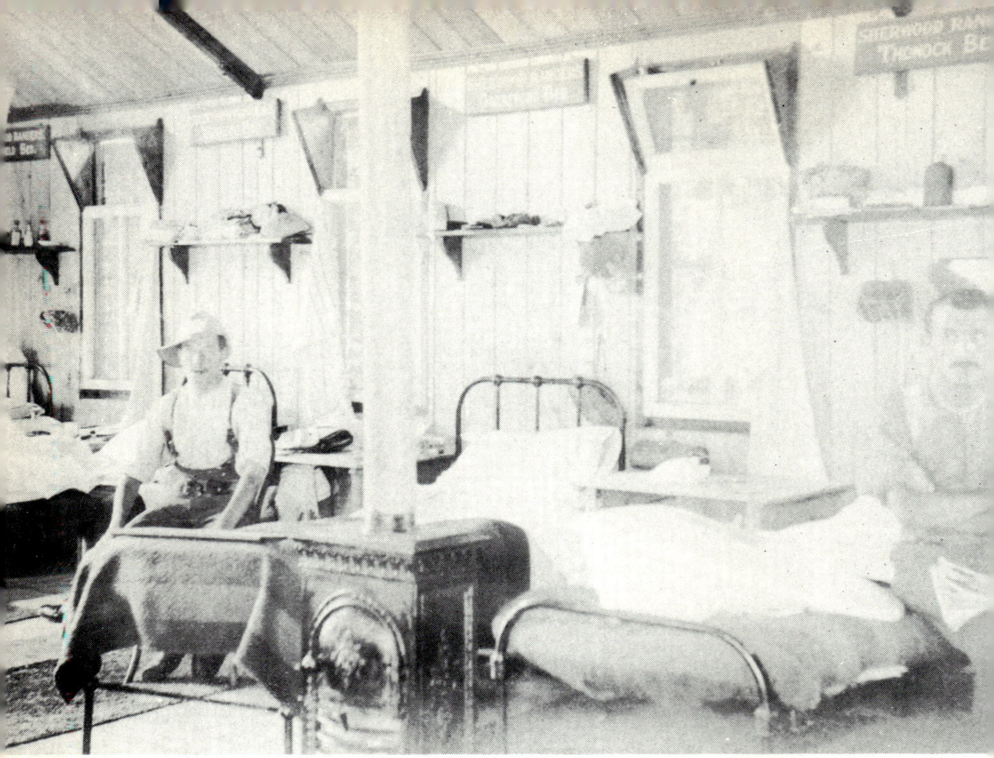

2 The base hospital at Deerfontein during the South African War, showing the dormitory of the Sherwood Rangers Yeomanry.

3 Bluejackets of HMS *Terrible* during the Boer War.

4 Lord Roberts visiting the Natal battlefields.

5 A Boer commando unit.

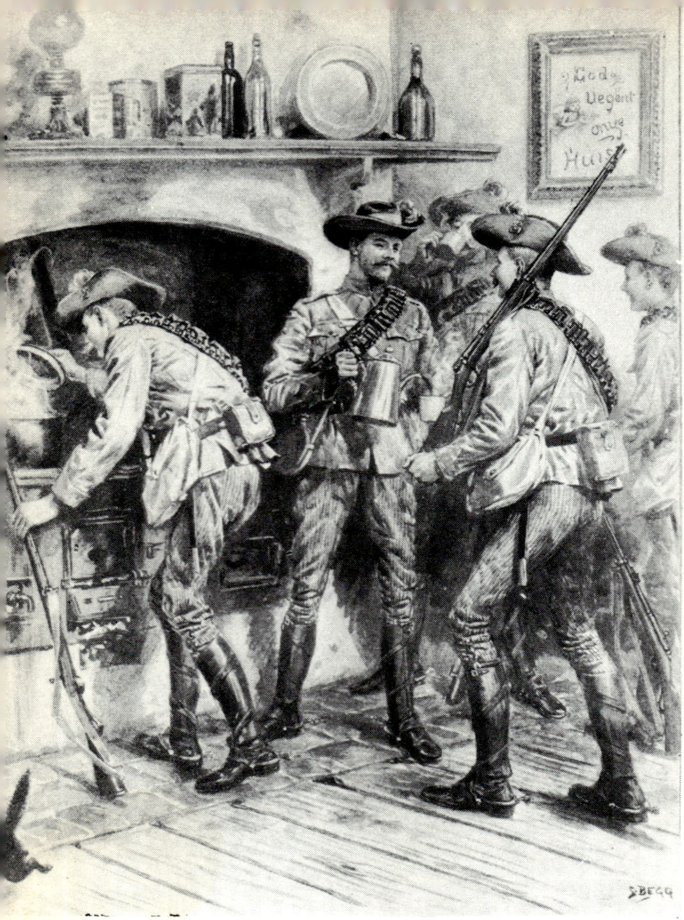
S.BEGG

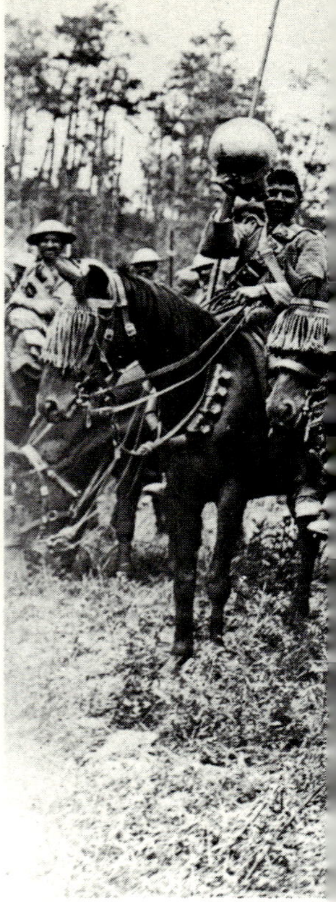

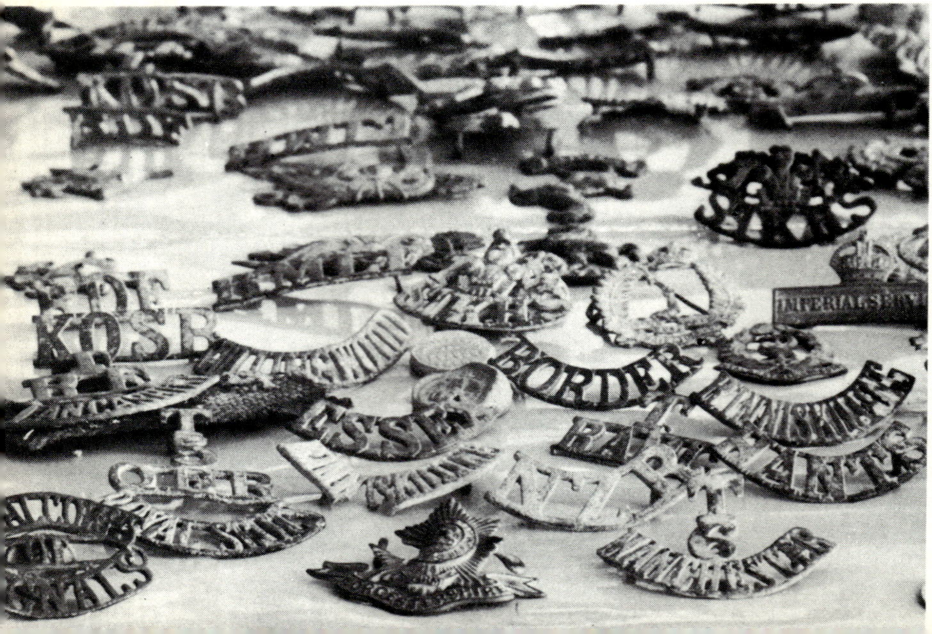
KOSB
BORDER
MANCHESTER

6 TOP LEFT: Boer War. Enemy troops fled so suddenly from Lubbes Hoop Farm when attacked by Colonial soldiers, that they left behind a hot meal.

7 LEFT: Regimental badges of the Allies who fought at Gallipoli now in the Alicitepe Museum.

8 TOP RIGHT: Deccan Horsemen, 1916.

9 RIGHT: Old guns at Gallipoli rotting away in the fort at Chanak (the Turks have no museum).

10 TOP: Alfred Deakin, Prime Minister of Australia, 1903–4, 1905–8, 1909–10.

11 BOTTOM LEFT: Sir Joseph Cook, Australian Prime Minister, later Australian High Commissioner in London.

12 BOTTOM RIGHT: John Curtin, Prime Minister of Australia, 1941–5.

13 TOP: HMS *Dreadnought*, 1906.

14 BOTTOM LEFT: Komiatum Ridge, New Guinea. Australian troops have driven out the Japanese garrison. At the end of this shaft is an elaborate underground shelter fitted with seats.

15 BOTTOM RIGHT: The first air raid on Darwin. An Australian ship watching the US destroyer *Peary* burning.

16 TOP: Winston S.
Churchill with Franklin D.
Roosevelt at Yalta, 1945.

17 BOTTOM: Field Marshal
the Viscount Montgomery
of Alamein by Sir Oswald
Birley.

but by mounting economic pressure, in which endurance would triumph: 'not by a complete and spectacular military victory, which is unlikely under modern conditions, but by convincing the Germans that they cannot win'.[40] It was therefore important for the British not to expend their financial resources too early by extravagant purchases in the United States. Cordell Hull noted bleakly in the margin: 'Interesting'.

North American businessmen had stronger terms. Total British war orders by the end of April 1940 amounted to only $81 million in Canada and $236 million in the United States: 'not worth a hoot in hell', as the Americans commented.[41] But the Allies did not appear to need even their own inadequate war production: the French sold to Eastern Europe half their output of their latest tanks, 830 anti-tank guns and 500 field guns, to go with the Hurricanes and Battles being sold by the British to these countries.[42] However at the same time that they were thus reducing their own capacity to deal with the immediate problem of Germany, the French at least were apparently prepared to multiply the odds indefinitely against themselves by inviting a confrontation with Russia. Chief of Imperial General Staff Ironside was entertaining the notion of an intensive air attack on Russian oil supplies at Baku, meantime securing the Middle East against Russian reprisal by using the Australian division, which he considered to be the best available.[43] This particular lurch into disaster was avoided. However the shock of the German invasion of Denmark and Norway on 9 April revealed suddenly the extraordinary inappropriateness of British as well as French military planning.

The campaign began promisingly, with a flourish of British exploits at sea. However most of Norway's cities had already been seized by the Germans by 11 April, while the British and French were still debating the composition of an expeditionary force to be sent to the new theatre. In the meantime another three-cornered wrangle had developed between the British, Australian and New Zealand governments over the reinforcement of the New Zealand First Echelon and the Australian 6th Division. Menzies had in fact already agreed with Labour support to raise a second division to keep the Australian Imperial Force supplied. The second and third convoys to complete 6th Division were due to sail, when the Admiralty suggested that the strength of the naval escort be reduced to meet the exigencies of the Norwegian campaign. It seemed

like 1914 all over again. The New Zealanders asked for maximum protection. The Australians suggested that the troops should in fact not be
embarked until the position had been clarified. The position was however immediately obscured by a British proposal that the convoys might
be diverted to the United Kingdom instead of the Middle East. The
Australian government protested against the possibility of the AIF being
divided and thereby getting out of their control. Once again the New
Zealanders forced the issue: they decided abruptly that they had no
time for further discussion, warned Canberra that it would be embarrassing 'if Australia were to take one course and New Zealand another', and
agreed on diversion of the convoy to the United Kingdom in return for
'the most explicit assurances re safety of convoy' from the Admiralty.[44]

Mackenzie King was closeted with Roosevelt during all this, attempting to determine what specific assistance the United States might be
prepared to let the British and French have if required, as it almost
certainly would be. Roosevelt was in fact extremely forthcoming: he
promised to send a Coastguard cutter to the Danish dependency of
Greenland, to reassure the local population and warn the Germans off;
spoke of letting the Canadians have some defence equipment belonging
to the US Navy 'at a nominal figure'; and even 'spoke of possibly finding
it necessary to send destroyers and cruisers to help the British'.[45] It
would hardly have seemed superfluous. The British and French were
bungling the campaign totally. A hammer-blow against Trondheim,
throwing the strength of the British Home Fleet against the *Luftwaffe*,
was countermanded, and smaller, more tentative, expeditions launched,
to be defeated in detail by smaller but more enterprising numbers of
Germans. Once again British and Commonwealth communications
seemed to be unfortunately lacking: after a British proposal that a force
from Canada's 1st Division should be committed to Norway, the Department of External Affairs protested bitterly:

We would have expected that Canadian Government would have been
informed by United Kingdom Government immediately . . . we are not
kept sufficiently informed. We are told what has happened; very seldom,
what will happen or may happen . . . we have no representative on the
War Cabinet or on the Cabinet Secretariat. . . . The Allied War Council
meets with Norwegian and Polish representatives, but not Canadian . . .
we do not seem to have been concerned at our exclusion from the Councils
of our Allies in a war in which our whole future is at stake.[46]

Concern might perhaps have been less marked if the Allied War Council had shown itself more competent to manage its affairs without help from the Dominions. The Norwegian experience was far from auguring well for the future. Many of its lessons were indeed obscure or ambiguous. It was none the less clear that the Germans had fought with far more dash and efficiency; that Allied strategy and tactics were alike inferior; that the anti-aircraft defences of British warships were utterly inappropriate and inadequate; and that some of the greatest tragedies arose from errors of judgement almost too bad to be true: troops were landed in arctic conditions without snowshoes or skis, aircraft were left to operate without lubricating oil, and in a weird reversal of the customary sea-versus-air situation, a British aircraft carrier was trapped at sea and sunk by a German battleship. At the same time any verdict on the Norwegian campaign had to be inconclusive. The fact was that the Allies had overwhelmed the German forces in the north before they were obliged to return to Britain; the British, French and Poles had in fact managed to commit some 24,500 men to the struggle against a mere 10,000 Germans; and the actual figures of casualties were not too depressing. The Allies lost 3,734 men, the Germans 5,296. At sea the Allies had sacrificed an aircraft carrier, a cruiser, an anti-aircraft cruiser, a sloop, 9 destroyers and 6 submarines against a loss of 3 cruisers, 10 destroyers, 8 submarines and a motor torpedo boat, which effectively put the German navy out of business as a fighting force. Even in the air, where the Germans had deployed an overwhelming force of 800 operational aircraft and 200 transports, the Allies had suffered in all a loss of 60 aircraft at most, including those lost with the aircraft carrier *Glorious*, against a total German loss of 242. The Norwegian disaster had at least some mitigating features.

It would have been hard to find any in the overshadowing calamity of the Battle of France. Here again the Allies had reasonable grounds initially to expect success. On almost every count the balance of arms was significantly in their favour. The German forces committed to the campaign in the west numbered approximately 136 divisions, with 7,700 guns and 2,693 tanks.[47] They confronted a French army of 94 divisions, with 11,200 guns and at least 2,800 tanks; a British army of 10 divisions, with 2,472 guns and 289 tanks; a Belgian army of 22 divisions, and a Dutch one of 10. The situation in the air was indeed less clear and probably different. The Germans committed somewhere between 2,670 and

3,534 aircraft out of a total availability of 4,549. Of the Allied air forces, the Dutch and Belgians between them could amass 309 aircraft, of which the latest Dutch Fokkers were certainly a match for the German Me110; the Royal Air Force had a total strength of 1,873 and the French of either 2,923 or 3,289 modern aircraft. On this basis the Germans might well have had to face odds of at least five to two against even in the air, had the Allies actually put their aircraft where they were most needed.[48]

What guaranteed German victory was the fact that the Allies did not put their superiority in anything where it was needed. The front in France was evidently crumbling by 13 May. On 14 May the British government decided that the Australian and New Zealand convoys already at sea should be diverted for the defence of the United Kingdom itself. On the same day the Germans breached the French defences on the Meuse. For the first time since 1805 it was possible to believe that Britain might actually be in imminent danger of military occupation. Churchill cabled Roosevelt on 15 May, asking directly for 'the loan of forty or fifty . . . older destroyers', as well as for 'several hundred of the latest types of aircraft, of which you are now getting delivery'.[49] In addition he suggested that the United States should 'keep the Japanese quiet in the Pacific, using Singapore in any way convenient'.[50] The last demand was particularly timely: political changes were already being mooted in Japan, tending towards a greater alignment with the totalitarian powers. Moreover, in an act of incredible prescience, United States Chief of Naval Operations Admiral Harold R. Stark had ordered the United States Fleet to remain at Pearl Harbour on 9 May, after completing its manoeuvres, instead of returning to San Diego. This however did not mean that the Americans would be justified in going any further at the moment to the assistance of France and the British Empire. Any movement as far east as Singapore would only leave continental America uncovered. Nor was it necessarily obvious that signing away two-fifths of the United States' destroyer strength to Britain would assist United States defence, when the ships were all too likely to fall into German hands in the event of British defeat.

Meanwhile the Commonwealth governments sought to face a situation for which nothing in their past experience had prepared them. The response to calamity was everywhere one of apparently renewed determination. The Governor-General of Canada affirmed in the Speech from the Throne on 17 May that Canada would stand shoulder to shoulder with Britain. On 21 May, as the Germans swept past Arras towards the sea, Menzies warned his Cabinet that the whole war situation had changed and that they could no longer count on getting help from the United Kingdom in the Pacific.[51] Despite this, as the situation worsened, the Australians decided to raise another division for overseas service; to send three of their remaining ships in Australian waters to relieve the East Indies Squadron of the Royal Navy; and, more than all, to release to the British the forty-nine Lockheed Hudsons building for Australia in the United States, despite British endeavours to prevent the contract from being fulfilled. At the same time another Australian Hudson squadron was sent to Singapore to replace one of the British Blenheim squadrons there.[52] Having made every possible sacrifice of Australian security to the cause of Britain, Menzies then appealed to Roosevelt not to cover Australia in the Pacific, but to 'rapidly and substantially increase British air power ... even if this means despatch to Great Britain of machines already in commission or designed for your own Air Force ...'.[53] Australia had itself done at least as much.

This was not indeed necessarily a universally popular policy in Australia. Nor was it yet certain that any efforts by the Dominions could do more than involve the Empire still more deeply in British catastrophe. Some kind of deliverance was achieved by the successful completion of the evacuation of Dunkirk on 4 June. The event supplied Mackenzie King with uniquely the correct rhetoric with which to rally his Quebecois supporters, already more reconciled to the war effort by the sufferings of France. Announcing that construction would begin on 100 ships and 300 tanks, and that the entire capacity of the Canadian automobile industry would be turned to the replacement of equipment lost by the British army in Flanders, King proclaimed that 'every fort in Canada will be another Calais and every harbor be another Dunkirk before the men and women of our land will allow the light and life of their Christian faith to be extinguished by the powers of evil ...'.[54] It was at least an attempt to prepare the Canadian people for the disconcerting prospect of having Winston Churchill himself arrive in their midst after the fall of Britain, determined to carry on the war against Germany.

The Canadians at all events could feel certain that any German strike

against their own territory would be overwhelmingly likely to lead to
direct United States intervention. Australia had no such assurance.
Moreover the Japanese were becoming increasingly restive. The British
Ambassador in Tokyo warned that 'unless some "positive" methods
were followed, he doubted whether it would be possible to prevent
Japan from being drawn into the war on the Axis side'.[55] Not surprisingly the Australian Railway Workers' Union protested that in this
situation the despatch of Australian troops overseas was contrary to the
preservation of the defence of their own country.[56] Anxiety mounted
when the Japanese demanded on 9 June that the Shanghai garrison be
withdrawn, the Hong Kong frontier closed, and supplies to China along
the Burma Road halted. On 11 June Menzies asked Churchill for an
appreciation of the alternatives with which the British Empire was confronted, while the Australian War Cabinet met grimly to consider
'whether or not we should continue to rely on the pre-war undertaking
that a British squadron of capital ships would proceed to Singapore
immediately on hostile action in the Pacific'.[57] The answer came flatly
on 13 June:

> In the unlikely event of Japan, in spite of the restraining influence of the
> United States, taking the opportunity to alter the status quo in the Far
> East, we should be faced with a naval situation in which, without the
> assistance of France, we should not have sufficient forces to meet the
> combined German and Italian Navies in European waters and the Japanese
> Fleet in the Far East. In the circumstances envisaged it is most im-
> probable that we could send adequate reinforcements to the Far East. We
> should therefore have to rely on the USA to safeguard our interests
> there.[58]

The Singapore Strategy was thus apparently over, if indeed it had
ever existed. It might be true that the British commitment had been
absolute,[59] although it had never been exactly precise or consistent; but
what mattered now was that it simply was not going to be fulfilled. The
New Zealanders replied furiously that

> a departure is made from the understanding, reinforced by repeated and
> most explicit assurances, that a strong British fleet would be available to,
> and would, proceed to Singapore should the circumstances so require,
> even if this involved the abandonment of British interests in the Mediter-
> ranean. . . . His Majesty's Government in New Zealand must observe

that the undertaking to despatch an adequate fleet to Singapore, if required, formed the basis of the whole of this Dominion's defence preparations.[60]

The New Zealanders' complaint was the more acute because the Anzac convoy was at that time about six days out of the Clyde. The troops actually arrived on the eve of the French surrender on 22 June. New Zealand General Freyberg commented that 'the arrival of the Australians and New Zealanders in the circumstances had been most opportune and had steadied the nation considerably'.[61] He added imperturbably on 15 June: 'I am sure Cabinet will agree with me, that New Zealand troops must be prepared to accept battle upon uneven terms in defence of Great Britain.'[62] He was quite right.

Nor was it only the New Zealanders and Australians who accepted the necessity of committing their only trained troops to a desperate defence of the Home Islands on the other side of the globe. Extraordinarily it was the Canadian 1st Division that was providing the key factor in the land defence of the United Kingdom. General McNaughton assured Chief of Imperial General Staff Sir John Dill on 29 June that 1st Division would prove 'a quick moving, hard hitting, determined force'.[63] This understated the case. Of the twenty-eight divisions in being in the Home Islands in one form or another, the Canadian 1st Division and the British 52nd Lowland Division were actually the only two both fully trained and at full strength. The 1st Division was the strongest piece on the British side of the board, and would have been relied upon to deliver the counter-attack to a German invasion.

The Canadians had the further satisfaction of being all together. The Australian and New Zealand forces in the British Isles were separated from the rest of the divisions in Egypt and Palestine. And now it was suggested by London that they should be divided still further. The proposal was that the newly formed 7th Division should be moved to Malaya, one brigade at a time. Meanwhile British Commander-in-Chief Middle East Sir Archibald Wavell planned a regroupment of his forces, which would fragment the New Zealand forces there, with the First Echelon scattered in six segments, only the headquarters staff actually remaining in Cairo. This at least was firmly opposed by New Zealand GOC Sir Bernard Freyberg, who warned Wavell that 'as no such change can be made without the approval of the New Zealand Government, I hope this proposal will not be proceeded with. I do not wish to disclose to the New Zealand Government the proposals as outlined by you to break up the New Zealand forces, as they would make a most unfavourable impression in New Zealand official circles with repercussions you probably have not foreseen.'[64] The New Zealand government was getting anxious in any case: on 9 July Prime Minister Fraser suggested to Churchill that perhaps he did not 'completely understand the point of view that is being forced by circumstances upon the Government and people of New Zealand, and, it is believed, Australia'.[65] Churchill promptly replied, reminding the New Zealanders that 'the immediate threat is to the United Kingdom, the security of which is vital', and hoping that it would be possible to reassemble the Australian 6th Division and the New Zealand 2nd Division later in the year.[66]

The New Zealand government still had the gravest misgivings about sending a Third Echelon away from the Pacific. It was decided in any case to divert a brigade group to garrison Fiji, the key to New Zealand's own security. A cable to London on 3 August began with the alarming suggestion that it 'might well be, in the existing circumstances, that the best contribution this Dominion could make to the common effort would be fully to ensure its own defence'. However it was characteristically admitted that 'a large view must be taken'; that in the last resort 'this Dominion must stand or fall according to the decision in the main theatres of war'; and that the Third Echelon would in fact be sent overseas. However Wellington took out some insurance by retaining 3,050 men for the defence of Fiji.[67] This concession was rewarded by an almost euphoric cable from Churchill expressing the view that Japan would not actually declare war unless Germany could first make a successful invasion of Britain itself, and promising that in the first phase of an Anglo-Japanese war

we should of course defend Singapore, which if attacked – which is unlikely – ought to stand a long siege. We should also be able to base on Ceylon a battlecruiser and a fast aircraft carrier which, with the Australian and New Zealand ships which would return to you, would exercise a very powerful deterrent upon any hostile raiding cruisers. . . . We are about to reinforce with more first-class units the Eastern Mediterranean Fleet. This Fleet could of course at any time be sent through the Canal into the Indian Ocean, or to relieve Singapore.[68]

It was accompanied by an even more enthusiastic missive to the Australians, which explained that we hope to maintain ourselves in Egypt and to keep the Eastern Fleet at Alexandria during the first phase of an Anglo-Japanese war should that occur. . . . If however, contrary to prudence and self-interest, Japan set about invading Australia or New Zealand on a large scale, I have the explicit authority of Cabinet to assure you that we should then cut our losses in the Mediterranean, and sacrifice every interest, save only the defence and feeding of this Island, on which all depends, and would proceed in good time to your aid with a fleet able to give battle to any Japanese force which could be placed in Australian waters, and able to parry any invading force, or certainly cut its communications with Japan. . . .[69]

Both these assurances had some extraordinary features. In the first place Churchill clearly had no idea at all whether Singapore could stand a siege or not. The fact was that the city could not resist a siege at all, because of the problems presented by its overcrowded civilian population. Nor was there any way in which a battlecruiser and an aircraft carrier could be expected to provide any kind of deterrent to the Japanese Combined Fleet. The cable to the Australians was wholly illogical. There was no chance of a British fleet's being able to arrive in Australian waters 'in good time' once the Japanese had actually 'set about invading Australia or New Zealand on a large scale'; and no chance that any fleet that the British would actually be able to send to the Pacific would be able to give battle on anything like equal terms to the Combined Fleet. But Churchill was contemplating at the time a quite different military venture.

On the same day that the reassuring cables were sent to Wellington and Canberra, the British Chiefs of Staff decided to send 102 tanks, 48 25-pounder field guns and 107 aircraft to Egypt to repel the Italian threat to the Suez Canal.[70] The decision to make this diversion of resources at a time when the air battle for Britain was mounting to a climax was probably the most heroic in the history of warfare. At the same time the decision for an offensive in the Middle East necessarily involved increasing the peril to Australia and the whole Eastern Empire. Naturally it was supported by the South Africans: Smuts, whose own South African Brigade was firmly retained in the continent, and indeed south of the Equator, in Kenya, assured Churchill reliably that diplomacy was the only weapon available to Britain in the Far East and that it was desirable at the moment to concentrate forces on the vital

British and Mediterranean fronts.[71] It was less easy for the Australians, for whom the Middle East strategy meant sending their armed forces around the world, and who were still convinced in any event that Singapore was the key to their security. On the other hand they were also convinced that garrison duties in Malaya would be unsuited to the Australian temperament. It was decided as a compromise to send another detachment of the RAAF to Singapore, but to send 7th Division to the Middle East.

The Australian decision might have been different had they known that at that time the Admiralty were explaining to United States Admiral Robert L. Ghormley that they had been forced to accept that events had invalidated the whole Far Eastern strategy. They could no longer assume that any threat to their interests there would necessarily be seaborne, or that they would be able to send a fleet to the Far East even within three months of an aggressive move by Japan. Nor could they station an adequate force there because their main concentration outside the United Kingdom was the Middle East.[72] It was accordingly suggested again that the United States should assume responsibility for Singapore, to which Ghormley could only point out again:

(a) the necessity for maintaining the concentration of US Naval forces, with the US Fleet in Hawaiian waters;
(b) the grave, and perhaps insuperable, logistic difficulties involved in operations of US forces six thousand miles from US repair and supply bases;
(c) the probability that US naval forces would be required in the Atlantic, if strategic priority in a two-ocean war were given to the defeat of Germany and Italy.[73]

For Churchill, of course, the Far East could be only a distraction. He promptly rejected an Indian request for anti-aircraft guns, pointing out the regrettable fact that in defence terms India, after a year of war, was still considerably more of a liability than an asset.[74] He similarly denounced the idea of using the Australian 7th Division to garrison the Malay Peninsula 'against a possible war with Japan, and a still more unlikely Japanese siege of Singapore'.[75] Churchill's own strategical vision was unclouded:

The Navy can lose us the war, but only the Air Force can win it. . . . The Fighters are our salvation, but the Bombers alone provide the means of victory. We must therefore develop the power to carry an ever-increasing volume of explosives to Germany, so as to pulverise the entire industry and scientific structure on which the war effort and economic life of the enemy depend. . . . In no other way at present visible can we hope to overcome the immense military power of Germany. . . . The Air Force and its action on the largest scale must therefore, subject to what is said later, claim the first place over the Navy or the Army.[76]

It can only be said that the concept was incredibly hazardous, the effort a failure and the reasoning unsupportable, on either logical or empirical grounds. It was in the first place difficult to see how Britain could hope to win a contest of aerial bombardment against a country with a greater population, twice its geographical size, even without its conquests, and a far greater industrial capacity. But in any case the sole unmistakable lesson of the war so far had been that battles were won as a consequence of securing mastery of the air over the battlefield, and this was achieved by fighters providing cover for light bombers. The Germans had lost the Battle of Britain, not because they needed more bombers, but because they did not have nearly enough fighters. The simple fact was that Britain could not possibly win a war against Germany with the resources available to it in 1940. What could be done was to hold the line with a deliberately defensive strategy until one or other of the great neutral powers of the United States or Russia became involved directly.

This was never to be Churchill's view. He had already agreed to a proposal by de Gaulle to land a Free French force in West Africa at Dakar. An expedition of 4,200 British and 2,700 French troops left on 31 August. The RAN flagship HMAS *Australia* was directed to accompany the expedition on 3 September. In an acutely unlucky affair, the landing was called off just at the moment when the French commander was about to surrender, having exhausted his ammunition. Two French submarines were sunk, as well as two destroyers, one by HMAS *Australia*. However sinking French warships had not exactly been the object of the exercise. Irritated at learning that an Australian ship had been involved in yet another unsuccessful British amphibious operation, Menzies cabled Churchill on 29 September protesting that it was 'absolutely wrong that Australian Government should know practically nothing of details of engagement and nothing at all of decision to abandon it until after newspaper publication. I have refrained from public criticism, but privately can tell you that absence of real official information from Great Britain has frequently proved humiliating.'[77] Churchill replied with equal annoyance, stressing the sacrifices that the British had made to strengthen their position in the Middle East.[78] Menzies in reply scouted the idea that Australia was 'shirking her share. . . . We have in camp in Australia further Expeditionary Force approximating 85,000 men, many of whom will shortly be moving to the Middle East. In spite of much public doubt caused by a real fear of what Japan may do, my Government has raised naval, air and military forces and pledged our resources to munitions production on a scale previously unknown and regarded only a year ago as impossible.'[79]

This was inevitably the crux of the matter. Churchill did not take up the issue of Japan with Menzies. Nor did he tell him that two days before he had written again to Roosevelt, suggesting that he 'send an American squadron, the bigger the better, to pay a friendly visit to Singapore' in the hope that it would have 'a marked deterrent effect upon a Japanese declaration of war upon us . . .'.[80] In a further attempt to put pressure on the United States, Churchill also instructed Eden to tell Ambassador Joseph P. Kennedy that 'if Japan attacked the United States without declaring war on us we should at once range ourselves on the side of the United States and declare war upon Japan'.[81] A gap was already apparent between what Churchill was prepared to tell Australia about the situation in the Far East and what British officials were telling the United States. And now a new and major distorting factor was introduced with the appointment of Air Vice-Marshal Sir Robert Brooke-Popham as Commander-in-Chief Far East. The first defence conference at Singapore started against a background of a fundamental disagreement on first principles between Brooke-Popham, who considered that 'the possibility of a major expedition against Australia or New Zealand may be ruled out initially'[82] and the New Zealanders, who argued indignantly that an attack against themselves was not 'without the bounds of possibility', and objected to the notion that the defence of New Zealand should be accorded 'a low degree of operational priority'.[83]

There were indeed obvious grounds for concern. Two days after 11,000 men of 7th Division had sailed from Australia for the Middle East, the conference decided that 'our ability to hold Malaya beyond the immediate vicinity of Singapore in the face of a determined attack is very problematical. Moreover, in the event of successful invasion, the survival of Singapore for more than a short period is very improbable.'[84] This was rather different from what Churchill had given the Dominion governments to understand on 11 August. It was however thoroughly consistent with the details provided of the actual military situation. It was for example calculated, though it is admittedly difficult to see on what grounds, that the 'minimum defence' of Singapore would require one battleship, one aircraft carrier, five cruisers and five destroyers on the naval side.[85] Even this force was, unhappily, not available. Eleven of the sixteen combat ships of the RAN were in fact serving in the Mediterranean and the Atlantic, including all the destroyer force and both the 8-inch-gun cruisers. The only warships left in Australian waters were two 6-inch-gun cruisers, two sloops and an armed merchant cruiser. The prospect in the air was worse. It was calculated that air defence requirements would be 582 modern aircraft in Burma and Malaya, 346 in the Netherlands East Indies, 312 in Australia, 60 in New Zealand and 104 on reconnaissance on the Fiji–New Hebrides line and in the Indian Ocean. The RAAF itself would need at least 320 modern aircraft.

The discrepancy between these requirements and reality was almost ludicrous. The British government had placed a complete embargo on the export of all military aircraft. It was lifted towards the end of the year sufficiently to provide Australia with eighty-eight Fairey Battles, unfit for action on any other front except possibly Abyssinia.[86] At this stage another development occurred certain to reduce still further the defence of the Eastern Empire in Churchill's list of strategic priorities. On 28 October the Italians invaded Greece, thereby opening up a new continental front. The Greek government invoked the unilateral guarantee made by the Chamberlain government. Churchill's response was immediate: 'One strategic salient fact leaped out upon us – CRETE! The Italians must not have it. We must get it first – and at once.'[87] Plans were set in train for the diversion of the York and Lancaster Regiment to the island. Meanwhile the Australians had made a decision. Following Churchill's decision to send a squadron of Blenheims to Greece, Sir John Latham, Australian minister-designate to Tokyo, had suggested rather despairingly that Australia try to buy military aircraft from Japan.[88] At the same time Australian naval officers were sent to Washington in mufti for consultations with the Americans, in an attempt to determine what the future intentions of the United States might actually be.

It would not have helped or encouraged them if they had known it, but the Australians arrived at precisely the time that United States grand strategy was being formulated by the War Plans Division in perhaps the most important military decision ever made. The United States was resolving to make its main military effort in the Atlantic and Europe, even as Churchill ordered a further four squadrons of Blenheims and four of Hurricanes to Greece. The British Empire was lost, in a quiet week in November 1940, by decisions made independently in Washington and London, without reference to the people directly concerned. This was indeed not the fault of the Americans, who could presume that His Majesty's governments across the globe shared confidences on matters of common life and death. What was apparent to the Australians however was the American concern that 'we should do more to show by deeds that Singapore means so much to us'.[89] The American dilemma was quite genuine: if Singapore were in fact important enough for Churchill to have suggested that the United States fleet should be despatched there, then a greater United States effort in the Atlantic could be expected to have the effect of releasing British forces for the Far East. What was not comprehensible was that the British should intensify their own effort in the Mediterranean, at the same time that the United States was redeploying for an Atlantic rather than a Pacific strategy.

This was indeed the essence of 'Plan Dog', formulated by Chief of Naval Operations Admiral Harold R. Stark on 4 November. Stark's analysis was basically that

purely naval assistance would not, in my opinion, *assure* final victory for Great Britain. . . . I believe that the United States, in addition to sending naval assistance, would also need to send large air and land forces to Europe or Africa, or both, and to participate strongly in this land offensive. . . . To carry out such tasks we should have to exert a major naval and military effort in the Atlantic. We should then be able to do little more in the Pacific than remain on a strict defensive. [This meant for Stark holding the Malay Barrier against Japan] denying access to other sources of supply in Malaysia, severing her lines of communication with the Western Hemisphere and raiding communications to the mid-Pacific, the Philippines, China and Indo-China. . . .

The critical conclusion was that: 'Any strength that we might send to the Far East would, by just so much, reduce the force of our blows against Germany and Italy.'[90] The 'Atlantic First' strategy was thus formulated.

Meanwhile Churchill asked the New Zealand government to approve the despatch of units of the New Zealand Division to Crete, having already obtained the approval of the rather excessively trusting New Zealand Commander-in-Chief Sir Bernard Freyberg. Wellington objected that the division was already split in three, between England, Egypt and Palestine. Churchill agreed to drop the plan. On 12 November Stark despatched Plan Dog to the Secretary of the Navy.[91] Two days later Sir Robert Brooke-Popham was told that because of the needs of other theatres of war he would have to reduce his minimum air defence capacity for the Far East to 336 aircraft, 'which would give a very fair degree of security'.[92]

Stark himself was subject to misgivings about the ability of the British to look after their own Empire. He wrote to Ghormley on 16 November that he was 'endeavouring to get hold of the British ideas as soon as I possibly can', and congratulating him on 'apparently beginning to convince the British that there is a Western Pacific in which the United States is interested and in which they also have a very great interest'. He added in a jovial mood that 'the fact that the British thought that we would be in [the war] within two or three days after election simply confirms my view of their political sense. . . . They might have known better, but, when I think over their diplomacy for the past several years, I am not surprised at their present guesswork.'[93] Stark may not have been actually clairvoyant, although there was very little reason to suspect that he was not. It may have just happened that on the day that he wrote to Ghormley, Wavell sent 'Barbarity' force, a brigade strong, to Crete. It contained units of the New Zealand Division, despatched without the knowledge – let alone the approval – of the New Zealand government or their commander-in-chief.

Confusion and obfuscation were almost total by now. The Australians in Washington were agreeably surprised to discover that the Americans had already made plans for the 'passage of units and their maintenance' for military co-operation with British Commonwealth forces in the Far East against Japan.[94] They however remained under the impression, in the absence of any information from London, that Ghormley's talks with the British Admiralty had 'not led us any further along the path of an agreed grand strategy in the event of American cooperation'.[95] The fact was that the Ghormley conversations had led directly to Plan Dog, which Ghormley then explained in full detail to the British Admiralty on 22 November. The British agreed that the 'primary object to be achieved by the Allies would be the defeat of Germany and Italy. Our main naval effort should therefore be so directed, and only sufficient naval forces disposed in the Pacific and the Far East as would prevent vital damage being caused to Allied interests.'[96] However the British also argued that even if all else had to be abandoned 'the security of Singapore must be ensured. . . . If Singapore were lost, it would not be possible to re-establish the position in the Far East.'[97] Churchill none the less endorsed Plan Dog in a memorandum to the Admiralty, stating that in his view 'Admiral Stark is right and Plan D is strategically sound and also most highly adapted to our interests. We should therefore, so far as opportunity serves, in every way contribute to strengthen the policy of Admiral Stark, and should not use arguments inconsistent with it. . . . A strict defensive in the Far East and the acceptance of its consequences is also our policy.'[98]

The trouble was that it was not necessarily going to be His Majesty's Government in London that would have to accept any unhappy consequences of Plan Dog. The Australians were becoming frantic. Labour leader John Curtin raised alarms in the Advisory War Cabinet about battleships cruising in the waters north of Australia. On 1 December Prime Minister Menzies asked Churchill for immediate action to be taken for the security of Singapore, after the Americans had asked point blank 'What Army reinforcements, if any, does Australia propose sending to Singapore?'[99] But Churchill's mind had never been further away from the problems of the Eastern Empire. Eden had told him on 8 November of the plans for a British offensive in Libya. He was already sufficiently engrossed with the prospect of expanding Italy's Greek adventure into a new continental front against the Axis. On 27 November he warned the Foreign Office to stall off the Dominions, telling them 'that we are waiting for the Greek situation to define itself more clearly'.[100] By 3 December he had become seized with the notion of an amphibious operation against the Italian island fortress of Pantelleria. Then on 9 December everything else was drowned for the moment by the echoes of what, as Mr Barnett suggests, many people had thought would never be heard again – 'The opening salvo of a British offensive', as 7th Armoured Division, 4th Indian and the 16th British Infantry Brigade dashed forward against Marshal Graziani's stranded army.

The campaign was a staggering demonstration of the manner in which a significant margin of technological superiority can upset almost any odds. The numerical balance against the British was indeed apparently hopeless. Graziani had about 250,000 men, of whom 80,000 were with the invasion force in Egypt or in direct support. Wavell had in the whole Middle East Command about 88,000, comprising 49,000 United Kingdom troops, 25,000 Australians, 8,400 Indians and 5,400 New Zealanders, only 36,000 of whom were in Egypt. The recipe for victory was provided by eighty-seven Hurricanes and fifty-two Matilda tanks, the real terror weapon of 1940, virtually impregnable to any Italian or German anti-tank gun except the cranked-down 88mm anti-aircraft gun. The Hurricanes drove the *Regia Aeronautica*'s biplane fighters from the sky, and the Matildas rumbled over the Italian ground defences. By 11 December the British had captured 38,300 Italian prisoners, at a total loss to themselves of 624. At this rate of exchange Libya could be expected to fall within a matter of weeks. But the first taste of success had dazzled Churchill with new visions. There was probably no less urgent threat to the British Empire anywhere than that posed by the Duke of Aosta in Abyssinia, with his 91,000 Italian and 191,000 native troops. Nor could the British Empire have found a more expendable ally than Haile Selassie, emperor-in-exile. However, Churchill approved Wavell's decision on 11 December to remove 4th Indian Division to the Sudan, replacing it with 6th Australian Division from Palestine.

The replacement did not indeed weaken the battle position of the British: 6th Australian were probably the most formidable shock troops in the Empire, inadequately equipped but totally fit, cocky, spoiling for a fight and not so much inspired by the Digger Legend as irreverently determined to eclipse it. The strategic effect of the replacement was however to delay offensive operations in the desert by nearly six weeks.[101] The commitment of their forces to the Mediterranean front also aggravated the anxieties of the Dominion governments, still without any assurances regarding Singapore or any clear idea of Churchill's strategic priorities. Churchill attempted to anticipate Australian objections by assuring Menzies that: 'We are planning to gather a very large army . . . and ample sea-power in the Middle East, which will face a German lurch that way, and at the same time give us a move eastward in your direction, if need be. Success always demands a greater effort.'[102] But the fact was that concentration in the Mediterranean could only mean deficiency in the Far East. This was pointed out to Churchill the very next day by the New Zealand government, in the tones of patient reproof peculiar to communications from Wellington: 'We have constantly borne in mind the necessity of taking a large view and of balancing our needs with those elsewhere in the common cause, but we wonder if it is fully realised in the United Kingdom how helpless this Dominion is against attack from seaward. As you know, the whole of our defence measures were built on the assumption that in time of potent trouble adequate naval forces would be available. They are not.'[103]

There was no answer to the New Zealand statement. In such a situation the simplest thing was to abuse the Australians. Churchill snappily reprimanded the Dominions Office for preparing a conciliatory cable to the Southern Dominions, affirming, 'I do not wish to commit myself to any serious dispersion of our forces in the Malay Peninsula and at Singapore.'[104] He sent instead a restrained vitriolic cable to Menzies, claiming that: 'The only way in which a naval squadron could be found for Singapore would be by ruining the Mediterranean situation. This I am sure you would not wish us to do unless or until the Japanese danger becomes far more menacing than at present.'[105] As a further precaution he then assailed the Dominions Office staff for getting 'into the habit of running a kind of newspaper full of deadly secrets, which are circularised to the four principal Governments with whom they deal'.[106] The Australians at least were already more or less resigned to the fact that there were some deadly secrets they were not going to know about: the War Cabinet in Canberra noted on 2 January that staff talks were going to be held between the British and Americans, but 'it is apparently not intended that Australia should participate in these'.[107] It was against this backdrop of thoroughly normal distrust and irritation between Britain and Australia that 6th Division went into action against the Libyan fortress of Bardia on 6 January, singing, of all improbable tunes, the theme from *The Wizard of Oz*.

No offensive operation was ever more remarkably successful: 45,000 Italians with 462 guns surrendered to an attacking force of about a third of their strength, who lost 500 casualties in the encounter. This was an even better ratio than that achieved in the original raid of 9 December.

Its effect was to convince Churchill even more strongly of the merits of dispersing British forces ever more widely over Africa and the Mediterranean. He was already demanding that 'every effort should be made to meet the Emperor of Ethiopia's wishes'.[108] He now proposed that 'supporting Greece must have priority after the western flank of Egypt has been made secure'.[109] This meant in effect that the British advance in Libya would have to stop at Benghazi at the furthest, leaving the western half of Libya in Italian hands, including the port of Tripoli, through which reinforcements could reach them from the Continent. Indeed 'it would not be right for the sake of Benghazi to lose the chance' of assisting the Greeks in their winter offensive in Albania. The strategic benefits of diversion were apparently limitless. 'The attitude of Yugoslavia may well be determined by the support we give to Greece. . . . If Yugoslavia stands firm and is not molested, if the Greeks take Valona and maintain themselves in Albania, if Turkey becomes an active ally, the attitude of Russia may be affected favourably.'[110]

The only thing more important than the Balkan front was apparently the defence of the United Kingdom itself: 'the task of preventing invasion, of feeding the Island and of speeding our armament production must in no way be compromised for the sake of any other objective whatsoever.'[111] Nor was there any doubt what speeding armament production meant: Churchill had already told everybody connected with aircraft strategy and production in the most unequivocal terms that he considered 'the rapid expansion of the bomber force one of the greatest military objectives now before us'.[112]

All this could be regarded as good news for the Emperor of Ethiopia and the Greeks. It did nothing for the Eastern Empire. It also set completely at defiance the fundamental military principle of the concentration of force. The fact was that Egypt could not be safe until all the ports of Libya were in British hands. Weakening the British forces in North Africa by the despatch of necessarily inadequate reinforcements to Greece, while still allowing the Germans and Italians access in North Africa, would simply expose the forces of the Empire to defeat severally in Europe, Africa and probably the Far East as well. It was a consideration that might have occurred to Churchill and his advisers – given time. But at this point the nemesis of the Eastern Empire intervened again.

With his virtually supernatural gift for offering the worst possible

advice at the worst possible time, Smuts assured Churchill that:
'Tripoli is much too far. Even Benghazi is as far beyond the frontier
as the frontier is from Alexandria. . . . Tobruk seems to me the ter-
minus.' On the other hand 'liquidation of the Abyssinian situation
should also be considered'. The fact that German troops and air force
personnel were already stationed in Bulgaria failed to terrify Smuts:
'the German concentrations may only be intended to pacify the Italians,
and to lure the British forces away from Britain, where the main attack
is intended and has to be made'.[113] This was much more inspiring than
lectures on imperial defence from Canberra, or bleats about lack of ships
from Wellington. Interestingly Smuts's views were shared by Wavell,
although he apparently drew different conclusions from them: he
argued rather that 'German concentration is move in war of nerves,
designed with object of helping Italy by upsetting Greek nerves, in-
ducing us to disperse our forces in Middle East and to stop advance in
Libya. Nothing we can do from here is likely to be in time to stop
German advance if really intended'.[114]

The Germans themselves provided fairly convincing evidence on the
same day that their eastward concentration was not all bluff: German
dive bombers operating from Sicily partially redressed the balance of
naval power in the Mediterranean by crippling the aircraft carrier
Illustrious and sinking the cruiser *Southampton*. Without adequate air
support the British could be facing a repetition of the Norwegian
disasters. However Churchill peremptorily ordered Wavell to 'conform
[his] plans to larger interests at stake. Nothing must hamper capture of
Tobruk, but thereafter all operations in Libya are subordinated to
aiding Greece. . . .'[115] It was perhaps surprising that a British Prime
Minister should have so unhesitatingly decided to overrule the advice
of the general who had presided over the most remarkable victories in
British military history. It was even more surprising that such a general
should have yielded so easily.

And meanwhile a whole new dimension of doom had become apparent
in the Far East. On 13 January the Australian Air Minister told his
Cabinet of an intelligence report of a new Japanese navy fighter '96' in
operation in China, with an armament of two 20mm cannon and two
7.7mm machine guns, and a speed in excess of 300 miles per hour.
The report came at the same time that the New Zealand government
appealed to Australia for three Catalina flying-boats for long-range

reconnaissance, as a previous order for five Catalinas from the United States had been pre-empted by British requirements.[116] Any complacency about the Far East was now logically impossible. One thing clear about the Second World War was that its battles were being decided by a few extra knots of speed, a few extra millimetres of armour, a slightly higher rate of fire. The new Japanese fighter had on the evidence exactly the same margin of superiority in both fire power and speed over the best British aircraft in the Far East – the Blenheim I – as the Hurricane had over the CR42 in North Africa. The Hurricanes had massacred the CR42s; the 96s would presumably massacre the Blenheims. It was however uniquely undesirable for the Australians to be encouraged to think along these lines, at a time when Churchill was set upon thrusting the only trained divisions of the Southern Dominions into a totally hazardous adventure on the Continent. British-born and trained Air Marshal Burnett assured the Australian War Cabinet that the new Japanese aircraft were few in number, which he had no reason to believe, and that in any case Australia's own Wirraway would 'put up a good show' against them, despite its having half the range, two-thirds of the speed, a third of the fire power and nothing like the manoeuvrability.[117] The indomitable Brooke-Popham seemed to be positively inspired by the reports of Japanese air supremacy: as he saw the situation, it was 'no longer a question of reducing our losses in Hong Kong but of ensuring the security of places that will be of great value in taking offensive action at a later stage of the war'.[118]

In desperation Menzies left Australia for London on 24 January, by way of Batavia and Singapore, in yet another attempt to discover for himself what the principles of imperial strategy actually were. He had every reason for concern. On the eve of staff talks with the Americans, the British asked for a modification of the promise to return Australian and New Zealand cruisers to home waters in the event of a southward move by Japan, preferring to retain them in the Indian Ocean. A final attempt was made to throw the responsibility for the defence of the Eastern Empire on to the United States on 29 January: the Americans were told that 'the security of the Far Eastern position, including Australia and New Zealand, is essential to the cohesion of the British Empire ... Singapore is the key to the defence of these interests. ... The loss of Singapore would be a disaster of the first magnitude, second only to the loss of the British Isles. ... '[119] Ghormley and Stark were shaken. Ghormley objected that 'the defence of the Far East should be built on the whole area of the Southwest Pacific instead of on the single objective of Singapore'. However he and Stark agreed to think about moving a strong United States naval force to the Atlantic, to enable the British Mediterranean Fleet to be sent to the Far East.[120] This was no t what the British wanted, either. They accordingly played their last trick, claiming quite without basis that 'after 1922, when Britain had given up the Alliance with Japan, . . . [it] had assumed that their interests in the Pacific would be protected against Japanese aggression by American Naval strength'.[121]

In the midst of this confusion Stark was presented with a request from the Admiralty to have the aircraft carriers *Furious* and *Illustrious* and the cruiser *Liverpool* repaired in United States yards. The Admiralty reluctantly admitted that the reason for their request was the lack of adequate repair facilities at Singapore or other British bases in the Far East.[122] The great naval base, useless as a deterrent without a fleet, would not have been able to service an adequate fleet, even had the Americans been prepared to project one there. The Singapore Strategy had never existed.

The Australians and New Zealanders were not going to be told this either. Instead they were assured by the indefatigable Brooke-Popham that 336 aircraft would give adequate security in Malaya; that the 'capacity of the Japanese should not be overestimated'; and that the Wirraway was a 'quite good machine for attacking ships over short distances', as indeed it was, given adequate fighter protection. There was none in the Far East. Burma possessed one squadron of Brewster Buffalo fighters and one flight of bombers; Malaya had 88 aircraft in all, comprising 24 Blenheims, 24 Vildebeestes and 4 Singapore flying-boats of the RAF, and 24 Lockheed Hudsons and 12 Wirraways from Australia. At a time when Churchill was proposing to send 15 squadrons of Hurricanes and Blenheims to Turkey,[123] there was still not a single modern fighter in the Eastern Empire. There never had been. By contrast the Australians had deduced from intelligence reports that the Japanese would have 650 aircraft available for an attack on the British Empire.[124]

Brooke-Popham simply ignored the Australian figures, which made his own simply nonsensical. Nor was Churchill moved by a renewed American refusal to base four heavy cruisers and an aircraft carrier on

Singapore, along with aircraft and submarines. Instead orders were sent to Wavell to abandon any serious effort against Tripoli, to 'concentrate all available forces in the Delta in preparation for movement to Europe', and to offer Greece 'the fighting portion of the Army which had hitherto defended Egypt . . .'.[125]

The available forces that Wavell could find comprised two British armoured brigades, a Polish brigade, the New Zealand Division and two Australian divisions. As the Greeks had themselves mobilized twenty-one divisions, it was unlikely that this small British force would be a decisive deterrent to any serious intentions the Germans might have. On the other hand the proposed expeditionary force represented all the available trained manpower of Australia and New Zealand. Wavell approached Menzies on 12 February, suggesting that he would be able to improve on the situation 'if [the] Australian Government will give me certain latitude as regards use of their troops'. Menzies according to Wavell 'was very ready to agree to what I suggest'.[126] However Wavell had not yet spoken to Australian Commander-in-Chief General Blamey when the latter met Menzies in Cairo.[127] Menzies indeed was impressed most strongly with the prospect that the Greeks might not resist a German attack at all, so the question of sending them help might not arise. In any event the Australian government would presumably have been far too concerned with the danger from Japan to have been en-thusiastic about a new continental commitment: the War Cabinet had decided on 13 February in Menzies's absence that: 'In plain words we find ourselves in serious danger of hostile action near if not upon our own coastline.'[128] An even more imminent danger to the Empire re-vealed itself on the same day: the desert flank had been turned: Germany was in Africa.

Wavell was fully aware of the dangers, except that he was not certain that the Germans had already arrived. He issued notes to his staff on 17 February, suggesting that the forces available for despatch to Greece were in fact 'very limited and it is doubtful whether they can arrive in time'.[129] He none the less summoned the Australian and New Zealand commanders, telling New Zealand General Freyberg, not the man most likely to question the orders of a superior officer, that the New Zealand Division was to be the vanguard of the imperial force to be sent to Greece, and that the New Zealand government had agreed to this. Freyberg was apparently given the impression that Wavell had 'established the right to deal directly with the New Zealand Government without letting me know what was happening . . .'.[130] The impression was in fact wrong: Wavell did not have the right and he had not consulted with the New Zealand government. Freyberg of course was not to know this. For him the situation was clear: 'We attended and were given orders to go.'

Blamey's position was even more invidious: he was told by Wavell that the question had already been discussed with the Australian government, although in fact all that had happened was that Wavell had discussed with Menzies the possibility of Australian forces being sent to Greece. The whole enterprise was the more repellent to Blamey because he had written to Menzies the previous November that

there is only one wise policy for us, and that is to endeavour to develop our maximum striking power with all possible rapidity . . . it does not seem possible that British military force alone without active American assistance can develop sufficient strength to overwhelm the Germans. . . . If international developments, for example in the Balkan countries, do not force us into the extremely dangerous position of participating piecemeal in land warfare, we must spend all our energies between now and the summer of 1942 in preparation.[131]

He was now being pitchforked into exactly the kind of piecemeal engagement he feared.

Blamey did not however tell the Australian government of his misgivings now. Canberra instead received on 23 February a soothing cable from Churchill explaining that the needs of the Southwest Pacific must be 'balanced in with the whole Empire war effort. . . . The invariable threat to the British Isles necessitates the holding of a certain number of forces in home waters. . . . Our war effort in the Mediterranean is likely to increase. . . .'[132] The Far East would accordingly simply have to wait a while. However he had assured Menzies the day before that if Japan attacked 'adequate naval reinforcements would at once be despatched to Australian waters', without admittedly saying where they were to come from.[133] He had also assured Menzies that if the expedition failed and there had to be an evacuation, 'the loss would be primarily one of material and that the bulk of the men could be got back to Egypt'.[134] Churchill then wrote to Acting Australian Prime Minister Arthur Fadden that 'we must take this only remaining chance of forming Balkan front and persuading Turkey and possibly Yugoslavia to enter the war on our side ... from the political point of view, failure to help this small nation putting up a gallant fight against one aggressor and willing to defy another would have grave effect on public opinion throughout the world. ...'[135] Menzies for his part told Fadden that 'though with some anxiety my own recommendation to my colleagues is that we should concur'.[136] But once again it was the New Zealanders who effectively took matters out of the control of the Australian government. On being informed that the New Zealand Division was an essential part of the plan and that Menzies had authorized the use of the Australian divisions, the New Zealand government immediately announced that its expeditionary force was 'ready to play the role for which it was formed', and expressed great satisfaction that an Australian and New Zealand force had been chosen to stand together.[137]

The New Zealand government naturally assumed that Freyberg had been consulted, and had no misgivings. He had not been consulted and had not felt it appropriate to tell Wellington that he had not been asked whether he had misgivings or not. Nor could the Australians know that the New Zealand commander had not communicated with his own government, any more than their own had. The situation abruptly altered when Blamey brought himself to write to Menzies that the whole plan 'is, of course, what I feared: piecemeal despatch to Europe. . . . I am not criticising the higher policy that has required it, but I regret that it has taken this dangerous form. . . . Past experience has taught me to look with misgivings on a situation where British leaders have control of first-class Dominion troops while Dominion commanders are excluded from all responsibility in contingency, planning and policy.'[138] This was indeed the case, but it was a little late: the first Australian units were due to leave for Greece in twenty-four hours.

At this point the whole conspiracy began to fall apart. Eden cabled to Churchill on the same day that the Greeks had made no attempt to transfer their forces to the Aliakhmon Line from the Albanian border to Mount Olympus, which it had been agreed offered the best prospects of a successful defence.[139] Churchill in return warned Eden: 'Grave Imperial issues are raised by committing New Zealand and Australian troops to an enterprise which, as you say, has become even more hazardous.' He even cautioned Eden against urging 'Greece against her better judgment into a hopeless resistance', suggesting that the loss of Greece and the Balkans would be 'by no means a major catastrophe for us, provided Turkey remains honest neutral. . . . We are advised from many quarters that our ignominious ejection from Greece would do us more harm in Spain and Vichy than the fact of submission of Balkans. . . .'[140] Menzies for his part repeated that he understood that Blamey and Freyberg were agreeable to the operation, although neither had been asked whether he agreed or not, and Menzies had convincing evidence that Blamey at least was wildly in disagreement with it.

It was certainly probable that the operation had progressed so far already that there was little practical possibility of halting it. Eden in any case was determined that it should not be halted: he had in fact been dedicating himself to urging the Greeks to a hopeless resistance, with the aid of impressively faked-up figures: he had promised on 22 February that Britain would provide 100,000 men with 240 field guns, 202 anti-tank guns, 32 medium guns, 192 anti-aircraft guns and 142 tanks.[141] And now the British Empire's voice of doom came to his support: Smuts, ever ready when a disastrous British policy required support, argued that it was 'too late to retreat . . . we cannot go back now . . . a German victory in the Balkans will result in a great setback to our cause; but the setback will probably be greater if we stand aside and don't help.'[142] Eden assured Churchill, with total disregard for military realities, 'Collapse of Greece without effort on our part to save her by intervention on land, after the Libyan victories had, as all the world knows, made forces available, would be the greatest calamity. . . .'[143] He could speak with the greater confidence of course now that, as Churchill put it in all sincerity, 'Smuts, with all his wisdom, and from his separate angle of thought and fresh eye, had concurred.'[144]

So, from their separate angle of complete misunderstanding, did the New Zealanders. Wellington affirmed that to abandon the Greeks 'would be to destroy the moral basis of our cause and invite results greater in their potential damage to us than any failure of the contemplated operation'.[145] But at this stage a cable from Blamey arrived, forecasting that 'within three or four months we must be prepared to meet overwhelming forces completely equipped and trained. . . . In view of the Germans' much proclaimed intention to drive us off the continent whenever we appear, landing of this small British force would be most welcome to them. . . .' He concluded: 'Military operation extremely hazardous in view of the disparity between opposing forces in numbers and training.'[146]

Eden of course had misrepresented things completely. The Libyan victories had not released British forces for service elsewhere. They had been a miraculous deliverance, possible only because of the extent to which technological superiority had redressed hopeless numerical odds. They were also incomplete, because the British forces had not been strong enough to overrun the whole of Libya before the Germans could arrive on the scene. On the other hand Blamey's excellent appraisal was delivered only after the Australian government had committed itself to the enterprise and Australian forces had begun to arrive in Greece. There was no time now for anything save anger. Fadden furiously cabled off to Wellington: 'Finally we protest against the actions of the Secretary of State for Foreign Affairs entering into an agreement affecting Dominion troops without prior consultation . . . repetition of such an action might well have far-reaching and unfortunate Imperial repercussions.'[147] The Greek venture had indeed all the earmarks of British Empire military co-operation: mutual distrust, deceit, amateurishness, confusion and defeat.

The principal actors could hardly be said to have earned much good fortune. Wavell had clearly sought to intimidate the Dominion commanders into accepting a plan that he did not believe in himself. Freyberg had not bothered to consult his own government before committing their forces to a venture any general must have known to be hazardous at least. Blamey had certainly warned his government, but only after it was too late to withdraw from the operation, as if he were concerned only to escape responsibility for a disaster he could not be troubled to avert. Eden had been prepared to delude the Greeks with exaggerated promises of help, and was now apparently concerned only that 'no difficulties will arise with regard to the despatch of Dominion forces as arranged'.[148] Churchill had shifted ground as the situation altered. At first it had been a question of forming a Balkan front of fifty divisions. Then, when it was apparent that Turkey was not coming to the party, it was a matter of fulfilling obligations to Greece for the sake of neutral opinion. Then the coup in Yugoslavia inspired Churchill again with the hope of collecting seventy divisions against the Germans' thirty. As he cabled Fadden, 'When a month ago we decided upon sending an army to Greece it looked rather a blank military adventure dictated by *noblesse oblige*. Thursday's events in Belgrade show the far-reaching effects of this and other measures we have taken on whole

Balkan situation. German plans have been upset, and we may cherish renewed hopes of forming a Balkan front with Turkey, comprising about seventy Allied divisions. . . .'[149] But the Turks were still showing no signs of responding. Moreover the German offensive in Libya was beginning to overrun the British defences, despite Wavell's forecast that it would be two months before the Germans could mount an effective campaign. The armies of the British Empire were facing another Sudan. Wavell decided on 4 April that the Australian 7th Division would have to remain in Africa, despite Blamey's protests that this would leave the Greek expedition seriously weakened.[150]

One more Australian division could not in fact have done more in Greece than add to the magnitude of the inevitable defeat. It left Wavell with a bare margin for manoeuvre in Africa. The German assault on Yugoslavia began on 6 April, four days after Rommel had broken through at Agedabia. In actual numbers the Germans were in fact probably fighting against odds again. Yugoslavia had in all twenty-four infantry and three cavalry divisions. The Greeks had twenty-one divisions, fifteen of which were containing the Italians in Albania, while six very understrength divisions were to co-operate with the British in the east. The British Expeditionary Force itself contrasted in many ways with Eden's assurances. Its total numerical strength was about 62,600, compared with the 100,000 he had promised. However the actual fighting component was little more than half this number, consisting of the 17,125 men of the incomplete Australian 6th Division, the 16,720 of the New Zealand Division and the British 1st Armoured Brigade. The remaining near-30,000 consisted of the enormous administrative tail of British base and supply units and Palestine and Cypriot labour gangs.[151] The armoured brigade indeed had 104 tanks, not too far short of Eden's figure of 142, but only half of these were cruisers, capable of fighting the German panzers. It could be said optimistically that something like thirty-five divisions in various stages of repair would be available against the twenty-six infantry, mountain and armoured divisions of the German Second and Twelfth armies. What upset the balance totally was the fact that the Germans could deploy about 800 tanks against 1st Armoured Brigade, and 1,158 planes against a British advanced air force of 80 serviceable aircraft.[152]

The greatest generalship in the world could have done little against such odds. The organization of the Greek campaign was rather less than that. As early as 22 March, a fortnight before the German attack actually developed, Blamey and Freyberg had wanted to pull the imperial forces back to the mountain passes south of Katerin. British General Wilson delayed the decision to withdraw until 9 April because of the determination of the Greeks to attempt to retain contact with the Yugoslavs. However this strategy, which in any case cost the Greeks four divisions and eliminated them as an effective element in resisting the German invasion, was never adequately explained to the Australian and New Zealand commanders.

Evacuation was accepted as virtually inevitable on 17 April. Meanwhile one unquestionable gleam of success lightened the scene of British Empire blunder and defeat. A German assault on Tobruk on 14 April was totally defeated by a combination of Australian infantry and British tanks and artillery, operating perfectly under the direction of Australian Major-General L. J. Morshead. The Australians fought resourcefully and aggressively even when the German tanks broke through the defence perimeter; the British artillerymen fought their guns until the panzers broke off the engagement; and the British tanks were deployed economically to harry the retreating Germans. The latter lost over 400 men and 17 tanks, the garrison only 90 men and 2 tanks. It was on a tiny scale, but it may have been the first time in the Second World War that a German offensive was totally defeated. On the following day the fantastic ratios of the December offensive were actually surpassed: an attack by Italian infantry with unenthusiastic German armoured support netted the garrison 803 prisoners for a total cost of one Australian killed and another wounded.

This was the good news. The Greek campaign showed the other side of the story: 16,111 members of the Expeditionary Force, over 25 per cent, had become casualties. Admittedly nearly 11,000 of this figure was made up by the British base units and the labour force captured by the Germans. Actual combat casualties, 90 per cent of which were Anzac, amounted to 2,092 against a total German casualty list for the campaign of 5,260. But the British had lost 209 aircraft and 104 tanks, while the Germans had lost not more than a quarter of these figures. The result was catastrophic. Wavell had in his whole command only at most 250 serviceable aircraft, at least a quarter of which were obsolete. His opponents had a total availability in the *Regia Aeronautica* and the *Luftwaffe* of 1,800, at least half of which were ready for immediate action.

One implication at least must have been obvious. Churchill had advocated the commitment to Greece in the first place, in order to make certain of the supreme strategic prize of the Mediterranean – Crete. But the Greek campaign itself had made certain that Crete could not be defended. The Royal Air Force would be overwhelmed even more quickly than in Greece, and the Royal Navy would be faced with a repetition of the Norwegian disasters, on an immensely greater scale. Churchill none the less decided that the defence of Crete 'ought to be a fine opportunity for killing the parachute troops'.[153] Wavell immediately gave the job to Freyberg. The New Zealand commander had apparently learned something from his Greek experience. He suggested to Wavell that 'the decision to defend the island be reconsidered if aircraft were not available'.[154] Wavell however assured him that the estimated scale of attack had been exaggerated and that the garrison would be equal to the task. Freyberg then informed the New Zealand government of his worries, chiefly that 'air forces in island consist of six Hurricanes and seventeen obsolete aircraft'.[155]

Freyberg's anxieties did not last long. Wavell repeated his conviction that the War Office estimate of the scale of attack was exaggerated.[156] Churchill sent off a fulsome cable to Wellington, suggesting that a German airborne attack 'ought to suit the New Zealanders down to the ground', and lauding 'the dignity and stoicism of New Zealand'.[157] Freyberg meanwhile recovered his confidence: as he now told Churchill: 'Cannot understand nervousness: am not in the least anxious about airborne attack: have made my dispositions and feel can cope adequately. . . .'[158] The fact of the matter was that he did not understand the situation and had been misled once more by Churchill and Wavell: as he subsequently informed his government: 'I did not know anything about the geography or physical characteristics of the island. I knew less about the condition of the force I was to command. Neither was I aware of the serious situation with regard to maintenance and, finally, I had not learnt the scale of attack which we were to be prepared to repel.'[159]

The Empire front almost collapsed on 1 May. A rebellion broke out in Iraq, garrisoned by the Royal Air Force with a quaint assortment of antiquated aircraft. On the same day a new German assault on Tobruk reached its height, with 91 tanks deployed against the fortress's strength of 35, in the first authentic blitzkrieg of the desert war. Again, the

Germans called off the fight, after losing 12 tanks against 4, and 954 casualties against 797. The 9th Division and the Royal Horse Artillery had proved their ability to hold down twice the strength of Rommel's forces in Africa. The Tobruk venture was succeeding.

Nor were the Iraqi rebels clearly going to present much threat to the Empire. Churchill began to show signs of optimism again: he congratulated the Australians, whom he had previously accused of 'making themselves comfortable' in Tobruk,[160] and advised the King to appoint Smuts 'Honorary Field-Marshal of the British Army', as a reward for 'the great part you are playing in our military affairs and the importance of the South African Army',[161] which had so far contributed 270 casualties to the conquest of Italian East Africa. Smuts responded by assiduously encouraging Churchill to persist in the defence of Crete, despite the urgent advice of Chief of Imperial General Staff Sir John Dill, who advised Churchill on 6 May that the Middle East should not be regarded as even second in the order of priorities after the United Kingdom, 'for it has been accepted principle in our strategy that in the last resort the security of Singapore comes before that of Egypt'.[162] This was of course the principle on which Australian and New Zealand defence planning had been based, and which had never been repudiated by Churchill himself. He now venomously replied to Dill, 'I gather you would be prepared to face the loss of Egypt and the Nile Valley, together with the surrender or ruin of the Army of half a million we have concentrated there, rather than lose Singapore. . . . The defence of Singapore is an operation requiring only a very small fraction of the troops required to defend the Nile Valley against the Germans and Italians . . . in any case Japan would not be likely to besiege Singapore at the outset. . . .'[163]

A new front in the Middle East had in fact already presented itself to Churchill. German aircraft had been using Syrian airfields during the Iraqi sideshow. The Gaullists were insisting that they be allowed to move into Syria to give the Vichyite forces there an opportunity to surrender to them. Wavell, attempting to plan an offensive to relieve Tobruk and awaiting a German descent on Crete, appealed against having to provide strong British support to a move by the Free French, which he was certain would be ineffective on its own.[164] The whole situation was becoming impossibly complicated. The British desert offensive fizzled out after a very small but not too unsatisfactory affair in which the British lost 160 men, 6 aircraft and 5 tanks, and the Germans 258 men and 3 tanks.

On 19 May the British Chiefs of Staff on Churchill's instructions ordered Wavell 'to improvise the largest force that you can manage without prejudice to security Western Desert and be prepared move into Syria at the earliest possible time . . .'.[165] The largest force meant the Australian 7th Division. Blamey had already warned Menzies on 18 May that it might be necessary to send this force to Palestine because of developments in Syria. Then on 20 May the German airborne attack on Crete began. The War Office estimate of the strength of the anticipated German attack was far from being exaggerated, as Wavell had suggested to Freyberg. The Germans in fact employed 23,000 men, or nearly three times the highest War Office estimate. On the following day Churchill invited Wavell to run the 'small-scale military risks' involved in an invasion of Syria, or resign, having already decided to sack him two days earlier.[166] The small-scale military risk was in fact to prove one of the most extraordinary campaigns of the war: a successful attack against a strongly motivated and well-equipped force by an army barely two-thirds its size in effective fighting strength, inferior in numbers of aircraft and guns, and wholly without armour.

It might have been imagined that the British leadership would have decided after the Greek affair to consult with Commonwealth governments before committing their divisions to perilous military ventures. This does not seem to have been the case. Wavell decided that he was ready to launch an invasion with 7th Division on 27 May. Menzies wrote on his own initiative to Churchill suggesting an occupation of Syria on 30 May.[167] Churchill informed him on 31 May that Syria would in fact be occupied as soon as possible. However the Australian government was not informed until 7 June that the invasion was to take place the next morning, using Australian forces.

Meanwhile the evacuation from Crete had begun on 27 May. The last fruits of the Churchill-Smuts strategy, acquiesced by Wavell, were the near-destruction of the British position in the Middle East by land, sea and air. Out of a total strength of 17,000 British, 7,700 New Zealand and 6,500 Australian troops, not counting 10,000 Cretan levies, 15,031 had become casualties; 3,787 had been killed or wounded, three-quarters of them New Zealanders or Australians, against German combat casualties of 6,580. The Royal Air Force had lost a further 46 aircraft, against a

German loss of 220 in all; and the Royal Navy had lost three cruisers and six destroyers sunk, leaving it outnumbered by the Italians by eleven to three in cruiser strength, and four to two in its battle force. The only possible hope for the future lay in the performance of the Dominion troops against the *Wehrmacht*, demonstrated in its most convincing form at Tobruk. It was the moment of all others in the history of the British Empire when mutual trust, recognition of efforts made and open dealing were called for. What the Southern Dominions were to get was more danger, deception, Brooke-Popham and acrimony, much of it over Tobruk.

9 Sinister twilight (1941–5)

Greece and Crete between them had virtually ruined Wavell's strategy in the Middle East. As the Australian official historian puts it:

In March he could deploy ten divisions – the 2nd Armoured; 1st Cavalry; 6th (British); 6th, 7th and 9th Australian; 4th and 5th Indian; New Zealand; 1st South African. Five of these had now either been broken up into small groups (as the 6th British and the Cavalry) or had lost their heavy weapons and were in need of rest and reinforcement (as the 6th Australian and the New Zealand). Of the divisions which remained, the 9th Australian was now besieged in Tobruk, the rearmed 7th Armoured (not included above), the 1st South African, and the 4th Indian were in process of concentrating on the Western Desert front, and the 5th Indian and the small British-African divisions were engaged in mopping-up in Abyssinia. The only substantial and ready reserve was the 7th Australian Division, in position about Mersa Matruh.[1]

This was the force that would have to act as the spearhead of the thrust into Syria which Churchill was now meditating.

Attempts had already been made to prepare the Australian government to accept yet another commitment of its trained manpower away from its own shores. Menzies was assured that the Japanese could marshal only 450 aircraft against the Malay Barrier, and that most of these would be obsolete, despite the fact that Australian intelligence had suggested three months before that the Japanese would have 650 modern aircraft available.[2] He was also told that the situation in Egypt made it impossible to send Hurricanes to the Far East, but that the American Brewster Buffalo would be more than a match for the best Japanese aircraft, despite its obvious inferiority to the new navy 96 fighter. This determination not to face facts in the Far East was shared unhesitatingly by the British Chiefs of Staff in Singapore: Brooke-Popham had already prepared an order of the day to be used in the event of a Japanese invasion, in which he claimed in advance that: 'We are ready. We have had plenty of warning and our preparations are made and tested. . . . We are quite confident. Our defences are strong and our weapons efficient. . . .[3] But he was having second thoughts about the Wirraway: in February he had affirmed that it would be quite good for attacking ships over short distances, but now he relegated it to being fit only for training. This might well have made the Australians less ready to co-operate in Churchill's Middle East strategy, but for a guarantee they fortuitously received from United States Admiral Harold R. Stark on 29 May that 'he would expect the US Pacific Fleet to take such steps as would prevent the overseas occupation and the permanent support of such garrisons as the Axis Powers might seek to establish' in the British and French Pacific Islands south of the Equator.[4]

Given this assurance the Australians were prepared to let their 6-inch gun cruiser *Hobart* go to the Mediterranean in response to a British request, and to endorse a British invasion of Syria, which began four days later on 8 June. This was again a misconceived venture: the Germans had already decided that it would make more sense for them to leave the defence of French colonies in French hands, and had actually withdrawn their military missions in Syria so as to remove any excuse for a British invasion.[5] The attack went on nevertheless. A mixed force of 18,000 Australians, 9,000 British tankers and artillerymen, 5,000 Free French and 2,000 Indians crossed the frontier, with about 70 guns and the same number of supporting aircraft. The Vichyite defenders numbered 37,000, not counting 10,000 local levies of dubious value, with 90 guns, 100 aircraft and 90 tanks. The British had no armour except Bren carriers and scout cars. It was clear from the start that nothing would go as planned. The Vichyites fought furiously; their tanks were an enormous problem for the invaders; a commando raid was a costly bungle; and the Free French forces were positively counter-productive, as their presence only inspired their compatriots to fight better than ever.

The bad news continued. In defiance of all principles of military strategy Wavell now divided his forces and launched his last big offensive in the Western Desert, 'Battleaxe', on 15 June, using 4th Indian Division, the Guards Brigade and 7th Armoured Division. The result was another costly failure: despite air superiority and a massive advantage in armour the British lost 969 men, 36 aircraft and 91 tanks, against German losses of 678, with 10 aircraft and 12 tanks. There could clearly

be little hope of an early relief of Tobruk. Menzies accordingly asked
Blamey if he expected the fortress would hold out, or if he should press
Churchill to evacuate 7th Division. Blamey himself was satisfied that
the garrison could hold their position. However he was also concerned
that the physical condition of the most formidable shock troops in the
Middle East was deteriorating rapidly under siege conditions. He was
anxious in any case to assemble the Australian units which were at the
time 'distributed among several forces and ten different areas'.[6] An
opportunity seemed to be provided by the surrender of the Vichyite
French in Syria on 12 July, after an intensely hard-fought struggle that
had cost the invaders more combat casualties than in the Greek campaign. The Australians had lost 1,465 killed and wounded, the British
and Indians 600 and the Free French 200. In addition 1,200 of the
British and Indians and 1,100 of the Free French had become prisoners
of the Vichyites, who themselves lost 3,348 killed or wounded. The
campaign had been an astonishing offensive operation, triumphing over
superior numbers, inadequate equipment, lack of battle experience,
hesitant leadership and allies of limited utility. It had also of course been
completely unnecessary.

Blamey now appealed directly to Wavell's successor, Sir Claude
Auchinleck, to pull out the Tobruk garrison and reorganize the frag-
mented Australian corps before it could be dispersed still further in
more military adventures. His request was backed by Menzies, who had
just approved the despatch of 27th Brigade, 8th Division, from Australia
to reinforce the garrison of Malaya. By pure coincidence the Australian
request for a reorganization of Middle East Command coincided with
a direct attack by the United States on the whole Middle East strategy
which Churchill was applying: presidential envoy Harry Hopkins told
Churchill and his Chiefs of Staff that 'in the Middle East the British
Empire had an indefensible position, in attempting to maintain which,
great sacrifices had been made. . . . No one in Great Britain appreciated
the feeling which existed throughout the US military command that the
Middle East was a liability from which the British should withdraw.'[7]
But Churchill was already pressing Auchinleck for an offensive in the
Middle East before the end of September, just as he was himself being
pressed by Stalin for a second front in Europe. Virtually all reinforcements that were not to be diverted to Russia would be allotted to the
new offensive. The Middle East had assumed a new importance: it was

literally the only front on which the British would be able to confront the Germans with a sufficient superiority of numbers to have some chance of defeating them.

This necessarily complicated the issue of the relief of 7th Division in Tobruk. Auchinleck had agreed on 1 August to replace the Australians in the fortress with the Polish brigade. Menzies urged on 7 August that the relief should be carried out promptly. It was indeed begun, but not promptly: Blamey protested in a letter to Army Minister Spender on 18 August that there had been 'a great deal of opposition to the relief of the troops in Tobruk and it certainly does present difficulties. . . . I am perfectly sure in my own mind that these are largely due to the Staff opposition to our desire to concentrate the three Australian divisions as a single command.'[8] Menzies resigned as Prime Minister of Australia on 28 August. Churchill wrote to his successor Fadden rejecting Menzies's notion of an Imperial War Cabinet and stressing the difficulties in the way even of a meeting of Dominion Prime Ministers.[9] Fadden's alarms were increased by a further cable from Blamey, suggesting that Auchinleck was now intending to send the artillery component of 9th Division to Tobruk. Fadden in his turn demanded the recall of the Australian forces. Churchill however assured Auchinleck that 'the Australians will play the game if the facts are put before them squarely'.[10] He had apparently convinced himself that the demand for the recall of the Tobruk garrison was simply a disagreeable characteristic of Menzies's political opponents, instead of a principle to which Menzies had explicitly committed himself. Blamey meanwhile continued to press for the relief, though admitting to Fadden that he was 'becoming personally the most unpopular man in the Middle East over the matter. . . . It is a short-sighted policy, but one that one frequently meets amongst the British, to use up a division until it is worthless for months afterwards.'[11] Churchill then assailed the unfortunate Fadden: 'I trust that you will weigh very carefully the immense responsibility which you would assume before history by depriving Australia of the glory of holding Tobruk till victory was won, which otherwise, by God's help, will be theirs forever.'[12]

The fact was that the Australians had had almost enough glory already. Churchill admitted in a cable to Auchinleck that he feared 'the dangerous reactions on Australian and world opinion of our seeming to fight all our battles in the Middle East only with Dominion troops'.[13] There could be no question that the Australians and New Zealanders had carried most of the fighting on land since Dunkirk and had borne most of the casualties. It was equally obvious that this kind of strategy had involved leaving the Southern Dominions totally exposed to any external threat. By the third quarter of 1941 the United Kingdom had enlisted some forty-one divisions, including armoured and home defence formations. Thirty-six of these were still in the Home Islands. The remaining five were in the Middle East, in Cyprus, Iran, or on the Libyan front. India had indeed organized seven divisions for overseas service, but only one, 4th Division, had seen serious combat; of the other six, one was in Cyprus, two in Persia, one in Iraq and two in Malaya. South Africa had produced two divisions, one of which had been through an arduous but almost bloodless campaign in Italian East Africa and was now awaiting a spell of more active operations against the Germans. The New Zealand Division had unquestionably been fully tried in Greece and Crete. There were three African colonial divisions, which in Churchill's own estimation could not possibly be deployed against a European army. Canada had four divisions in the United Kingdom, none of which, through no fault of their own, had yet seen action at all. By contrast Australia had so far only one division overseas, 8th Division in Malaya, which had not experienced intense combat; 6th Division had fought through Libya, Greece and Crete; 9th Division had outfought the Germans at Tobruk; and 7th Division had experienced one of the toughest campaigns of the war in Syria.

In these circumstances the Australians and New Zealanders were entitled to feel that they had made an adequate contribution to the security of the Empire on the other side of the world. They were the more encouraged to think along these lines by the horrifying reports that began to stream back to Canberra from Australia's minister-designate to Chungking, Frederic Eggleston, who had arrived in Singapore just as Churchill was assuring the New Zealand government that he could 'not believe that the Japanese will face the combination now developing around them'.[14] Eggleston's first discovery was that even the British Commander-in-Chief China Station, Admiral Sir Geoffrey Layton, was 'afraid of the absolute control of war strategy by Churchill'.[15] This was only the beginning of the horror story. The more Eggleston saw of the combination facing Japan, the less he became convinced of its capacity to deter anything. The Dutch navy, for example, was only 'a very small affair'.[16] The land forces in the Netherlands East Indies, 'like all weak armies make up in uniforms what they lacked in power'.[17] He was on strong ground here: by far the largest Dutch force, the Java garrison, consisted of only 25,000 men, only one in forty of whom were Dutch. Moreover this diminutive strength had been weakened still further by inappropriate strategy: the Dutch had originally wanted to abandon the outlying islands and concentrate on the defence of Java, but had been persuaded by Brooke-Popham to try to hold all their territories in the Indies.[18] The mood in Singapore itself was Wagnerian without grandeur. Churchill's envoy, Duff Cooper, nicknamed resentfully by the locals 'Tough Snooper', was 'grumpy and silent' at dinner, as indeed he had cause to be;[19] the Australian commander 8th Division, Lieutenant-General Gordon Bennett, did not seem to want to talk to Eggleston either, and kept pretending to be distracted by the passing show in the streets; Brooke-Popham himself was 'not a commanding figure', but kept exuding optimism for which Eggleston could see no justification.[20] He scouted a Dutch report that the Japanese had 91,000 men in Indo-China, asserting that they had landed only one division as far as he could see; he was certain that they would not expose their battleships to aerial bombardment; and he now said that they had only 100–200 aircraft available for operations against the Malay Barrier. Brooke-Popham's euphoria was shared by the British Chiefs of Staff, who reported on 26 September that 'Japan is now concentrating her forces against the Russians and cannot suddenly change this into a concentration in the south . . . she must therefore be anxious to avoid a war in the south in the next few months'.[21]

Churchill was only too glad to accept this view as well. In pursuance of a policy of deterrence rather than defence against Japan, he reversed his former opinion of Hong Kong, which he had believed could neither be held nor relieved in the event of war with Japan,[22] and asked the Canadian government to provide one or two battalions to reinforce the present garrison. This was justified on the grounds that there were 'signs of a certain weakening in attitude of Japan towards United States and ourselves', and because of the need to 'reassure Chiang Kai Shek as to genuineness of our intention to hold the colony and in addition would have a very great moral effect throughout the Far East'.[23] By contrast Churchill was more opposed than ever to the relief of Tobruk, asking the new Australian Labour Prime Minister John Curtin to 'consider

once again' the issue of relief already discussed with Menzies and
Fadden.[24] Curtin's insistence on the acceptance of a request that
Menzies had made three months before precipitated the completion of
the relief, despite two cables from Churchill that exceeded in bitterness
anything sent so far from London to the government of the Dominion
that had sacrificed more lives to the British cause than the rest of the
Empire put together.[25] Relations of trust and goodwill between Britain
and the Southern Dominions had dropped to their lowest point at precisely the moment in imperial history when such emotions were going
to be most required for the survival of the Empire.

Meanwhile Brooke-Popham was in Canberra, attempting to allay the
effects of Eggleston's horror stories. He had received on 6 October a
report from RAAF intelligence pointing out the obvious deficiencies of
the Buffalo, as compared with the new Japanese navy fighter 96. Since
the report could not be answered, Brooke-Popham ignored it. Everything was looking up in the Far East. 'Malaya was growing from strength
to strength.'[26] Its strength was in fact about 88,600 men, of whom 19,600
were British, 15,200 Australian, 37,000 Indian and 16,800 locally
enlisted.[27] This might have seemed quite formidable, and the Australians
at least were fit and hard-trained. However nobody had confidence in
the local levies, and the Indians were at a level of efficiency even lower
than that of the Indian army in 1938, which Auchinleck had judged to be
'showing a tendency to fall behind the forces of such minor states as
Egypt, Iraq and Afghanistan'.[28] This was indeed a consequence of the
sheer growth of the Indian army: the needs of training a force
approaching a strength of some 984,514 men were being met by
relocating the best men and NCOs from combat divisions back to base
camps to act as drill instructors. The unfortunate result was that the
units that would actually be doing the fighting were the ones that had
been deliberately denuded of their most promising leadership material.
Nor did the Malayan garrison yet possess any tanks at all.

On the other hand, according to Brooke-Popham, 'our existing air
forces could cope with any aircraft the Japanese could bring against us'.
He had now raised his estimates of potential Japanese air strength to
500, but believed that lack of landing facilities 'would reduce the availability of aircraft for operational use to 250'.[29] Even this might have
been considered enough for an air defence establishment consisting of
5 British and 3 Dutch Catalina flying-boats; 36 British Vildebeestes; 83

British, 16 Australian and 15 New Zealand Buffaloes, 21 of which were temporarily unserviceable; 31 British Blenheim Is; 31 British Blenheim IVs; 31 Australian Hudsons; and one solitary Australian Beaufort, which was the only genuinely first-class modern aircraft in the lot. There was no doubt that this collection of exhibits of aviation history could have added up to a formidable striking force, especially if there had been sufficient torpedoes to equip them with, which there were not, if only they could have been given anything like adequate fighter protection. There were in the United Kingdom 1,800 modern fighters that could have held their own against the Japanese; there were another 500 in the Middle East; and a further 676 had been either despatched to Russia, or were about to leave. There was not one such aircraft in the British Empire beyond the Mediterranean.

Brooke-Popham had more good news, however. Burma, for example, was 'being strengthened with a view to its being capable of defending itself on the land'. What it actually had was one Burma division, one Indian division, no tanks, no anti-aircraft guns and sixteen Buffaloes. Hong Kong was also being strengthened, and it and the Philippines would 'form a pincers which could be brought into operation if Japan comes south'.[30] The striking arm of the Hong Kong part of the pincers at this time consisted of three Walrus amphibians, four Vildebeestes, one gunboat and four motor torpedo boats. Churchill at least was prepared to offer something more substantial than hopes, although he assured Curtin again that Japan would not go to war 'unless or until Russia is broken'. However, he added, 'in order further to deter Japan, we are sending forthwith our newest battleship, *Prince of Wales*, to join *Repulse* in the Indian Ocean. This is done in spite of protests from the Commander-in-Chief Home Fleet, and is a serious risk for us to run. . . . In addition the four 'R' battleships are being moved as they become ready to Eastern waters.'[31] In a more genial note to Wellington, he told the New Zealanders that the particular merit of the *Prince of Wales* was that 'nothing is so good as having something that can catch and kill anything',[32] although a bare couple of months before he had told the First Sea Lord that 'sorrow rises to the heart, or ought to', when comparing the inadequate armament of *Prince of Wales* and her sisters with that of other modern battleships.[33] Then on 10 November Churchill told the Lord Mayor's luncheon at the Guildhall that: 'We now feel ourselves strong enough to provide a powerful naval force of heavy ships, with its necessary ancillary vessels, for service if needed in the Indian and Pacific Oceans. Thus we stretch out the long arm of brotherhood and motherhood to the Australian and New Zealand peoples and to the peoples of India. . . .'[34]

This was a quite misleading account of what had been done. But any chance that an effective battle force might still be sent to the Far East was lost when the battleship *Barham* was torpedoed in the Mediterranean on 11 November. *Prince of Wales* and *Repulse* on their own could be viewed only as liabilities rather than as assets to the situation. The Australians, who had not been told of the loss of *Barham*, none the less agreed to detach five of their own destroyers to provide a screen for the British ships. Then on 7 December the moment of truth came. Battle Force Pacific Fleet was put out of action at Pearl Harbour; Hong Kong was attacked by land and air; and the Japanese xxv Army, 125,400 strong, with 168 guns, 179 tanks and 534 aircraft, moved against the garrison of Malaya, two-thirds its size, inexperienced, largely unreliable, with no tanks and 161 aircraft. The Singapore Strategy had run out of time.

The position of the Southern Dominions was desperate. The Royal Australian Navy was scattered all the way from Sydney to the Mediterranean. Only the 8-inch gun cruiser *Canberra* and the two 6-inch gun cruisers *Adelaide* and *Perth* were in Australian waters, along with two destroyers, two sloops and an armed merchant cruiser. Five more destroyers, two armed merchant cruisers and seven corvettes were at Singapore; one 8-inch gun and one 6-inch gun cruiser were in the Indian Ocean; and one sloop was on patrol in the Red Sea. The total air defence of the Australian Continent consisted of 101 Wirraways, 53 Hudsons, 12 Catalina flying boats and 11 Seagull amphibians in service; and 126 Ansons, 108 Wirraways and 72 Fairey Battles in reserve. Moreover only 40 Hudson and 45 Wirraway flying crews were fully trained; and 10 of the Hudsons and 12 of the Wirraways had already been earmarked for service in the islands. The position as regards armour was hardly more satisfactory: some 185 tanks were assembled over the next few months, but only 12 of these were Matildas, capable of actually fighting other modern tanks. The situation was not quite as bad as Curtin pretended it was three years later, when he told the Canadians that there was not one tank in Australia at the time of Pearl Harbour, although he was strictly correct when he said that there was 'not one of any kind of fighter aircraft in Australia'.[35]

In this situation it seemed best to try to stop the invader as far away from the Dominions themselves as possible. Curtin ordered on 8 December that Australian garrisons should be sent to the Netherlands East Indies. Then on 10 December *Prince of Wales* and *Repulse* were sunk by Japanese air attack. In possibly the worst moment in the history of the British Empire, Churchill cabled to Curtin that it was not considered in London that there was 'any immediate large scale threat to Australia and much less New Zealand'. Germany on this view was still the main enemy.[36] It was an unfortunate time to point this out to the Australians, as the last shreds of British guarantees of protection were torn apart by the Japanese xxv Army. The Australian commander in Malaya, General Bennett, cabled to Curtin that he saw in Malaya 'a total absence of the offensive spirit. . . . The position has arrived when something must be done – urgently. I strongly urge that, should the request be made, at least one division of the A.I.F. from the Middle East be transferred to Malaya.'[37] Menzies himself dismissed Churchill's viewpoint as fatuous. The decision was taken immediately to stop Australian participation in the Empire Air Training Scheme, in an attempt to build up the number of trained air crews in Australia itself. The British Chiefs of Staff however reiterated their view on 22 December that only the minimum of force necessary for the safeguarding of vital interests in other theatres should be diverted from the operations against Germany, and insisted that it was essential to maintain the outward flow of air trainees from Australia and New Zealand.

At this point Curtin appealed to the only possible alternative source of assistance. The United States Joint Chiefs of Staff had in fact already decided to reroute to Brisbane a convoy originally intended for Manila. On 22 December Curtin told President Roosevelt that 'reinforcements earmarked by the United Kingdom for despatch to Malaya seem to us to be utterly inadequate, especially in relation to aircraft and more particularly fighting aircraft. . . . We have three divisions in the Middle East. Our airmen are fighting in Britain, Middle East and training in Canada. We have sent great quantities of supplies to Britain, to the Middle East and to India. Our resources here are very limited indeed. It is in your power to meet the situation.'[38] His arguments were made the more urgent by the news of another great British defeat: the garrison of Hong Kong was forced to surrender, after suffering some 1,224 battle casualties against a Japanese loss of 2,754. None the less the British mission to the staff conferences with the Americans was still primarily concerned to stop the United States from becoming 'too Pacific-minded', and opposed a suggestion by United States Admiral Ernest J. King to set up a South-West Pacific War Council, 'because of their unwillingness to see Dominion representatives on a body with powers of controlling strategy'.[39]

Meanwhile Bennett had asked again for 'Australian division from Middle East by fastest means' as 'essential to save situation'.[40] Nothing else was likely to. At this point the Admiralty asked the Australian government to send *Australia* and *Perth* from their own waters to Singapore, even though the British Chiefs of Staff were convinced by now that a major defeat of the United States Navy could take place within a matter of hours, leaving Australia and New Zealand open to invasion. For the first time an Australian government flatly rejected a British request for assistance. Within two days they had repented: *Australia* and *Perth* sailed for the West Java Sea on 31 December, the latter never to return.[41]

Churchill had no thanks for the Australians, but he still had kind words for the New Zealanders, whom he praised for their splendid courage and loyalty to the Mother Country'.[42] But even the New Zealanders were becoming dissatisfied: their Chiefs of Staff now pointed out that the 'successful conduct of war depends still, as it always has, upon (i) secure resources (ii) secure bases and (iii) secure lines of communication. . . . The British Empire has hitherto subsisted on these three aspects of security . . . if the Japanese Navy can finally defeat Allied Naval Power – and this might *happen at any time* – Japan will be strategically in a position to cut all Pacific communications. . . .'[43] In this dark hour the Australians in Malaya provided virtually the only source of encouragement: over 14–15 January Bennett's 8th Division ambushed and smashed a Japanese attack at Gemas, using against the enemy the methods that they had themselves employed brilliantly against the British and Indians. The Australians repeated the perform-ance two days later at Muar, destroying eight Japanese tanks. This did not however elicit congratulations from London. Instead the Dominions Office warned Churchill about 'the present rather cantankerous attitude of the Commonwealth Government', and advised that it might be as well to be careful about what was said to the New Zealanders, because of the 'danger that Mr Fraser might communicate' with the Australians, who apparently should be kept in the dark about everything as much as possible.[44] Mutual trust was not flourishing in adversity.

It fell apart completely after the German General Rommel launched a counter-attack in Libya on 21 January, hurling the British Eighth Army back from Benghazi. On 23 January a Japanese force of 5,300 overran the Australian garrison of 1,390 on Rabaul, killing or capturing nearly 1,000 of the defenders for a loss of only 65. In this situation Curtin learned from Earle Page that the British had been 'considering the evacuation of Malaya and Singapore. After all the assurances we have been given the evacuation of Singapore would be regarded here and elsewhere as an inexcusable betrayal ... the more so since the Australian people, having volunteered for service overseas in large numbers, find it difficult to understand why they must wait so long for an improvement in the situation when irreparable damage may have been done to their power to resist, the prestige of Empire, and the solidarity of the Allied cause.'[45] The unforgiveable words had been spoken. Nor was this merely a display of Australian cantankerousness : the New Zealand government warned Churchill again on 30 January that 'without fighter defence for Wellington and Auckland the Government may have to face serious repercussions in the morale of the people, which may lead to an appreciable diminution in the total war effort'.[46] The situation worsened when the island of Ambon fell on 3 February, with the loss of 400 of its Australian garrison of 1,100.

But it was not only in the Far East that the imperial front was collapsing : by 6 February the Eighth Army was back at Gazala, after a retreat of some 250 miles along the coast of Cyrenaica. The British Chiefs of Staff accordingly opposed more determinedly than ever American suggestions to divert supplies for the relief of Australia.[47] The New Zealanders in their turn began to protest against the continued use of the much-tried New Zealand Division in an operational role in the Western Desert. It was suggested in fact that public opinion might 'point to a demand that New Zealand forces should be returned to the Pacific Area to meet the danger nearer home'. In the meantime they asked for 'as far as possible for public use, a full statement of the number of troops at present held in the United Kingdom and of the reasons, which I do not for a moment suggest are not completely conclusive, for their retention'.[48] The Admiralty in return asked in a remarkably aberrant mood that the only large warship that the New Zealanders had kept in home waters, the armed merchant cruiser *Rangitira*, should be sent to Vancouver for conversion as a commerce raider, 'as under present circumstances and having regard to the wide dispersion of enemy-occupied territories and the length of his sea communications ... serious damage could be inflicted on Japanese interests by one or more fast vessels acting as commerce raiders and capable of undertaking minor landing operations against outlying bases'.[49]

Even the New Zealanders finally jibbed at this. Meanwhile the Australians had not surprisingly devised a schedule for the massive diversion of relief to their threatened continent. On 15 February their Chief of Staff, Lieutenant-General Sturdee, proposed to Curtin that 'the Govt give immediate consideration to':

(a) The diversion to Australia of:—
    (i) that portion of the A.I.F. now at Bombay and en route to Java;
    (ii) the British Armoured Bde in the same convoy.
(b) The diversion of the remaining two flights to Australia.
(c) The recall of 9 Aust Div and remaining A.I.F. in M.E. at an early date.[50]

Sturdee's appreciation was completed on the day that Singapore fell. This was by any calculation the greatest and most disgraceful defeat in British military history: 67,340 Indian troops, 38,496 British, 18,490 Australians and 14,382 local volunteers, 138,708 in all, were killed or captured in the course of a campaign that had cost the Japanese only 9,824 battle casualties. It was a thought-provoking response to Churchill's exhortations that there should be 'no question of surrender ... entertained until after protracted fighting among the ruins of Singapore City ... the city of Singapore must be converted into a citadel and defended to the death'.[51] In fact nobody should have expected that a huge Asian city without food or water would be defended to anything like the death by an inadequately trained and ill-equipped army, three-fifths of whom were themselves Asians. An analysis of the battle casualties made the implications quite plain. Total Empire killed or wounded amounted to 4,676. Of these, 3,195, or about 70 per cent, were provided by 8th Australian Division, which comprised only 13 per cent of the total imperial force. By contrast the Indians made up 45 per cent of the total force, but accounted for only 21 per cent of the battle casualties. They also provided the Japanese with a rather unexpected bonus, when 25,000 of them went over to the Axis after surrendering and enlisted in the Indian National Army.[52] Of the 14,382 local volunteers, ten in all shed their blood for the Empire.

The Australian effort had been admittedly perhaps the least impressive in the history of the AIF, but was still beyond comparison superior to that of the other units involved. Yet again the Australians had made a combat contribution out of all proportion to their actual numbers. Yet again there was not the slightest indication that the British leadership appreciated this fact, or was even aware of its existence.

Wavell's Chief of Staff, Lieutenant-General Sir Henry Pownall, was unfortunately another member of the long line of British commanders who happened to find Australia and the Australians simply detestable. The Curtin government in his estimation was actuated 'by a mixture of public opinion in Australia and common funk'. He found every reason to endorse Wavell's own view that the Australians 'would be the most difficult of our allies'. Even Winston Churchill 'had little enough use for them before', except presumably when it came to actual fighting. Pownall's own verdict was that the Australians were 'the most egotistical, conceited people imaginable. I sincerely hope I shall have nothing further to do with them.' The RAAF 'did not show up well. . . . Right away, from the first day, they showed signs of not being at all gallant.'[53] Churchill himself assiduously sought to shift the blame for the Malayan catastrophe from the Indians to the Australians, assuring the House of Commons in secret session on 23 April that 'credible witnesses disparage the Australians'. There was truly plenty to disparage.[54] On the other hand it was equally obvious that the Australians had with the New Zealanders borne a wholly disproportionate share of the combat effort of the British Empire to date; that they were with all their faults the only troops who had made an effective showing against the Japanese in Malaya; and that the survival of the British Eastern Empire might very well depend on their will and ability to go on resisting the Japanese southward drive. There had never been a time when the need to maintain sympathetic relations between London and Canberra might have seemed so imperative.

Relations were in fact allowed to deteriorate beyond anything previously experienced. The Australian government was understandably no more enthusiastic about British leadership than the British were about Australian fighting ability. Curtin remarked bitterly though correctly that Wavell's past successes had been 'mainly against Italians or black troops'. On 17 February, the day that Sumatra fell, he again requested the return of 6th, 7th and 9th Australian divisions from the Middle East. However Wavell wanted 6th and 8th divisions in Burma, and Churchill wanted 7th Division there as well. On 20 February, while Japanese aircraft made a devastating attack on Darwin, Australia's northernmost capital, Churchill angrily told Curtin that:

> I suppose you realise that your leading division . . . is the only force that can reach Rangoon in time to prevent its loss and the severance of communication with China. . . . There is nothing else in the world that can fill the gap. . . . I am quite sure that if you refuse to allow your troops which are actually passing to stop this gap, and if, in consequence, the above evils, affecting the whole course of the war, follow, a very grave effect will be produced upon the President, and the Washington circle, on whom you are so largely dependent.[55]

It was a rather disingenuous threat, as it was the Americans who were resolved to try to hold Australia, despite British objections to any diversion of forces from the Mediterranean front. Curtin replied with commendable restraint on 22 February, as Timor, Australia's last overseas garrison, fell to the Japanese, pointing out that Australia had sent troops to Malaya and the Pacific Islands on the understanding that the divisions would be returned from the Middle East. It was also impossible to send just one division to Burma, as 'it could not be left unsupported . . . or there might be a recurrence of the experiences of the Greek and Malayan campaigns'.[56] However Churchill had already cabled to Curtin to tell him that Australian demands had once again been totally disregarded: 'We could not contemplate that you would refuse our request and that of the President of the United States. . . . We therefore decided that the convoy should be temporarily diverted to the northward. The convoy is now too far north for some of the ships in it to reach Australia without refuelling.'[57]

The news caused sheer astonishment in Canberra where the War Cabinet was already faced with the report of Japanese preparations for an invasion of Java, where 3,000 Australian troops were still deployed, while the commanding officer at Port Moresby in New Guinea warned of the low morale of the troops there in view of their lack of naval, air and political support. Again Curtin responded with moderation to Churchill's provocations: 'Wavell's message . . . reveals that Java faces imminent invasion. Australia's outer defences are now quickly vanishing and our vulnerability is completely exposed. With A.I.F. troops we sought to save Malaya and Singapore, falling back on Netherlands East Indies. All these northern defences are gone or going. Now you contemplate using the A.I.F. to save Burma. All this has been done, as in Greece, without adequate air support.'[58]

Again New Zealand provided timely support for the Australian argument: the New Zealand Prime Minister warned Churchill that he and his colleagues 'were appalled by this attempt to think in terms of the past, and if this line of thought is persisted in we must brace ourselves to meet the fate of Malaya, with infinitely less excuse'.[59] Curtin in fact was still prepared to try to meet the British position: he offered two brigade groups for the defence of Ceylon, on condition that 9th Division should be released from the Middle East as quickly as possible. Churchill as usual attempted to split the two Dominions, telling the New Zealanders that: 'You have never asked for the withdrawal of your Division, and we have admired the constancy of spirit and devotion to the cause which has animated your Government and people.'[60] However the New Zealand government promptly pointed out that they had become aware of 'a feeling which . . . is becoming marked in the Division, that their proper place when their own country is in danger is in the Pacific theatre . . . we have a lot of sympathy for that point of view.'[61]

Meanwhile Churchill successfully opposed a suggestion by the Americans that an advisory war council should be established in Washington, on which Australia and New Zealand would be represented. Instead he assured Curtin that:

During the latter part of April and the beginning of May, one of our armoured divisions will be rounding the Cape. If, by that time, Australia is being heavily invaded, I should certainly divert it to your aid. This would not apply in the case of localised attacks in the north. . . . But I wish to let you know that you could count on this help should invasion by, say, eight or ten Japanese divisions occur. . . . I am still by no means sure that the need would arise especially in view of the energetic measures you are taking and the United States help.[62]

The fact was that Churchill was already becoming preoccupied with the prospect of opening a new front, once more against his hapless former ally France, by seizing the island of Madagascar. This exploit, enthusiastically supported by Smuts, would necessarily require a diversion of shipping and resources that otherwise would have been available for the defence of the Southern Dominions. However Churchill was still firm in his resolve not to be shaken by anything that might happen to the Eastern Empire: as he told the Dominions Secretary: 'I do not see much use in pumping all this pessimism [appreciation of situation in the Far East] throughout the Empire. . . . Altogether there is too much talk. A very different picture and mood may be with us in a couple of months.'[63] But they were not going to come as a result of any decisions taken in London. The British commitment to Australia had finally been spelt out as a promise of one division in the event of invasion by ten times that number of Japanese. Curtin wrote back, pointing out that this would indeed be a case of too little arriving too late.

But it was not only Australia that was apparently to be sacrificed in the interests of a wider view: on 6 April Sir Stafford Cripps, Churchill's own representative in India, told the Americans that

last night the Japanese Navy . . . sank all shipping between Madras and Calcutta . . . the Japanese Fleet is between the inferior British Fleet and its base, and that in a few hours engagement is certain with the British in most critical situation . . . there will then be nothing left to protect route from Persia to India. . . . Sir Stafford says, 'if we had 30 heavy bombers in Ceylon the British Fleet could be saved. Nothing else can save it. The bombers are not available.' Sir Stafford says there is only one bomber in the Near East which could fly to Tripoli; that heavy bombers in unjustified numbers are being held in England; that his efforts with Churchill to have some of the 'surplus' bombers sent to the Far East have been unavailing. . . . Sir Stafford further says we have reached the military crisis here and implores our aid in getting heavy bombers from England to this area without delay.[64]

Admiral Somerville in fact managed to extricate his imperilled Far Eastern Fleet, leaving the Japanese masters of the Bay of Bengal after sinking two British cruisers, two destroyers, an aircraft carrier and a corvette, without the loss of any of their own ships. A bitter commentary on Cripps's appeal was provided by the news that 234 British heavy bombers had raided the historic and militarily unimportant German town of Rostock on 24 April in preparation for Sir Arthur Harris's projected offensive against the German civilian population. Nor were appeals to the Americans necessarily going to be rewarding: a request from General Douglas MacArthur himself for an aircraft in the South-West Pacific drew the comment from United States Chief of Staff General Arnold that it would 'take a lot more than this one cablegram to get a carrier for MacArthur, regardless of the rights and wrongs of the case'.[65] Curtin's Minister for External Affairs Herbert Evatt reported from Washington, in reply to Curtin's letter, hoping that 'there is a full appreciation in London and Washington of grave threat with which we were confronted', that the Allied Service chiefs who laid down a general strategic policy were loath to admit any fundamental error: the determination in Washington was still to fight a holding war in the Pacific, and make the major military effort in Europe, in the hope that the Japanese gains could be recovered after the defeat of Germany.[66]

It was at this point of mounting Australian disillusionment about Allied strategic priorities that Churchill at last became concerned that relations between the Eastern Empire and the United Kingdom might become permanently impaired: as he pointed out to the First Sea Lord: 'Dr Evatt has made me the strongest appeals about an aircraft carrier. We had of course promised them *Hermes* but she was sunk on our business before being sent to them. . . . I have been wondering whether the *Furious* could be spared. . . . We have to consider our permanent relationship with Australia and it seems very detrimental to the future of the Empire for us not to be represented in any way in her defence.'[67] Here at least Canberra and London could agree, even though they were actually viewing the problem from differing perspectives: there was no question of Australia's shifting allegiance from the United Kingdom to the United States, but it was certainly going to be hard for the Australians to retain the desired relationship with the British unless the British actually re-established a presence in the Pacific.

This was made more unlikely than ever when Rommel launched his new offensive on the Gazala Line on 26 May. Numerically the odds favoured the British impressively: 100,000 infantry to 90,000; and 849 tanks to 560. Moreover the British armoured force included 167 of the American Grants, armed with a 75mm gun, while only 40 German tanks possessed a comparable weapon. However the Axis had recovered air supremacy over the battlefield, deploying a total of 704 aircraft, including the excellent Me109s, against a total British availability of 320. This last discrepancy was certainly due in part to the diversion of British aircraft to Russia and the Far East. It also reflected the extent to which

British air production had been diverted to supplying the needs of the bomber offensive against Germany. The bomber barons acted effectively to ensure that there would be no modification of this strategy. On the night of 30–31 May, while the Stukas smashed a way for the Afrika Korps through the British defences in Libya, 1,134 bombers, comprising literally all aircraft available for the purpose, headed for the city of Cologne. Churchill was convinced: as the British defences collapsed in Africa for want of adequate air cover, he congratulated Sir Arthur Harris, Chief of Bomber Command, announcing that the raids marked the introduction of a new phase in the British air offensive against Germany.[68] There would be no diversion of air production to the fighters and dive-bombers that were winning the war for the Axis.

Meanwhile Rommel swept on to his greatest victory: by 30 June the British were back at El Alamein, the last possible line of defence before the Nile delta. The German victory had been overwhelming: for a cost of about 6,000 casualties in all, Rommel had annihilated the equivalent of some three complete British divisions. Once again a British army in the field had been reduced to about half its strength by successive military disasters. In May 1942 Eighth Army comprised two armoured divisions, with two tank brigades, two South African infantry divisions, one Indian and one British. Another Indian division, an Indian brigade and an armoured brigade were in support. By the end of June, Auchinleck was left with only the New Zealand Division, the battered South African 1st Division, two Indian brigade groups and one armoured division, accompanied by the assorted remnants of three other divisions. As in May 1941 the only intact and effective reserve available was an Australian division. The 9th Division had to be moved from Syria to play the role acted by 7th Division the year before. The Eastern Empire, at a time of infinitely more immediate peril to itself, was again standing guard in the Middle East. Rommel at this time had four armoured divisions (two German and two Italian) and six other infantry divisions.

This situation understandably was not entirely approved by the Australian and New Zealand governments. Curtin had asked in April that two of the British divisions earmarked for India should be diverted to Burma, 'until such time as the 9th Division AIF and the remainder of 6th Division are returned'.[69] Instead two Indian divisions were diverted to the Middle East, which Curtin considered should have been sent to

Burma. However certain developments had helped to allay Australian fears: by the beginning of June the whole of the RAN was back in Australian waters, apart from four destroyers and three corvettes; and on 6 June the Americans won a victory over the Japanese at Midway, which has as much claim as any encounter to be regarded as the genuine turning-point of the Second World War. This was of course not certain at the time. Curtin however was sufficiently reassured to agree not to press in the meantime for the return of 9th Division, even though Stanley Bruce still appeared gloomy about the prospects of holding Egypt, and Eggleston suggested that the lack of public reaction in Britain against the fall of the Eastern Empire 'appears to suggest that the British people have lost the sense of Empire: a foolish thing, for Britain can no more do without her Empire than it can do without her.'[70]

It was at least clear that Britain could not hold Egypt without the Eastern Empire. Under intense artillery preparation the Australian and New Zealand forces thrust by night at Rommel over 10 and 12 July. However the New Zealand Division suffered heavy casualties from a counter-attack by German armour when the numerically stronger British tanks failed to give them support. Churchill thereupon asked the New Zealand government to send reinforcements 'to keep this splendid unit in its present basis'.[71] The 9th Australian Division shared the same experience on 27 July, when again British armour failed to advance to assist the Australians in holding the ground they had won. Mutual confidence between Canberra and London plummeted again. Curtin complained bitterly that the AIF 'was being made a chopping block in Africa when there were 900,000 other troops in the Middle East'.[72] Morshead warned that it was 'vital that on the next occasion our armour restores our lost faith in them . . .'.[73] It was indeed true that the armour had many reasons for caution: they lacked a tank to match the German MkIV, or an anti-tank gun to compare with the 88mm, and they had a long record of defeat at German hands to look back on. On the other hand they still had far more heavy tanks than Romel; the Grant was comparable to anything except the MkIV; and the unhappy fact remained that 'the British won most of their successes by infantry attacks, the Germans most of theirs by armoured counter-attacks. German armoured formations almost always arrived where most needed, British almost never.'[74] The least one could say was that something would have to be done to break this pattern if the Empire was to survive the war.

This was the more serious in that gains won by Dominion infantry were being lost through lack of support from British tank crews. Most unfortunately the next trial of Dominion infantry and British armour provided an even greater disaster. On 19 August a raiding force of 6,086 men, including 5,000 Canadians, carried out a 'reconnaissance in force' at Dieppe, losing some 4,384 casualties, 3,379 of them Canadian, along with a destroyer and 106 aircraft, including 88 Spitfires. The Germans lost a submarine-chaser, 591 men and 48 aircraft. The Allies had gained at least invaluable guidance on how not to invade the Continent. Considering the quality of the troops involved, the Germans had gained perhaps their most remarkably one-sided victory of the war.

The extent of the Dieppe disaster was not fully known in the Eastern Empire. There were in any case more serious problems closer to hand. The victory of Midway had not apparently halted the Japanese advance towards Port Moresby in New Guinea, Australia's last island bastion. Another Japanese invasion force landed in the east of the island at Milne Bay on 26 August. Meanwhile Morshead appealed for 6,113 reinforcements to bring 9th Division back to strength. The New Zealanders had already decided in response to Churchill's plea to send a further 5,500 to the Middle East. Evatt asked with understandable bitterness for some reciprocity: 'There is not one British soldier in Australia; the British Navy, on which we relied, has disappeared; except for a few trainer types, there is not a British plane in Australia. Where do we stand with you?'[75] Curtin none the less approved despatch of the reinforcements sought by Morshead. He did however find cause for complaint when Morshead was passed over as commander Eighth Army in favour of Sir Bernard Montgomery. The threat to Australia was briefly lightened by a total victory over the Japanese at Milne Bay on 5 September. But the Japanese advance towards Port Moresby continued across the Owen Stanley mountains. Curtin appealed to both Churchill and Roosevelt for help, telling the former that he was 'surprised that naval strength to build up the Eastern Fleet to a point where it could help in the Pacific is being disposed elsewhere'.

On 23 September the Japanese offensive faltered and began to recoil in the face of desperate resistance from 6th Australian Division, back from the Middle East. The Japanese tide was ebbing at last. Then Curtin launched his bombshell. He told Churchill and Roosevelt on 22 October that a manpower deficiency of 22,000 existed in Australia and that the best way to remedy it would be to recall 9th Division from Egypt.[76] The timing was unfortunate to say the least. Eighth Army was due to start its new offensive against Rommel on the following day, with an infantry attack delivered by 9th Division, the New Zealand Division, 1st South African and 51st Highland Division. It was also less than three weeks before D-Day for a new American assault in the Solomons, which would presumably require all available shipping. Curtin of course knew nothing of the impending El Alamein offensive. Here at last were the conditions for total military victory against a German command. Montgomery and Alexander could deploy 220,000 men against 96,000; 1,029 tanks, with 200 more in reserve, and 1,000 under repair, against 489, with 21 under repair; 2,311 guns against 1,219; and 530 aircraft against 350.

This may have been 'the last purely British victory in the war against Germany; it was the swansong of Britain as a great independent power'.[77] It was certainly disenchanting that, unlike the victories of the RAF and the navy, it should have been won by overwhelming numbers in a battle in which lack of imagination was carried to the point of inspiration. Auchinleck had fought his battles against the Germans like a master duellist, infinitely responsive to the parry and thrust of combat. His misfortune had been that his rapier tended to develop flaws, and he was prone to leave the fighting at first to more or less inadequate subordinates, incapable of performing the drills he had explained to them. Montgomery was an executioner rather than a swordsman, resolute in wielding an axe, but rather at a loss if the victim insisted on getting up from the block, as at Arnhem.

El Alamein in any case was clearly going to be another battle in which the main shock would have to be borne by the Australian and New Zealand divisions. Roosevelt told Curtin on 16 September that he could not 'too strongly stress that leaving the 9th AIF Division in the Middle East will best serve our common cause'.[78] This was no more than the truth, apart from the obvious fact that it would be impossible to pull the major attacking division out from the line in the middle of an offensive. General Alexander's view that 9th Division was the one that he could least afford to do without was given strong corroboration by the casualty figures. Eighth Army at the opening of the battle comprised three British armoured divisions, three British infantry divisions, 4th Indian Division, 1st South African Division, the New Zealanders, and 9th

Australian Division, as well as the Greeks and the Free French. Of 13,500 casualties lost by Eighth Army in the whole battle, 9th Division supplied 5,800.[79]

At this point the long-suffering New Zealand government, whose division was providing the other main element in Eighth Army's infantry attack, also decided to raise with Churchill 'the question of the return of the 2nd New Zealand Division from the Middle East'. They pointed out the threat of a further Japanese offensive, the fact that the Dominion's manpower resources 'have now reached straining point', the extremely heavy casualties that the division had suffered, and especially that 'it would be absolutely impossible for the New Zealand Government to resist the strong feeling to which I have referred should it become known that all three Australian Divisions have returned'.[80] Prime Minister Fraser went on to say in the New Zealand Parliament that he did not 'believe in the theory of a holding war in the Pacific while the fullest efforts are concentrated on one second front in Europe. If we have our eyes at the ends of the earth and the campaigns waged there, and not at our own door, then we are heading for disaster.'[81]

It was a strong view, but the New Zealanders were capable of being turned from it. On the very next day Fraser informed Churchill that he and his colleagues had been 'greatly impressed' by Churchill's arguments that it would be dangerous to remove the New Zealand Division in present circumstances, and accordingly they decided that they could not take the responsibility of pressing for the return of their troops.[82] Churchill did not even attempt to argue with the Australians. He decided unilaterally that all Australian troops remaining in the Middle East should be returned home by early 1943. This was too late to placate Curtin, who still referred sarcastically to Australia as 'WSC's forgotten land', and grumbled that Churchill and Roosevelt had long since made their minds up 'that if the British Empire in the Far East had to go then it had to go. The only part which had not gone was Australia.'[83] But the Australians had a new concern, as the Americans began to drive to victory in the Pacific. It was an anxiety shared by the New Zealanders, that 'it would be neither wise nor proper to allow the offensive against the Japanese in the South Pacific to be conducted entirely by the Americans without substantial British collaboration'. So far, British Commonwealth ground forces, in the form of the Australian army, had indeed borne the brunt of the fighting at least in the South-West Pacific area, crushing Japanese resistance in Papua, after a six months' campaign costing 5,698 Australian battle casualties and 2,848 American, in return for the destruction of 12,000 Japanese. By contrast a British offensive in Burma floundered to total defeat in the same period, despite 'temporary local air superiority over Arakan . . . overwhelming numerical superiority in the early stages, preponderance in artillery and a monopoly in armour . . .'.[84]

At the same time a renewed British military effort seemed demanded for political reasons, if British imperial authority were to be reasserted successfully after victory. This was the more important in view of remarks made by Roosevelt at a meeting of the Pacific War Council on 31 March 1943, when he referred to possible changes of sovereignty affecting the various island territories in the Pacific.[85] This however was still insufficient to shake British commitment to the 'Atlantic First' strategy: the British Chiefs of Staff continued to deny that any extension of the pressure against Japan at the expense of the war against Germany could be regarded as justifiable. Even the Americans were surprised at this concentration on the European theatre: Marshall remarked cynically that the British 'were all for a heavy war in the Pacific before Singapore but now they are naturally more interested in Europe'.[86] There was admittedly no doubt that Europe was now the more rewarding theatre, and the British were still playing a leading role in the Anglo-American thrust. The North African campaign came to an end on 13 May, when 240,000 Axis troops surrendered to the British Eighth and United States Fifth armies. In July the Allies landed in Sicily, deploying 250,000 British and 217,000 United States troops from an invasion fleet of 1,614 British ships and 945 American. The surrender of the Italian fleet on 9 September gave the British the opportunity to despatch naval forces to the Far East, while holding their army back to try to maintain parity with the Americans. But this 'first serious move by the British to participate with a sizeable force in the War in the Pacific' was aborted too.[87] United States Admiral Ernest J. King objected that 'no useful purpose would be served by the employment of the British units in the Pacific'.[88] The British did not plan to send out enough destroyers to safeguard the larger vessels; they were too heavy for use in the waters in the Solomons and New Britain; they were unnecessary, in view of United States naval superiority; and they would be a further drain on the trooplift supply. In addition it would complicate the logistic problem if they just went to Australia and New Zealand 'to stay in port and show the flag'.

On the other hand King was happy to see the British ships operating in the Bay of Bengal. But this was not what the Australians wanted. Roosevelt had spoken again at the Pacific War Council about the need to establish new bases in the Pacific Islands, to be developed 'for all nations not for any single nation'.[89] Plans for the survey of islands in the South-East Pacific for their development as future air bases were already under way. In some alarm the Australian War Cabinet decided that it had now become

of vital importance to the future of Australia and her status at the peace talks in regard to the settlement in the Pacific that the *military effort* should be concentrated as far as possible in the Pacific, and that it should be on a scale to guarantee her an effective voice in the peace settlement. If necessary, the extent of this effort should be maintained at the expense of commitments in other theatres. In the interests of Australia and the British Empire in the Pacific, it is imperative that this view should be accepted by the United Kingdom and the other Dominions, especially New Zealand and Canada.[90]

It was at least accepted by the British Foreign Office, which commented on the Pacific situation that 'if there is to be no major British role in the Eastern War, then it is no exaggeration to say that the solidarity of the British Commonwealth and its role in the maintenance of peace in the Far East will be irretrievably damaged'.[91] For the first time British and Australian views on diplomacy in the Pacific seemed to coincide. Evatt triumphantly affirmed that in whatever claims 'this country has made in relation to the prosecution of the war against Japan we have been animated by not merely a resolution to defend Australia and its territories, but also a determination to maintain the prestige of the British Commonwealth in areas where Japanese military occupation and political infiltration have subjected the United Nations to tremendous risks.'[92] He and Curtin were in fact already considering the possibility that 'possessing powers which haven't the means adequately to defend the islands should be supported by Britain and America assisting in their defence . . .'.[93] On 20 October Evatt invited the New Zealanders to attend a conference in Canberra to consider the postwar situation in the Pacific, including the proposition that 'it would be wise for Great Britain to transfer all British colonies in these areas to Australia and

New Zealand'.[94] American control of trans-Pacific air routes should be adamantly opposed.

Curtin had originally been hoping that the Australian and New Zealand governments would be able to count on British support. But the hopes of an increased British military effort in the Far East were shattered when Chief of Imperial General Staff Sir Alan Brooke refused even to discuss operations in South-East Asia before agreement had been reached on the assault on the European continent. 'Buccaneer', the first amphibious commitment that the British had been prepared to make in the Far East, was abandoned on 5 December. Meanwhile the Australians discovered to their fury that a conference had been held at Cairo, attended by Churchill, Roosevelt and Chiang Kai-shek, at which decisions had apparently been made about the disposal of mandated territories in the Pacific. Curtin complained that the only information he had received had been relayed to him by Stanley Bruce, who had 'picked it up off his own bat'.[95]

All this gave particular point to a speech made by Curtin on 14 December to a conference of the Australian Labour Party, where he argued that

in the Fourth Empire which is approaching, the trend [must be] to augment an association of independent sovereign people by a common policy in matters that concern the Empire as a whole. . . . The Australian and other Dominion Governments should have full knowledge of all essential facts, developments and trends of policy; they should obtain this knowledge in time to express their views before decisions are taken; they should have the opportunity, through their accredited representatives, of presenting to and discussing with the War Cabinet . . . any suggestions . . . that the Governments may . . . desire to submit.[96]

He did not effectively develop this theme in his opening address to the Australian–New Zealand conference in Canberra on 17 January, stressing instead the need for the two countries 'to take the primary part in applying to the countries of the South and South-West Pacific the principles of freedom from fear, freedom from want and freedom from oppression'. However the New Zealanders themselves expressed the wish to 'discuss closer liaison in defence between Australia, the United Kingdom and ourselves, and with the other South Pacific Powers'.

The agreement signed between the two countries on 21 January

constituted an unqualified assertion of the interests of British Commonwealth countries in the region in any postwar settlement in the Pacific.
The two governments declared that 'they have vital interests in all
preparations for any armistice . . . and agree that their interests should
be protected by representation at the highest level on all armistice planning and executive bodies'. Further, 'it would be proper for Australia
and New Zealand to assume full responsibility for policing or sharing in
policing such areas in the South West and South Pacific as may from
time to time be agreed upon'. They accepted 'as a recognised principle
of international practice that the construction and use, in time of war,
by any Power, of naval, military or air installations, in any territory
under the sovereignty or control of another Power, does not, in itself,
afford any basis for territorial claims or rights of sovereignty or control
after the conclusion of hostilities'. Most impressively and unequivocally
they declared 'that no change in the sovereignty or system of control of
any of the islands of the Pacific should be effected as a result of an
agreement to which they are parties or in the terms of which they have
both concurred'.[97] Curtin and Fraser had declared a Monroe Doctrine
for the South Pacific.

It was not surprising that the Australian–New Zealand Agreement
should have been interpreted by the Americans as a deliberate blow at
themselves. Evatt indeed strengthened this impression by reminding
the Americans of his anger at not having been invited to the Cairo
conference.[98] There was however reason to suspect that the Australians
had overlooked some aspects. The Dutch for example expressed irritation to the Americans at not having been informed or consulted, although the conference discussed 'territory and peoples over which the
Netherlands claimed complete sovereignty'. The British had not been
consulted either, although only because they had declined an invitation
to attend on the grounds that it was 'understood that . . . [the Con-
ference] is designed to effect an exchange of views between the Commonwealth and New Zealand Governments on Pacific questions as a
preliminary to further consultation with His Majesty's Government in
Great Britain and other interested Governments'.[99] The Americans
however assumed that in fact

it seems all too likely that the British may heartily support the Australian
and New Zealand proposals. . . . For some time it has been evident that
the British Government is apprehensive lest Australia and New Zealand

come too closely under American influence. This apprehension has found outward expression in . . . the despatch of a recent mission headed by Sir Walter Layton. Although Sir Walter has come back with the report that 'the feeling Australia has towards the Empire is in no way changed by what has happened in the Pacific', the apprehension still remains. It is very likely therefore that the British Government warmly welcomes this Australian-New Zealand Agreement as it demonstrates that these two members of the Empire do not intend to be subservient to the United States.[100]

The trouble was, as Australian representatives in Washington pointed out, that 'while the United Kingdom holds different views from the United States on many matters and is occasionally annoyed at American policy, nevertheless the United Kingdom still feels herself unable to resist American pressure on major matters'.[101] The fact was that nothing could any longer conceal the reality that the United States was by far the senior partner in the wartime alliance. Halifax warned Eden from Washington of the tacit assumption in the United States that 'without possibility of question, the United States has taken Great Britain's place as mistress of the seas'.[102]

Whatever else this might imply, one thing was obvious: the role of the British Empire in the international scene could only be significantly altered. A common realization of this brought the ends of the Empire together again. Curtin and Churchill renewed their correspondence as if the confrontations of the past three years had never happened. Churchill agreed fully that a British force based in Australia for use in the Pacific would 'produce good results upon Australian sentiment toward the Mother Country. . . . If the Japanese should withdraw from Malaya or make peace as a result of the main American thrust, the United States Government would after the victory feel greatly strengthened in its view that all possessions in the East Indian Archipelago should be placed under some international body upon which the United States would exercise a decisive control.'[103] But as always there were problems. Curtin pointed out that it would be necessary for any British forces operating in the South-West Pacific to be assigned to the commander-in-chief of that theatre, like the Australian forces.[104] There could be no question of a separate British Commonwealth command, even apart from the problem of who would command it. Objections and incompatible solutions multiplied. The Americans wanted the main

British effort to be made in Burma and towards China, to take Japanese pressure off Chiang Kai-shek. Curtin favoured a drive towards Malaya and the Indies. The British Chiefs of Staff wanted a roving naval task force to operate in the Pacific, with Nimitz's command. Churchill wanted a northward but independent thrust from Australia.

Curtin in London renewed his invitation to have British troops stationed in Australia, emphasizing the extent to which the Commonwealth military effort in the Pacific had so far been sustained by Australia and New Zealand virtually alone. The British suggested some six divisions, twenty squadrons of aircraft and a fleet of six battleships, ten aircraft carriers and twenty-five cruisers, for operations against Japan in 1945. The Australian Chiefs of Staff now reacted with horror at the thought of the added strain upon Australia's fully stretched manpower and supply resources of having an enormous British force of some 675,000 men based on their continent. But a solution could not be delayed. The last phase of the war was already unfolding. On 6 June an Allied invasion force, roughly equally divided between the United States and the British Empire, and covered by 6,080 American and 5,510 British aircraft, landed in France. A month later the tide began to turn slowly in Burma with the Japanese defeat at Imphal. Curtin eagerly pressed Churchill for any kind of early British participation in the Pacific War. The increasing pace of the American thrust might make the use of large Commonwealth land forces superfluous, but a British naval task force would be 'the only effective means for placing the Union Jack in the Pacific alongside the Australian and American flags. It would evoke great public enthusiasm in Australia and contribute greatly to the restoration of Empire prestige in the Far East . . . the pace of events here demands immediate action. . . .'[105]

Back in Australia, Curtin ruefully informed Parliament of the limited success of his attempts to improve the machinery for 'full and continuous consultation' among the governments of the Commonwealth. The Canadians had been very polite, but said only that proposals for postwar military co-operation would 'have to be considered carefully along with the whole range of matters concerned with world security'. Smuts said nothing. Curtin recognized that Canadian defence was essentially a matter for co-operation with the United States, and that the South Africans viewed their national defence as part of the general European scene. He could 'envy our sister Dominions the good fortune of their geographical and strategic locations, but our experience has been entirely different from this'.[106] Nor could Curtin endorse the Canadian view that the existing system of consultation worked well enough. Indeed it seemed almost impossible to make it work at all, when it was a matter of getting the British committed to the Eastern Empire. Churchill and the British Chiefs of Staff now proposed to Washington that there should be formed 'a British Empire task force under a British commander, consisting of British, Australian and New Zealand land, sea and air forces, to operate under General MacArthur's Supreme Command'.[107] Churchill put this to Curtin on 23 August, suggesting as an alternative that the main British effort should be made in Burma. Curtin objected that he should have been consulted before the proposal was made to the United States, and that in any case the Australian government would not agree to having their forces taken away from MacArthur and placed under a British commander. The Americans for their part were showing rapidly decreasing enthusiasm for British participation at all.

Victory seemed to be bringing only more problems. Curtin reiterated that he did not care what the United States did north of the Equator so long as it did not trespass on British territories in Hong Kong, Singapore or Malaya.[108] General Blamey now noted that the Americans were building up enormous stocks under Recriprocal Lend-Lease from Australia, 'far in excess of legitimate operational requirements, with the object of making them available in the Philippines, China or America itself . . . thus buying favourable publicity for American interests, both Government and private, at the expense of our sadly strained and depleted Australian resources'.[109] Eggleston attacked a speech of Churchill's, referring to the mighty war that the United States was fighting in the Pacific, on the grounds that the Americans 'will consider that they have won the war in the Pacific and they will insist on dominating the peace. In British circles I see almost complete acquiescence in this position and in addition a tendency to resent any criticism of the inertia on the Burma side.'[110] Evatt for his part rather indiscreetly told the Americans that

Australia was on the horns of a dilemma: they were bound to the Empire by ties of blood, and by economic ties, but that more and more they were coming to the realization that their political future as a people was cast in the Pacific; they found little sympathy with that point of view in London, which was mostly concerned with India, or in Canada, which was preoccupied with the United States, or in South Africa. Australia felt very much alone, and they realised they had a part to play in the Pacific.[111]

But at last, and for the last time, the Empire was on the march, even in the Far East. The British offensive at last opened in Burma on 10 December. The maximum deployment of British strength in the Second World War had been achieved. In Europe, 12 United Kingdom and 5 Canadian divisions stood beside 61 American, 12 half-strength French, and 1 Polish. In Italy, Alexander commanded 3 United Kingdom divisions, 2 Indian, 1 New Zealand and 1 South African, along with 2 Polish and the 7 United States and 1 Brazilian division of the Fifth Army.[112] In Burma, 2 United Kingdom divisions, with 7 Indian and 3 African, were engaging 10 under-strength Japanese divisions, who in their turn had the support of the 2 divisions of the Indian National Army. In the Pacific, 7 Australian divisions and 1 New Zealand division fought alongside 24 United States army and marine divisions. Indeed in the South-West Pacific area the Commonwealth forces maintained almost numerical parity with the Americans: the Australians and New Zealanders together deployed 668,617 army and air force personnel, not counting Home Guards and militia, and the Americans 688,739. It was indeed an imperial effort, however calculated: of the forty-five British divisions actually deployed on the battlefront or in campaign areas in all four main theatres of combat, twenty-eight came from the Empire overseas. Eggleston's words were demonstrably true: the Empire could not have done without Britain, but neither certainly could Britain have done without the Empire.[113]

The immediate problem was still to get the British effectively involved in the Pacific campaign. It was clear that this would be resolved only by the usual experience of confrontation between Canberra and London. Australian hopes for more effective consultation among the various Commonwealth countries had failed again in face of Canadian opposition and South African lack of interest. Nor was New Zealand any more concerned to support an Australian initiative without support from the other Dominions or the United Kingdom: the Australians noted regretfully that 'Canada and South Africa do not favour proceeding with your proposal [for joint discussions on defence co-operation] at present, and that New Zealand considers that the matter should be postponed. It is agreed that there is no alternative to the course.'[114] But traditional forms of communication were hardly succeeding in resolving the wrangles that were developing. On the one hand the Australian government wished to reduce the size of the army, to relieve the manpower shortage; but it also wanted its forces to continue to be associated with MacArthur's command in the forward movement against Japan, especially since Blamey had pointed out that 'the increased prestige of the Australians in the native mind brought about since the commencement of operations . . . has been considerable'; while to revert to a defensive role 'would, in the native mind, lower the prestige of the Government to such an extent that it might be difficult to recover on the termination of hostilities . . .'. MacArthur however now suggested that 'all Australian formations would come under British command for operations to the south'.[115] Churchill proposed the formation of a British Commonwealth force 'of British, Australian, New Zealand, British-Indian and possibly Canadian divisions' as 'a striking demonstration of Commonwealth solidarity'.[116]

This indeed was what the Australians had been after all along. However, Blamey pointed out that although it was most desirable, it was unfortunately unrealistic and impracticable, as such a force would not be ready for action before August 1946, by which time the Americans would long since have been in Tokyo. Blamey was indeed certain that the Americans would do everything to ensure that they alone dictated peace terms in the Japanese capital: he told a press conference on 9 July that he was quite convinced in his own mind that no British troops would be allowed to take part in the final move against Japan. This was unfair. Churchill told Curtin's successor Chifley on 26 July that the Combined Chiefs of Staff had agreed in principle to allow a British Commonwealth land force and possibly a small tactical air force to take part in the main operations against Japan. Appropriate British commanders and staff would accordingly visit Nimitz and MacArthur to draw up plans for British participation. The implications of the wording gave the Australians something new to worry about. Chifley warned Attlee, who had succeeded Churchill, that 'you refer to "British Commanders". This expression is taken to mean officers of the United Kingdom Forces and not officers of British Commonwealth Forces. . . . There are, of course, in the Australian Forces, officers who have distinguished themselves in the campaigns in the Middle East and the Pacific who have claims for consideration in the appointment of Commanders and Staffs.' He added that it had been 'necessary to make representations on the claims of Australian senior Commanders to command formations comprising British Commonwealth Forces when the AIF was serving in the Middle East'.[117]

Chifley's protestations had of course no effect. Attlee proposed two British officers to command the British Commonwealth forces on land and sea. It was however suggested that an Australian might be appointed to command the air component, since it would consist mainly of RAAF squadrons. Concerning the proposed land commander, the British government explained that: 'We do not think that the fact that this officer has not yet fought the Jap should be considered a handicap, since the terrain of the mainland of Japan is very different from that in which Jap has hitherto been engaged.'[118] It was perhaps logical, but unlikely to be accepted by the nation that had indeed fought the Jap constantly for over three and a half years, and regarded itself 'not as a subsidiary but as the principal Pacific power which has for so long borne the heat and burden of the struggle against Japan'.[119] The wrangling over command between the two Labour governments continued even after the defeat of Japan, Attlee insisting that Dominion forces in the Far East should remain under British command, and Chifley maintaining that Australian units would participate in a Commonwealth force only under Australian command. In fact a British force did participate in the final offensives against Japan; a well-integrated British Pacific Fleet with 2 battleships, 4 fleet carriers, 6 cruisers, 15 destroyers, and 218 aircraft contributed effectively to strikes against the Japanese garrisons in the East Indies, to the Okinawa campaign and to the final bombardment of the Home Islands.

It could however be only a token contribution, even if the Americans had been less determined to reserve for themselves the satisfaction of annihilating the navy that had challenged them in 1941: the United States admirals in the Pacific had available from their own navy some 23 battleships, 90 aircraft carriers, 52 cruisers, 323 destroyers, and 15,000 aircraft. British Admiral Rawlings told Nimitz that 'looking back on all that has happened, I begin to see that what matters is not the size of the British contribution, or what we were able to do, but that it is our being a part of that forging which overshadows everything else'.[120] But understandable tendencies to downgrade the British effort as that of a second-rate power only tended to obscure the reality of a complex situation. The productive output of the British Empire had been truly fantastic: the

Empire in fact outproduced Germany in aircraft and tank production, and even Russia in the latter. Nor had this been wholly a British effort: 11 per cent of the total output of guns, 12 per cent of the aircraft, and 45 per cent of the armoured fighting vehicles were produced outside of Britain, almost all in the Dominions.[121]

The imperial role had also been enhanced in the actual fighting: in the First World War Britain had supplied 78 per cent of the fatal casualties, the Dominions 14 per cent and India and the colonial Empire 8 per cent. In 1939–45 the relative figures were 73 per cent, 19 per cent and again 8 per cent. There could be no question as to either the magnitude of the effort or who had helped most to make it. Once again commanders on both sides rushed to do full justice to the Canadian achievement. Montgomery explained to the men of 1st Infantry and 5th Armoured divisions in Italy that 'when I say you did magnificently, I mean magnificently'.[122] On the other side German General von Vietinghoff commented that 'though not strong in numbers, the Canadians are right good soldiers', and that 'only Canadians attack like that!'[123] The most convincing proof of the Germans' regard for these particular opponents was noted by the official Canadian historian, Colonel G. W. L. Nicholson: 'The reported appearance of Canadians in a given sector was frequently the signal for the Germans to commit there the best formations in the theatre.'[124] The Canadians similarly noted with satisfaction that in the victory campaign in Europe the German High Command 'has paid First Canadian Army the compliment of consistently opposing our forces with some of the best troops available to them',[125] although they were compelled to admit that the best German troops were usually far more formidable than they were themselves.

This was not important. What was of real significance was the fact that despite British misgivings, pretended or real, about Canadian reliability before the war, Canadian divisions were again spearheading a British advance in a European war and accepting losses more severe than those suffered by any other units under Eisenhower's command. By the same token even the unspeakable Australians, whom General Pownall apparently expected to leave the Empire after Singapore, had been going to all lengths to reaffirm the authority of the British Empire in the Pacific. The Southern Dominions continued to do so for the next twenty years. The Australian Labour government continued after victory in its efforts to discover 'which measures for cooperation in the British Commonwealth could best be undertaken by us to assist the United Kingdom in the burden which she is carrying'.[126] As late as 1954 Freyberg, ever the incurable optimist, was arguing in the House of Lords that in any future war 'at least one third of the British forces will be from Commonwealth countries overseas. These forces must be used in the best way possible', implying that they had possibly not been used in such a way on previous occasions.[127]

But it was an impossible dream. There were flickers of Commonwealth military solidarity from time to time, in Korea, in Malaya, in the years of the Indonesian confrontation, in the token relationships of Australian and New Zealand units with British in Singapore, the former symbol of the idea of imperial defence. But the whole concept of an imperial military effort uniting the British peoples in a common front was already dying as the governments of the United Kingdom continued their policy of commitment to Europe. It was to disappear totally with the 1960s, vanishing beneath the incredibly shrunken horizons of the British people: gone forever with the memories of southern stars on a naval ensign, of a deeper shade of air force blue, of slouch hats in Trafalgar Square.

Conclusion

The South African War proved beyond question that the various elements of the British Empire beyond the seas were prepared to co-ordinate their military efforts with those of Britain in a common cause, and that they could do so with great success in the field. The effect of the First World War was to leave the British Empire for a brief period the strongest military power in the world, by air, land, and sea. The Second World War brought defeat, subordination and eventual dis-integration.

There are obvious tangible and impersonal reasons for this striking reversal of the status of British power. Most comprehensible of these is perhaps the decline in British economic performance relative to that of other major powers, itself largely a consequence of the imperial expansion of the late nineteenth century, which provided traditional British industries with short-term assured access to underdeveloped markets. However the remarkable expansion of British productive capacity under wartime conditions indicates that this decline could have been arrested at any stage by appropriate governmental policies. Again, there can be no question that the sheer magnitude of the British effort on these occasions placed great and damaging strains on British social and economic institutions. But once more it could be argued that both world wars might have been averted by more forcible and also more honest diplomacy on the part of the United Kingdom, and that perhaps the main contributing factor to the outbreak of the Second World War was the adoption by the British government of a policy of disarmament more extreme than was found necessary by any other major power.

What does emerge with almost embarrassing consistency from all the available evidence is an inability amounting almost to a refusal on the part of successive British governments to organize the military resources of the overseas Empire in any effective sense. It is admittedly true that the enormous diversity of the Empire put great practical difficulties in the way of such an organization. It is also true that many elements within the Empire would have been unsuited, and other elements would have been violently opposed, to being organized in this way. But other important elements would not. The African, Asian and West Indian colonies could make no significant contribution to Britain's ability to fight a major war against a modern power. India could at most be described as a marginal asset. Much the same could be said of South Africa, and even more strongly of Quebec. But English-speaking Canada was prepared to contribute, in terms of both manpower and economic production, more substantially than any other part of the Empire; and Ontario's imperial loyalty drew a positive inspiration from Quebec's ethnic nationalism. Similarly, Australia and New Zealand were on the other side of the globe from Europe, confronted by unique strategic problems of their own; but New Zealand identified its own national interests with the views of the British government on almost every occasion and the Australians in fact played a combatant role in both world wars second only to that of the United Kingdom itself. There was more than sufficient goodwill and material capacity in the English-speaking parts of the Empire to provide a power base for the United Kingdom to continue to play the part of a global power.

What was always lacking was the readiness on the part of the British to play such a role, with the resources available to them. The British were indeed always ready to employ the resources of the overseas Empire to support their role as a European power. But this was a viewpoint that consistently disregarded the interests and potentialities of the Empire itself. The British vision remained rigorously Eurocentric, apart from an emotive concern with the peculiar problems of the Indian Empire. Genuine attention was paid in London only to viewpoints that harmonized with this continental preoccupation. British ministers welcomed the comments of Canadian Liberals dependent on the support of Quebecois regionalists. They positively courted the Afrikaaner Jan Smuts. But Canada, assured of the protection of the United States, could not involve the British in any defence responsibilities at all; and the security of South Africa depended essentially on the success of British European strategy. The views of the Eastern Empire, concerned with threats to its security from outside Europe, were consistently treated very differently.

It was perhaps unfortunate that the main spokesmen for the interests of the Eastern Empire necessarily had to be Australians. New Zealand shared the same anxieties, but in the last issue New Zealand could usually be counted upon to accept British guidance. Australia, far closer geographically to Asia, could not. But Australia was not only speaking for itself. The strategic concerns of successive Australian governments were applicable to the whole Empire east of Suez. They were in fact shared by British naval officers who spent sufficient time in the South Pacific to become aware that its security problems were different from those of the North Sea. Creswell, Tryon, Fanshawe and even Jellicoe gave full support to Australian attitudes on imperial defence. Their submissions also were invariably set aside in London, or at best acted upon imperfectly and inadequately.

Even an Australian can accept that Britain's rulers might well have found Australians unlovable, on the whole. There is no doubt that many of them seemed to find Australians detestable. Crewe, Grey, Haig, Jellicoe, Churchill, Wavell, Pownall among others seem to have literally found it impossible to say anything good about Australians. But personal attitudes really do not seem to have been fundamental here. The most Anglophile and obviously imperial-minded Australians were treated with the same disregard as their more abrasive and apparently nationalistic compatriots. Deakin's proposals were taken no more seriously than those of Hughes. Bruce, Lyons, Menzies and Page were no more successful in attaining a genuine meeting of minds with the British than Curtin or Evatt.

Yet Australia did not only have a case to present. It also had a certain moral claim to be heard. Australia had eagerly sought to co-operate in every British foreign war since 1883; it made a greater combat contribution and suffered more combat casualties than any other part of the overseas Empire in the South African War, and the two world wars; and Australian governments of whatever political complexion showed themselves committed to the idea of Empire so long as there was any framework of reality to found that idea upon. It all made no difference. Stanley Bruce's boast that the heart of the Empire had been moved from the North Sea to the Pacific never had any basis in fact. The heart of the Empire was where the military resources of the Empire were concentrated, and this certainly never changed. The only British battleship outside European waters in 1914 was HMAS *Australia*; there was not one capital ship, not one 3.7-inch anti-aircraft gun, not one modern tank, not one single-seat monoplane fighter in the overseas Empire in 1939; and the only combat tanks east of Suez in December 1941 were Australian-made Matildas, and the only single-seat fighters were United States Navy Buffaloes, incapable of taking an effective front-line role against the *Luftwaffe*. The Empire was defended with equipment that could not have been usefully employed in the war against Germany.

The British may not have been fully conscious of the fact that the effect of their defence policy decisions from the 1890s on would be to leave the overseas Empire helplessly exposed to any threat emanating from outside the European continent. There can be no question that this is what actually happened. Nor is there any real doubt as to the motivation for such a policy. The name of the game as always was the balance of power in Europe. Considerations of imperial defence were accorded no weight at all compared with the overriding concern to preserve a leading role for Britain in the affairs of the Continent, with the basic objective of preventing any single state from acquiring hegemony over Europe. It became fashionable to talk of a 'decision for Europe' in the 1960s, in the context of British relations with the European Economic Community. But the decision for Europe had been taken at least seventy years before. Despite the fact that they possessed the biggest Empire in history, Britain's leaders still interpreted the international role of the United Kingdom as that of a European great power, not as that of part of a global empire. It was too narrow a vision, even in terms of the commitment that it implied. The fact was that the United Kingdom could continue to function as a great power at all only if it could augment its own demographic and economic resources with those of the other British peoples beyond the seas. To do so, it would have been necessary for British governments to have recognized what the interests of those peoples were, and to have adopted the policies necessary to reconcile those interests with their own preoccupations in London. It would have required an effort to display genuinely imperial qualities of sympathy and imagination, fully befitting the heirs of Rome, as imperial-minded Englishmen were sometimes pleased to describe themselves. The tragedy of the British Empire is that these qualities were more likely to be glimpsed on the frontiers of the Empire – in Toronto, Vancouver, Wellington or Melbourne – than in the Home Islands themselves.

Notes

Chapter 1

1 Henry James, *English Hours* (New York 1960), p. 108. For a general discussion of the demographic ambitions of some colonial imperialists, see A. Ross, *New Zealand Aspirations in the Pacific in the Nineteenth Century* (Oxford 1964).

2 C. Barnett, *The Swordbearers* (London 1963), pp. 215–16; see also Barnett, *The Collapse of British Power* (London 1972), *passim*, especially pp. 19–47, and C. Chisholm, *A Handbook of Commercial Geography* (London 1916), pp. 287–92.

3 H. W. Richardson, 'Retardation in Britain's Industrial Growth', *Scottish Journal of Political Economy* (June 1965), p. 125.

4 C. P. Kindleberger, *Economic Growth in France and Britain* (Cambridge 1964), p. 146.

5 *Ibid.*, p. 272.

6 A. M. Imlah, 'British Balance of Payments and Export of Capital 1866–1913', *The Economic History Review* (1952–3), pp. 208–9.

7 Richardson, 'Retardation in Britain's Industrial Growth', p. 146.

8 Colonel W. Waters, trans., *The German Official Account of the War in South Africa* (London 1904), p. 23.

9 D. MacCallum, 'The Early "Volunteer" Associations in New South Wales and the Proposals in the First Quarter of the Nineteenth Century', Royal Australian Historical Society, *Journal* (December 1961), pp. 352–67.

10 See C. Hermon Gill, Commander, 'The Origins of the Royal Australian Navy', *ibid.* (November 1959), p. 140.

11 George F. G. Stanley, *Canada's Soldiers* (Toronto 1960), p. 179.

12 New South Wales, *Votes and Proceedings*, 1854, *Report from the Select Committee on the Volunteer and Yeomanry Corps Bill*, 78–A, p. 11.

13 Great Britain, *Hansard Parliamentary Debates*, 3rd ser. CLV 4 April 1860, p. 9395.

14 Queensland, *Journals of the Legislative Council*, 1882, XXXI, pt 1, *Report of the Military Committee of Inquiry*, p. 227.

15 D. MacCallum, 'Some Aspects of Defence in the Eighteen Fifties in New South Wales', RAHS, *Journal* (1958), pp. 71–115.

16 Great Britain, *Report of the Select Committee, Evidence*, 27 May 1861.

17 Agent-General Queensland to Secretary of State for the Colonies, 28 November 1884, COL/92, no. 84/1262, App. 1; see also D. MacCallum, 'The Alleged Russian Plans for the Invasion of Australia, 1864', RAHS, *Journal* (November 1958), pp. 301–21.

18 V. Fitzhardinge, 'Russian Naval Visitors to Australia, 1862–88', *ibid.* (June 1966), pp. 129–58.
19 Gill, 'The Origins of the Royal Australian Navy', p. 142; see also B. A. Knox, 'Colonial Influences on Imperial Policy, 1858–66', *Historical Studies, Australia and New Zealand* (1964), pp. 61–79.
20 Queensland, V. and P., 1865, I, *Statistics on the Volunteer Corps*, pp. 461–3; see also D. Anderson, 'Queensland's Colonial Defence Policies', unpublished thesis (University of Queensland), chap. 4.
21 Queensland, V. and P., 1878, I, *Queensland Defences – First Progress Report and Second Progress Report*, pp. 529–32.
22 *Ibid.*, 1882, I, *Report on the Defence Force*, p. 560.
23 *Confidential Despatches from Secretary of State*, GOV/11, 20 March 1878, no. 366.
24 *Ibid.*, 22 October 1879, no. 389.
25 Secretary of State for the Colonies to Governor New South Wales, 11 May 1881, NSW, 1881, II, *Report of the Intercolonial Conference*, p. 3.
26 AGVic to PremVic, 2 July 1883, Victoria, Papers presented to Parliament by Command, 1884, III, *Annexation, Federation and Foreign Convicts.*
27 Gill, 'The Origins of the Royal Australian Navy', p. 144.
28 C. P. Stacey, 'John A. MacDonald on Raising Troops in Canada for Imperial Service', *Canadian Historical Review* (March 1957), pp. 37–40.
29 S. Brogden, *The Sudan Contingent* (Melbourne 1943), p. 12.
30 C. P. Stacey, 'Canada and the Nile Expedition of 1884–5', *CHR* (December 1952), pp. 319–40.
31 *Ibid.*, p. 324.
32 Stanley, *Canada's Soldiers*, p. 272.
33 Lord Melgund, 'The Recent Rebellion in North-West Canada', *Nineteenth Century* (August 1885), pp. 312–27.
34 AGNSW to SSC, 16 May 1885, NSW V. and P., 2nd session 1885, II, *Australian Contingent for the Soudan*, p. 620.
35 Barbara Penney, 'The Age of Empire', *HSANZ* (November 1963), pp. 32–42.
36 General H. Essame, *The Battle for Europe 1918* (London 1972), p. 3.

Chapter 2
1 Tryon to Loch, 7 March 1885, NSW V. and P., 1885–6, II, *Colonial Naval Defences*, p. 281.
2 Dalley to Stout, 16 April 1885, *ibid.*
3 Tryon to Dalley, 4 May 1885, *ibid.*
4 PMNZ to GovNZ, 6 May 1885, *ibid.*
5 GOV/11, 19 June 1885, no. 489.
6 PRE/21, *Premier and Chief Secretary's Dept., Correspondence and Associated Papers Relating to the Naval Defence of Queensland, June 1885–August 1902.*
7 GovNSW to PremNSW, 7 March 1886, NSW V. and P., *Naval Defences of Australia*, p. 272.
8 *Ibid.*, 11 March 1886.
9 GOV/11, 18 November 1886, no. 470.

10 GOV/35, *Confidential Despatches for the Secretary of State for the Colonies, January 29, 1868–October 1, 1904*, 25 March 1887.
11 O'Rourke, 'Problems of Queensland Defence', p. 157.
12 SSC to GovVic, P.87/2291, 16 June 1887, Victoria, *Parliamentary Papers*, 1889, III, no. 57, *Inspection of Colonial Forces by an Imperial General Officer*.
13 *Ibid.*, Memorandum by General Steward for the Minister of Defence, 1 March 1889.
14 A. Deakin, *The Federal Story* (Melbourne 1963), p. 25.
15 *Ibid.*
16 Victoria, *Parl. Pap.*, *supra*, 18 April 1889.
17 Queensland, V. and P., 1889, I, *Report of Major-General Edwards*, pp. 1351–5.
18 South Australia, *Parl. Pap.*, 1890, IV, no. 145, *Remarks by the Colonial Defence Committee on Major-General Edwards' Report*.
19 M. Hooper, 'The Naval Defence Agreement 1887', *Australian Journal of Politics and History* (April 1968), pp. 52–75.
20 *Ibid.*
21 Trainor, 'British Imperial Defence Policy', p. 206.
22 *Ibid.*, p. 216.
23 South Australia, *Parl. Pap.*, 1897, II, no. 89, *Memorandum re the Conference of Premiers in London and the Report of the South Australian Naval Commandant*.
24 Great Britain, House of Commons, Select Committee on Naval Estimates (1888), *3rd Report*, p. vi.
25 Great Britain, *Hansard Parl. Deb.*, 3rd ser., CCCXXXIII, p. 1171.
26 *Ibid.*
27 A. J. Marder, *From the Dreadnought to Scapa Flow; I, The Road to War* (Toronto 1961), p. 6.
28 South Australia, *Parl. Pap.*, 1897, II, no. 89.
29 The words attributed to Laurier by Tupper did not in fact appear in the published version of Laurier's address. See Preston, *Canada and Imperial Defense* (Durham 1967), p. 240.
30 N. Penlington, 'General Hutton and the Problems of Military Imperialism in Canada, 1898–1900', Cook, Brown, Berger, eds, *Imperial Relations in the Age of Laurier* (Toronto 1969), pp. 45–60.
31 GOV/14, *Report of the 1897 Colonial Conference*.
32 Great Britain, *Hansard Parl. Deb.*, 4th ser. LXII, p. 860.
33 Outen J. Clinard, *Japan's Influence on American Naval Power 1897–1917* (Berkeley 1947), p. 19.
34 Major-General Sir Frederick Maurice, *History of the War in South Africa, 1899–1902* (London 1906), p. 95.
35 Salisbury to O'Connor, 25 January 1898, *British Documents on the Origins of the War 1898–1914*, G. P. Gooch and H. Temperley (London 1937), I, no. 8.
36 J. L. Garvin, *The Life of Joseph Chamberlain* (London 1934), III, p. 259.
37 *Ibid.*, p. 271.
38 NSW V. and P., 1900, IV, app. K, *Conference of Naval Officers*, 5 August 1899, pp. 346–8.

Chapter 3

1 See L. S. Amery, ed., *The Times History of the War in South Africa, 1900–1902*, V, p. 505; also Wayne Kruger, *Good-bye Dolly Gray* (London 1959), for an authoritative contemporary account of the whole conflict.

2 Hubert du Cane, *The German Official Account of the War in South Africa, March 1900 to September 1900* (London 1906), pp. 326–7.

3 W. H. H. Waters, *The German Official Account of the War in South Africa, October 1899 to February 1900* (London 1904), p. 221n.

4 Great Britain, *Hansard Parl. Pap.*, 1904, XL, p. 262.

5 *Ibid.*, I, paras 8019, 8021, 8025; see also Preston, *Canada and Imperial Defense*, p. 261.

6 Berger, *Imperial Relations*, p. 25.

7 PremQld to PremNSW, 1 August 1899, NSW V. and P., 1901, III, pp. 981–1044.

8 A. P. Haydon, 'South Australia's First War', *HSANZ* (April 1964), pp. 222–33.

9 PremVic to PremNSW, 20 September 1899, *ibid.*

10 Colonel Commanding Artillery to Assistant Adjutant-General, 21 September 1899, *ibid.*

11 PremNZ to AGNZ, 22 May 1885, NZ, *Appendix to the Journals of the House of Representatives*, 1885, A–7.

12 Berger, *Imperial Relations*, p. 26.

13 NSW, *Parl. Pap.*, 1901, III, p. 559.

14 Penlington, 'Military Imperialism in Canada', app. H.

15 Waters, *German Official Account*, p. 47.

16 B. Gardner, *The Lion's Cage* (London 1969), p. 147.

17 *The Times History of the War in South Africa*, III, p. 307.

18 *Ibid.*, pp. 326–7.

19 Commonwealth Archives Office, Defence Department, File 01/1953.

20 Victoria State Archives, Defence Department, File 00/10105.

21 Commonwealth of Australia, *Parl. Pap.*, 1901–2, I, *Contingents (Australian) in China*, p. 38.

22 G. H. L. Le May, *British Supremacy in South Africa 1899–1907* (Oxford 1965), p. 86.

23 The New Zealanders lost 293 killed, wounded and missing; the Canadians, 407; the Australians, 1,029.

24 *Times History*, III, pp. 37–8.

25 D. O. W. Wall, *The New Zealanders in South Africa, 1899–1902* (Wellington 1949), p. 88.

26 Penney, 'Australia's Reactions to the Boer War', p. 123.

27 *Commonwealth Parl. Deb.*, IV, pp. 5405–6.

28 *Ibid.*, pp. 11250–1, 11380–1.

Chapter 4

1 Penney, 'Australian Reactions to the Boer War', p. 126.

2 *Commonwealth Parl. Pap.*, 1903, *Colonial Conference 1902*, pp. 949–1126.

3 *Ibid., Naval Defence of the Commonwealth*, p. 1034.
4 *Ibid.*, p. 1903.
5 La Nauze, *Deakin*, p. 441.
6 Commonwealth Archives Office, CP 290, set 26, *Secret and confidential letters despatched by the Prime Minister's Office, 1903–10*. (See bibliography for list of CAO documents consulted.)
7 ROM CRS A1108 Prime Minister's Dept, Correspondence with British Government, Prime Minister and Governor-General.
8 Preston, *Canada and Imperial Defense*, p. 342.
9 *Ibid.*, pp. 330–2.
10 William R. Braisted, *The United States Navy in the Pacific, 1909–22* (Austin 1971), p. 5.
11 Clinard, *Japan's Influence on American Naval Power*, p. 33.
12 *BDD*, II, p. xv.
13 CP 290.
14 La Nauze, *Deakin*, p. 447 fn.
15 Roosevelt to Spring-Rice, 13 June 1904, in Elting E. Morison, *The Letters of Theodore Roosevelt* (Cambridge 1951), IV, no. 3096.
16 *Commonwealth Parl. Pap.*, 1906, II, *Report of the Director of the Naval Forces on the Defence of the Commonwealth of Australia for the Year 1905*, pp. 53–7.
17 Grey to Bertie, 15 January 1906, *BDD*, III, pp. 177–8.
18 G. Macandie, *The Genesis of the Royal Australian Navy* (Sydney 1949).
19 *BDD*, VI, pp. 201–26.
20 Great Britain, *Hansard Parl. Deb.*, 4th ser., CXCVI, p. 560.
21 *Commonwealth Parl. Pap.*, 1908, II, *The Defence of Australia by Colonel H. Foster, together with Remarks Thereon by Captain W. R. Creswell, Naval Director*, pp. 363–79.
22 *Ibid.*, 1909, *Defence: Correspondence Regarding a Conference between the Representatives of His Majesty's Government and the Governments of the Self-Governing Dominions on the Subject of Naval and Military Defence*, pp. 147–80.
23 *Ibid.*
24 *Ibid.*
25 *Ibid.*
26 SSC to GGAust, 30 April 1909, *ibid.*
27 Woodward, *Great Britain and the German Navy*, p. 465.
28 Macandie, *Genesis of the Royal Australian Navy*, p. 253.
29 Deakin to Crewe, 27 September 1909, F. O. 800/91, Public Records Office. (See bibliography for full list of PRO documents consulted.)
30 Crewe to Grey, 3 November 1909, *ibid.*
31 Crewe to Deakin, 15 December 1909, Deakin Papers, MS.
32 *Commonwealth Parl. Deb.*, LIV, p. 6252.
33 GGAust to SSC, 9 December 1909, in Macandie, *Genesis of the Royal Australian Navy*, p. 246.
34 MP/729/2, file 1856/4/155 Schemes of Defence – Mobile Forces of Australia, VII, pp. 626–7.
35 I. H. Nish, *Alliance in Decline* (London 1972), p. 66.
36 *BDD*, VII, pp. 629–32.

37 Nicholson to Grey, 4 May 1912, Navy Records Society, *Policy and Operations in the Mediterranean, 1912–14* (London 1970), p. 10.
38 Memorandum by McKenna, 24 June 1912, *ibid.*, pp. 37–42.
39 D. Dignan, *New Perspectives on British Far Eastern Policy, 1913–19* (Brisbane 1969), p. 277.
40 D. C. Sissons, 'Attitudes to Japan and Defence', unpublished thesis (University of Melbourne), p. 145.
41 CID, Minutes of 117th Meeting, 4 July 1912, *Policy and Operations in the Mediterranean*, pp. 60–83.
42 Memorandum by Churchill, 17 July 1912, *ibid.*, pp. 90–1.
43 *Commonwealth Parl. Pap.*, 1912, II, *Naval Defence of the Empire*, pp. 117–19.
44 Jerram Papers, cited in Nish, *Alliance in Decline*, p. 95.
45 Jose, *Royal Australian Navy*, p. xli.
46 Barnett, *Collapse of British Power*, p. 81.
47 Macandie, *Genesis of the Royal Australian Navy*, p. 289.

Chapter 5
1 SSC to GGAust, 29 July 1914, in E. Scott, *Australia during the War* (Melbourne 1936), p. 6.
2 GGAust to PMAust, 31 July 1914, *ibid.*, p. 8.
3 Population 3,554.
4 Population 3,992. Horsham and Colac were hardly major centres of population. However, the press blazed the words of Cook and Fisher across the Empire in a few days. Fisher in any case repeated the phrase in subsequent speeches at Benalla in Queensland, and in his address to the new Federal Parliament.
5 Scott, *Australia During the War*, p. 11.
6 SSC to GGAust, 14 August 1914, in Scott, *ibid.*, p. 12.
7 *Ibid.*, 6 August 1914, in Scott, *ibid.*, p. 13.
8 GGAust to SSC, *ibid.*
9 SSC to GGAust, 11 August 1914, in Jose, *Royal Australian Navy*, p. 5.
10 Jose, *ibid.*, p. 136.
11 See correspondence between SSDA, GGAust and GNZ in Files of the Governor, G48, W/2.
12 B. Liddell Hart, *History of the First World War* (London 1970), p. 91.
13 See for example CAB 19/33, First Report of the Dardanelles Commission, pp. 3–9, 47; Public Record Office (see bibliography for list of Cabinet papers consulted); M. Hankey, *The Supreme Command* (London 1961), pp. 244–50.
14 See R. Kermer, 'Russia, the Straits and Constantinople', *Journal of Modern History* (1920), pp. 400–15.
15 CAB 19/33, p. 15.
16 Churchill to Kitchener, 8 February 1915, cited in Churchill, *The World Crisis* (London 1933), II, p. 615.
17 Churchill, *ibid.*, p. 182.
18 George H. Cassar, *The French and the Dardanelles* (London 1971), p. 78.
19 For basic reading on the Battle of Jutland see Barnett, *The Sword-*

bearers, pp. 121–218; Churchill, *The World Crisis*; Hart, *History of the First World War*, pp. 357–406; Marder, *From the Dreadnought to Scapa Flow*.

20 C. E. W. Bean, III, p. 7.
21 *Ibid.*, pp. 56–7.
22 See for example J. Terraine, *The Western Front* (London 1964); and M. J. Williams, 'The Treatment of the German Losses in the Somme in the British Official History' (February 1966), *Journal of the Royal United Services Institute*, pp. 22–32.
23 P. Guinn, *British Strategy and Politics, 1914 to 1918* (Oxford 1965), p. 178.
24 Bean, III, p. 995.
25 V. Bonham-Carter, *Soldier True* (London 1963), pp. 144–5.
26 Cited in L. C. F. Turner, *The Great War, 1914–1918* (Melbourne 1971), p. 44.
27 R. Blake, ed., *The Private Papers of Douglas Haig, 1914–1919* (London 1952), p. 157.
28 *Ibid.*
29 Bean, v, p. 27.
30 *Ibid.*, pp. 26–37.
31 *Ibid.* See also W. Moore, *The Thin Yellow Line* (London 1975).
32 D. J. Murphy, 'Religion, Race and Conscription in World War I', *AJPH* (1974), pp. 155–63.
33 Turner suggests that this may have been at least partially due to the fact that 'the AIF prided itself on being an élite volunteer force'. Turner, *The Great War*, p. 32.
34 Rawlinson to PMAust, 8 February 1917, cited in Bean, IV, p. 16.
35 L. S. Amery to PMUK, cited in Amery, *My Political Life* (London 1955), II, p. 91.
36 UK, Govt, Cd. 856, *Imperial War Conference. Selections from Minutes of Proceedings and Papers Laid before the Conference*.
37 *Ibid.*
38 W. K. Hancock and J. van der Poel, eds, *Selections from the Smuts Papers* (Cambridge 1966), I, pp. 427–30.
39 Relative casualties at Arras seem singularly indefinite: C. Falls, in *Military Operations in Flanders and Belgium* (London 1940), pp. 556–61, indicates a range of between 140,000 and 158,000 for the British and between 79,418 and about 100,000 for the Germans.
40 Bean, IV, p. 542.
41 See Chapter 9.
42 William S. Sims, *Victory at Sea* (New York 1920), pp. 6–7.
43 Wilson to Sims, 4 July 1917, cited in Tracy B. Kittredge, *Naval Lessons of the Great War* (Garden City 1921), p. 438.
44 *Ibid.*, p. 454.
45 C. R. M. F. Cruttwell, *A History of the Great War* (Oxford 1934), p. 438.
46 Bean, IV, p. 876.
47 See Mason Wade, *The French Canadians, 1760–1967* (Toronto 1968), especially chaps XI and XII, for the fullest available account of the impact of the war on Canada.

48 Essame, *Battle for Europe*, p. 113.
49 L. Hart, *Through the Fog of War* (London 1938), p. 149.
50 Monash to Pearce, 5 November 1918, Pearce Papers, bundle 7.
51 Bean, IV, p. 618, and V, p. 118.
52 *Ibid.*, V, p. 676.
53 Blake, *Private Papers of Douglas Haig*, p. 290.
54 *Ibid.*, p. 291.
55 *Ibid.*
56 United States War Office, *Report of the Military Board of Allied Supply* (Washington 1924), I, pt one, pp. 57–60.
57 Bean, V, p. 177.
58 C. E. W. Bean, *The A.I.F. in France, 1918* (Sydney 1942), p. 906.
59 *Ibid.*, pp. 485 and 873.
60 Blake, *Private Papers of Douglas Haig*, p. 319.
61 *Ibid.*, p. 327.
62 Bean, VI, pp. 875–6.
63 *Ibid.*, p. 876.
64 Scott, *Australia During the War*, p. 751. Among those present were H. C. Bailey, Robert Blatchford, Neil Munro, Frank Anstey, Gilbert Parker, Ian Hay and Conan Doyle.
65 Bean, *The A.I.F. in France, 1918*, pp. 878–9.
66 S. W. Roskill, *Naval Policy Between the Wars: The Period of Anglo-American Antagonism, 1919–1929* (London 1968), I, p. 71.
67 *Report of the Military Board of Allied Supply*, pp. 57–60.
68 H. A. Jones, *The War in the Air* (London 1937), app. XXXI.
69 Bean, VI, pp. 1098–9.

Chapter 6
1 Cited in Hancock and van der Poel, *Selections from the Smuts Papers*, III, pp. 506–17.
2 Harcourt to Ferguson, 6 December 1914, Novar Papers, 4, NLA.
3 Ferguson to Harcourt, 13 May 1915, *ibid.*
4 Naval Records Collection, WA5, file, NA, RG45, cited in W. R. Braisted, *The United States Navy in the Pacific, 1909–1922* (Austin 1971), p. 163.
5 F.O. 371/2647.
6 *Australia During the War* CP 360/8, vol. 4.
7 *Ibid.*, vol. 3.
8 External Affairs II, CRS A981, item *Japan 101*, pt. 1
9 Sir John Jordan to Arthur Balfour, 23 December 1918, F.O. 371/3693 [3057].
10 Memorandum by Max Muller on Japanese Policy in Korea, *DBFP*, 1st ser., VI, no. 419.
11 Alston to Curzon, 18 July 1919, *ibid.*, no. 431.
12 Geddes to Walter Long, 25 November 1918, in L. A. Temple Patterson, ed., *The Jellicoe Papers*, II, 1916–35 (London 1968), pp. 287–8; also Murray to Jellicoe, 23 December 1918, *ibid.*, p. 289.
13 Jellicoe to the First Lord, 3 March 1919, *ibid.*, pp. 290–5.
14 Jellicoe to Long, 2 May 1919, *ibid.*, pp. 296–7.

15 Jellicoe to GGAust, 12 August 1919, *ibid.*, IV, chap. I, p. 347.
16 *Ibid.*, chap. I, p. 326.
17 *Ibid.*, p. 338.
18 *Ibid.*, p. 347.
19 Jellicoe to Long, 20 August 1919, *ibid.*; also Jellicoe to the Secretary of the Admiralty, August 1919, *ibid.*; see also Roskill, *Naval Policy Between the Wars*, I, p. 116, for another view of the quality of Australian naval personnel.
20 J. M. McCarthy, 'Australia and Imperial Defence: Co-operation and Conflict, 1918–1939', *AJPH* (April 1971), pp. 19–32.
21 Temple Patterson, *Jellicoe Papers*, p. 338.
22 Foreign Office to Admiralty, 21 January 1920, *DBFP*, 1st ser., VI, pp. 1053–4.
23 Admiralty to Foreign Office, 12 February 1920, *ibid.*, p. 1054.
24 *Ibid.*
25 Eliot to Curzon, 17 June 1920, *ibid.*, XIV, no. 52.
26 Alston to Curzon, 23 January 1920, *ibid.*, VI, no. 695.
27 Memorandum on Effect of Anglo-Japanese Alliance upon Foreign Relationships, 28 February 1920, *ibid.*, no. 761.
28 *Report of the Department of Defence on the Military Defence of Australia, 1920*, Pearce Papers, MS 1827, pp. 7–10.
29 J. R. Poynter, 'The Yo-Yo Variations: Initiative and Dependence in Australia's External Relations, 1918–1923', *HSANZ* (1967), nos 53–6, pp. 231–49.
30 Memorandum by Sir B. Alston respecting suggestions for an Anglo-Saxon Policy for the Far East, 1 August 1920, *ibid.*, no. 80.
31 Poynter, 'Yo-Yo Variations', p. 239.
32 AGNZ to GGAust, 27 August 1920, *Naval Defence of the Pacific (Australian Scheme)*, G48 N/22.
33 GGAust to AGNZ, 3 September 1920, *ibid.*
34 P.R.O., Memorandum no. 30–C, September 1920 (Washington Conference).
35 Riddell, *Documents on Canadian Foreign Policy*, p. 12.
36 *Ibid.*, p. 13.
37 *Ibid.*, p. 692.
38 See for example Meaney, 'The British Empire in the American Rejection of the Treaty of Versailles', pp. 213—34.
39 GGCan to SSDA, 15 February 1921, Department of External Affairs, *Documents on Canadian External Relations, 1919–1939* (Ottawa 1970), pp. 162–3.
40 SSDA to GGCan, 26 February 1921, *ibid.*, pp. 163–4.
41 GGCan to SSDA, 1 April 1921, *ibid.*, pp. 166–7.
42 *Commonwealth Parl. Deb.*, 7 April 1921, XCIV, p. 6899.
43 See G. Hermon Gill, *Australia in the War of 1939–1945, Royal Australian Navy, 1939–1942* (Canberra 1957), p. 16, n. 3.
44 SSDA to GGCan, 26 April 1921, DCER.
45 Roskill, *Naval Policy Between the Wars*, I, p. 290.
46 *Ibid.*, p. 339.
47 Gill, I, p. 15.

48 *Commonwealth Parl. Deb.*, 24 July 1923, vol. 104, pp. 1485–7.
49 Canada, *Deb.*, 4 May 1923.
50 *Ibid.*, 20 May 1924.
51 CAB 32/9, 1923 Imperial Conference, Stenog. Notes, 8th mtg., pp. 19–20.
52 *Commonwealth Parl. Pap.*, 1923–4, *Summary of Proceedings of the Imperial Conference*, p. 634.
53 SSC to GGNZ, 20 February 1924, N.A. 10/2.
54 *Commonwealth Parl. Pap.*, 1923–4, *Report of the Inspector-General* of the Australian Military Forces, p. 159.
55 *Commonwealth Parl. Deb.*, 27 June 1924, vol. 107, p. 1702.
56 Paper 900–B, *Imperial Defence Policy*, July 1928, PM 156/6/19, pt 1, *Defence: CID B Papers*.
57 COS 372 of April 1935 (CID), *ibid.*
58 External Affairs 11, CRS A981, item Japan 101, pt 1.
59 Roskill, *Naval Policy Between the Wars*, 1, p. 461.
60 *Commonwealth Parl. Pap.*, 1924–5, *Report of the Inspector-General of the Australian Military Forces*, p. 194.
61 Memorandum by the Secretary, Department of Defence, 'Co-operation in Empire Defence', War Cab. Minute no. (4591), of 18 December 1945, Dedman Papers.

Chapter 7

1 *Commonwealth Parl. Pap.*, 1926–8, *Report of the Inspector-General of the Australian Military Forces*, p. 167.
2 Great Britain, Cmd. 2769, *Imperial Conference, 1926. Appendices to the Summary of the Proceedings*, pp. 181–2.
3 *Ibid.*, pp. 165–6.
4 R. Higham, *Armed Forces in Peacetime: Britain, 1918–1940, A Case Study* (Hamden 1940), app. 11, pp. 326–7; see also D. John, 'The Debate on British Military Air Policy', unpublished thesis (University of Kentucky 1969).
5 *New York Times*, 8 January 1927.
6 *Ibid.*, 4 February 1927.
7 *Ibid.*
8 *Ibid.*
9 S. W. Roskill, ed., *Documents Relating to the Naval Air Service*, 1, 1908–18, Navy Records Society (London 1969), app. 1; Charles C. Bright, 'Britain's Search for Security, 1930–1936', unpublished thesis (Yale University 1970), p. 23.
10 Roskill, *Naval Policy Between the Wars*, 1, p. 525.
11 Paper 900–B, Imperial Defence Policy, July 1927, PM 156/6/19, pt 1, *Defence: CID B Papers*.
12 Barnett, *Collapse of British Power*, pp. 277–8.
13 Great Britain, Cmd. 3718, *Imperial Conference 1930, Appendices to the Summary of Proceedings*, p. 11.
14 *DBFP*, 2nd ser., IX, pp. 282–3, n. 2.
15 J. Eayrs, *In Defence of Canada* (Toronto 1964), p. 300.
16 CAB 21–397, Cabinet: Registered Files. Defence of Australia 1935.

17 *Aerial Defence of NZ – Report of Air Marshal Sir John Salmond*, Naval Dept N.A. 5/4/2.

18 CID 1009–B, PM 156/1/1, pt IA.

19 *DBFP*, XIII, 2nd ser., no. 926.

20 Sir John Pratt, 'His Majesty's Government's Policy in the Far East', C.P. 77(34) CAB 24/248, *Foreign Office Survey of Situation in the Far East*, 1 December 1933.

21 Bright, 'Britain's Search for Security', p. 84.

22 CAB 19(32)2.

23 Memorandum to Cabinet on the Development of Australia, Pearce Papers, MS 1827/30.

24 Hankey to Chamberlain, 30 October 1933, CAB 21–396, Imperial Defence, General Annual Review, 1933.

25 Bruce to Pearce, 8 December 1933, Pearce Papers, MS 1827/2.

26 Bright, 'Britain's Search for Security', pp. 175–80.

27 *DBFP*, 2nd ser., VI, no. 363.

28 Bright, 'Britain's Search for Security', p. 210.

29 *Ibid.*, p. 214.

30 *Ibid.*, p. 226.

31 PM 156/6/18, pt I, *Defence: CID A Papers*, 200–A of December 1934. The visionaries exaggerated the physical as well as the moral effects of aerial bombing to an extent sufficient to render their calculations totally misleading: for example, in the raid on Cologne on 30 May 1942 some 3,000 tons of bombs killed 469 people and wounded 5,027.

32 COS 372 of April 1935 (CID), PM 156/1/1.

33 See for example George W. Baer, *The Coming of the Italo-Ethiopian War* (Cambridge 1967); J. B. Hoptner, *Yugoslavia in Crisis, 1934–1941* (New York 1963); F. Y. Laurens, *France and the Italo-Ethiopian Crisis, 1935–1936* (The Hague 1967).

34 CAB 27–476, C.P. (4)32, *Minutes and Memoranda of the Committee on the Preparations for the League of Nations Disarmament Conference, 1931–2*.

35 Barnett, *Collapse of British Power*, p. 348.

36 The negotiations on the agreement have been covered at great length, though with little reference to the diplomatic implications in Bright, 'Britain's Search for Security', pp. 321–66; see also D. C. Watt, 'The Anglo-German Naval Agreement of 1935', *Journal of Modern History* (June 1956); *DGFP*, Series C 1933–7. *The Third Reich: First Phase* (Washington 1962), IV, pp. 329–470.

37 Simon to Clerk, 9 May 1935, F.O. 371/19108; J1711/1/1.

38 C. P. Stacey, *Six Years of War* (Toronto 1970), pp. 6–7.

39 External Affairs II, CRS A981, item *Review of World Situation*.

40 CAB 27/596, C.P. (8)35, Memorandum by C. W. Orde, 7 January 1935.

41 F.O. 371/19120: J3292/1/1.

42 F. L. W. Wood, *The New Zealand People at War* (Wellington 1958), p. 27.

43 Memorandum by Mounsey, F.O. 371/19130; J4358/1/1.

44 Cabinet Conclusions, no. 1 (42/35), F.O. 371/19127.

45 Minute by Thompson, 22 August 1935, F.O. 371/19130; J4329/1/1.
46 D. G. Carmichael, 'Australia and the Italo-Ethiopian War, 1935–1936', unpublished thesis (University of Queensland), p. 84.
47 SSDA to Dominion Prime Ministers, 17 September 1935, F.O. 371/19145; J5992/1/1.
48 Minute by Thompson, 27 August 1935, F.O. 371/19129; J4578/1/1.
49 SSDA to PMNZ, 23 August 1935, cited in Wood, *The New Zealand People at War*, p. 35.
50 F.O. 371/19129; J4565/1/1.
51 Minute by Garran, 29 August 1935, F.O. 371/19129; J 4165/1/1.
52 *Ibid.*
53 F.O. 371/19130; J4358/1/1.
54 *Ibid.*
55 GGCan to SSDA, 4 September 1935, D.O. 114/67.
56 GGNZ to SSDA, 5 September 1935, F.O. 371/19131; J4434/1/1.
57 F.O. 371/19132; J4670/1/1; also League of Nations *Official Journal*, Special Supplement no. 138, pp. 65–79.
58 F.O. 371/19137; J5234/1/1.
59 External Affairs II, CRS A981, item *Abyssinia-Italy 14, Annexation by Italy*.
60 *The Bulletin*, 25 September 1935.
61 *Commonwealth Parl. Deb.*, 9 October 1935, vol. 147, p. 579.
62 *Ibid.*, 10 October 1935.
63 See Carolyn Ayling, 'Australia's Attitude towards Europe between the Two World Wars', unpublished thesis (University of Queensland), p. 290.
64 Cabinet Minutes, 50(35)2, CAB 23–82.
65 D.O. 114/66.
66 F.O. 371/20155; J493/7/1.
67 Te Water to MacDonald, 14 December 1935, D.O. 114/67.
68 GGNZ to SSDA, 14 December 1935, *ibid.*
69 C.P. 26(36).
70 UK Gov. White Paper, Cmd. 5107.
71 CAB 16/112, 10(36).
72 CAB 23/83, 15(36)1.
73 Parr to Savage, 6 March 1936, PM 201/11/1.
74 GGNZ to SSDA, 11 March 1936, *ibid.*
75 D. Gillison, *Australia in the War of 1939–1945*; *Royal Australian Air Force*, I (Canberra 1962), p. 42.
76 Ayling, 'Australia's Attitude towards Europe between the Two World Wars', p. 320; also McCarthy, 'Australia and Imperial Defence: Co-operation and Conflict, 1918–1930', pp. 19–32.
77 CID, 1256–B, PM 156/6/19, pt 6, Defence: CID B Papers: *Holland and the NEI: Defence Problems*.
78 S. Woodburn Kirby, *History of the Second World War*, *United Kingdom Military Series: The War Against Japan* (London 1957), I, p. 12.
79 Ayling, 'Australia's Attitude towards Europe', p. 320.
80 McCarthy, 'Australia and Imperial Defence', p. 31. The Battle

would not go away, however: the RAAF eventually acquired 366 *faute de mieux*, long after they had become quite obsolete for combat.

81 Canada, *Deb.*, 14 February 1937, IV, pp. 3862–73.
82 *The Times*, 30 January 1937.
83 *Ibid.*, 31 January 1937.
84 Kirby, *The War Against Japan*, p. 17.
85 COS 539 (JP), CAB 53/29.
86 McCarthy, 'Australia and Imperial Defence', p. 29.
87 *Ibid.*, p. 34.
88 CRS A461, A 326/1/4, item *Imperial Conference of 1937*. Briefs prepared for delegates to the Imperial Conference.
89 F.O. 371/21172; R3892.
90 PM 156/1/1, pt 1A, Imperial Defence: General.
91 *Ibid.*
92 CAB 32/128, Imperial Conference, 1937, Stenog. notes, 10th mtg, 1 June 1937.
93 P. C. Hasluck, *Australia in the War of 1939–1945. The Government and the People, 1939–1942* (Canberra 1970), I, p. 573.
94 PM 156/1/1.
95 Saionji-Harada Memoirs, p. 1818, GHQ, United States Armed Forces, Pacific, Far East Command, Military Intelligence Section, General Staff, Special Studies no. 161, Microfilm; also James B. Crowley, 'A Reconsideration of the Marco Polo Bridge Incident', *Journal of Asian Studies* (May 1963), pp. 277–92.
96 Saionji-Harada Memoirs, pp. 1825–45.
97 Dedman Papers, N.L.A. MS 987.
98 CRS A461, A326/1/4, C.P. ser. 4, bundle 3.
99 CAB 3–7, 271–A; also Barnett, *Collapse of British Power*, chap. V, *passim*; and D. Divine, *The Blunted Sword* (London 1964), pp. 184–209.
100 Great Britain, *Hansard Parl. Deb.*, 5th ser., 17 November 1937, vol. CCCXXIX, p. 409.
101 J. Harvey, ed., *The Diplomatic Diaries of Oliver Harvey, 1937–1940* (London 1970), p. 49.
102 *Ibid.*, p. 55.
103 Tracy B. Kittredge, Capt, Comnaveu Historical Monograph, *United States-British Naval Cooperation, 1940–1945*, MS, Microfilm job no. 1, sec. III, pt C (Chap. 12), p. 263, A–9506.
104 Saionji-Harada Memoirs, pp. 2019–24.
105 AA 1971/216.
106 *Commonwealth Parl. Deb.*, 24 August 1937, vol. 154, p. 26.
107 CRS A816, item 19/301/437.
108 CRS A1608, item SCO15.
109 *Ibid.*
110 Great Britain, *Hansard Parl. Deb.*, 24 March 1938, vol. CCCXXXIII, pp. 1405–6.
111 *The Times*, 25 March 1938.
112 CRS A1608, item SCO15.

113 GGNZ to SSDA, 12 May 1938, cited in Wood, *The New Zealand People at War.*
114 See for example L. Mosley, *On Borrowed Time* (London 1972).
115 See for example J. W. Wheeler-Bennett, *Prologue to Tragedy: Munich* (London 1948).
116 *Commonwealth Parl. Deb.*, 25 May 1938, vol. 157, p. 432.
117 *The Times*, 26 May 1938.
118 *Commonwealth Parl. Deb.*, 28 September 1938, vol. 157, p. 432.
119 *The Times*, 2 July 1938.
120 Saionji-Harada Memoirs, p. 2023.
121 *Ibid.*, p. 2236.
122 J. MacVickar Haight, 'Franklin D. Roosevelt and Naval Quarantine of Japan', *Pacific Historical Review* (May 1971), pp. 203–26.
123 D. C. Watt, *Personalities and Politics* (London 1965), p. 169.
124 See for example CAB 23/93, *Conclusions of the Cabinet Meetings, 1926–39*, 27(38)2; also Robert J. O'Neill, *The German Army and the Nazi Party, 1933–9* (London 1966), pp. 152–7.
125 D. Richards and H. Saunders, *Royal Air Force*, I, *1939–1945* (London 1953), app. 5.
126 Mosley, *On Borrowed Time*, p. 76. This figure, drawn from the Czech military archives, may include some 200 Russian aircraft stationed in Czechoslovakia during the crisis.
127 On the argument that Chamberlain's suspicions of the Russians' intentions were justified 'because the Russians made no military moves whatsoever during the crisis' (John, *Debate on British Air Policy*, p. 292), see *inter alia* Mosley, *On Borrowed Time*, pp. 54 and 82.
128 D.O. 114/94.
129 *The Times*, 13 September 1938.
130 *Ibid.*, 16 September 1938.
131 *Ibid.*
132 B. Hutchinson, *The Incredible Canadian* (Toronto 1952), p. 237.
133 *The Times*, 1 October 1938.
134 *Commonwealth Parl. Deb.*, 5 October 1938, vol. 157, p. 388.
135 *Ibid.*, p. 399.
136 Files of the Governor, G48 D/6, Defence Conference, Wellington, April 1939, ON.S., COS 15.
137 *Ibid.*
138 *Ibid.*, CID Paper 682–M.
139 *Ibid.*, pt v (e).
140 CRS A981, item USA. 15.
141 *Commonwealth Parl. Deb.*, 12 December 1938, vol. 158, p. 2761.
142 Ayling, 'Australia's Attitude towards Europe', p. 362.
143 McCarthy, 'Australia and Imperial Defence', p. 30.
144 *Sydney Morning Herald*, 7 December 1938.
145 *The Times*, 23 December 1938.
146 Kirby, *The War Against Japan*, p. 19.
147 Saionji-Harada Memoirs, p. 2358.
148 *Ibid.*, p. 2390.
149 *Ibid.*, p. 2411.

150 *Ibid.*, p. 2437.
151 *Ibid., Report to the Throne*, p. 2432.
152 *Ibid.*, p. 2511.
153 A. Chanady and J. Jensen, 'Germany, Rumania and the British Guarantees of March–April 1939', *AJPH* (August 1970), pp. 201–17.
154 Kirby, *The War Against Japan*, p. 20.
155 *Ibid.*
156 Canada, *Deb.*, 20 March 1939, III, p. 2434.
157 *Sydney Morning Herald*, 21 March 1939.
158 CRS A816, item 11/301/213.
159 UKHCNZ to SSDA, 23 April 1939, CAB 21/497/22.
160 Chatfield to Ismay (undated), *ibid.*
161 Files of the Governor, G48 D/6, Defence Conference, Wellington, April 1939: Defence of the South-West Pacific, D.C.1.
162 *Ibid.*, D.C.3.
163 *Ibid.*
164 *Sydney Morning Herald*, 25 April 1939.
165 Kittredge MS, p. 264, A–9506.
166 *Ibid.*, p. 58, A–5774. The United States Fleet comprised Battle Force US Navy with its supporting units, based upon San Diego, California.
167 PMAust to HCAustUK, 22 May 1939, External Affairs II, CRS A981, item Australian Foreign Policy.
168 CAB 21/495/32, CID, COS Sub-Committee, COS 793.
169 PMAust to PMUK, CRS A981, item Great Britain, 8B.
170 CRS AA1971/216.
171 See for example B. Collier, *The Defence of the United Kingdom* (London 1957), pp. 77–8; David E. Griffin, 'The Role of the French Air Force, the Battle of France, 1940', *Aerospace Historian*, vol. 21 (1974), pp. 144–53; Shirer, *Collapse of the Third Republic*, pp. 700–5.
172 *Pace* Mr Barnett, who draws completely opposite conclusions from the data. See especially, *Collapse of British Power*, pp. 7–11 and 585.
173 AA 1971/216.
174 *Sydney Morning Herald*, 25 August 1939.
175 Although to be fair it must be remembered that neither Britain nor France had any plans for concerted action with Poland either.
176 Stacey, *Six Years of War*, p. 45
177 External Affairs, II, CRS A981, Australian Foreign Policy 39.
178 Hasluck, *Government and the People*, I, p. 153.
179 J. W. Pickersgill, ed., *The Mackenzie King Record* (Toronto 1960), I, p. 15.
180 External Affairs II, CRS A981, item Australian Foreign Policy 39.
181 *Sydney Morning Herald*, 4 September 1939.

Chapter 8

1 *Sydney Morning Herald*, 3 September 1939.
2 PMCan to PMUK, 3 September 1939, in Stacey, *Six Years of War*, p. 59.
3 GGNZ to SSDA, 4 September 1939, in Dept. of Internal Affairs,

Documents relating to New Zealand's participation in the Second World War (Wellington 1972), I, pp. 6–7.
4 Pickersgill, *Mackenzie King Record*, pp. 30–1.
5 Hasluck, I, p. 158.
6 *Ibid.*, p. 159.
7 Stacey, *Six Years of War*, p. 59.
8 *Ibid.*, p. 60.
9 Canada, *Deb.*, 7 September 1939, II, p. 1.
10 *Ibid.*
11 Gillison, I, pp. 61–4.
12 The proposal was the more remarkable in that the British Chiefs of Staff had already decided in December 1938 that they did not believe 'although of course they could not say so, that Australian troops would settle down in peacetime to garrison duties ...' (Ismay to Harding, 13 December 1938, CAB 21/496/32).
13 CAB 65/1, War Cab 4(39).
14 CAB 65/1, War Cab 8(39).
15 F. Feiling, *The Life of Neville Chamberlain* (London 1946), p. 419.
16 CRS A2671, item 15/1939.
17 *Ibid.*, item 14/1939.
18 R. Parkinson, *Peace for Our Time* (London 1971), p. 255.
19 *The Times*, 13 October 1939.
20 GGNZ to SSDA, 12 October 1939, Wood, *The New Zealand People at War*, pp. 106–7.
21 *Ibid.*, p. 107.
22 Lothian to Halifax, 10 November 1939, *NZ Docs*, III, p. 534.
23 Kittredge MS, p. 268, A–9506.
24 *NZ Docs*, I, app. II, *New Zealand Forces: Note of a Meeting Held at the War Office at 5.30 p.m. on Monday 6 November 1939.*
25 Nash to Fraser, 29 November 1939, *NZ Docs*, I, pp. 47–8.
26 Hasluck, I, p. 171.
27 Officer to Bruce, CP 447/2, item SC292.
28 CRS A816, item 52/302/135.
29 CP 290/6, bundle 2, item 35.
30 PMAust to PMNZ, 21 November 1939, *NZ Docs*, I, pp. 42–3.
31 CRS A816, item 52/302/135.
32 GGNZ to SSDA, 20 November 1939, *NZ Docs*, I, pp. 41–2.
33 ActPMNZ to PMAust, 21 November 1939, *ibid.*
34 PMAust to PMNZ, 28 November 1939, *ibid.*
35 CRS A816, item 52/302/135.
36 CP 290/6, bundle 2, item 35.
37 *Ibid.*
38 Pickersgill, *Mackenzie King Record*, p. 39.
39 Roosevelt to Chamberlain, 11 September 1939, in Dept of State, *Foreign Relations of the United States, British Commonwealth, 1939–1945* (Washington 1958–70), I, p. 671.
40 Chamberlain to Roosevelt, 4 October, *ibid.*, pp. 674–5.
41 H. Duncan Hall, *History of the Second World War: North American Supply* (London 1955), pp. 8–17.

42 This would have amounted to more than the whole anti-tank capacity and more than a third of the artillery capacity of the defeated Polish army.

43 CRS A2671, item 55/1940.

44 GGNZ to SSDA, 2 May 1940, *NZ Docs*, I, p. 97.

45 Pickersgill, *Mackenzie King Record*, pp. 107–8.

46 Stacey, *Six Years of War*, p. 141.

47 See for example the exhaustive study in Shirer, *Collapse of the Third Republic*, pp. 695–709.

48 *Ibid*. The whole problem of the discrepancy between Allied availability and deployment in the air can neither be summarized nor, probably, solved. All that can be affirmed is that although the British had only 416 aircraft actually based in France, they committed about 90 per cent of their total operational strength to the fighting over France, and lost some 808 aircraft in all. Since the French lost fewer aircraft, they presumably must have committed fewer. The fact is that some 2,000 French aircraft, more than the total operational strength of the RAF, seem to have been withheld from the decisive combat.

49 Churchill to Roosevelt, 15 May 1940, in Churchill, *The Second World War*, II, pp. 35–6.

50 *Ibid*.

51 Hasluck, I, pp. 213–14.

52 *Ibid*., p. 215.

53 Menzies to Roosevelt, 29 May 1940, *FRUS*, 1940, III, pp. 5–6.

54 *The Times*, 6 June 1940.

55 CP 290/6, item 54.

56 CRS A1608, A45/2/1.

57 Gill, I, p. 129.

58 SSDA to GGNZ, 13 June 1940, *NZ Docs*, III, p. 206.

59 M. Howard, *The Continental Commitment* (London 1972), p. 102.

60 GGNZ to SSDA, 15 June 1940, *NZ Docs*, III, pp. 206–7.

61 Freyberg to Minister of Defence, 22 June 1940, *ibid*., I, pp. 136–44.

62 *Ibid*., 27 June 1940, I, pp. 131–2.

63 McNaughton to Dill, 29 June 1940, in Stacey, *Six Years of War*, p. 285.

64 Wood, *New Zealand People at War*, p. 175.

65 GGNZ to SSDA, 9 July 1940, *NZ Docs*, III, pp. 14–15.

66 SSDA to UKHCNZ, 13 July 1940, *ibid*., I, pp. 163–4.

67 GGNZ to SSDA, 3 August 1940, *ibid*., pp. 170–3.

68 SSDA to UKHCNZ, 11 August 1940, *ibid*., III, pp. 17–20.

69 PMUK to PMAust, *ibid*., pp. 21–2.

70 Churchill, *The Second World War*, II, p. 345.

71 Gill, I, p. 256.

72 Kittredge MS, pp. 277–8, A–9506.

73 *Ibid*., p. 280. It is perhaps worth noting that the fact of United States neutrality was not regarded by Ghormley as a relevant objection to the Singapore project.

74 PMUK to SS India, 1 September 1940, Churchill, *The Second World War*, II, p. 524.

75 PMUK to SS War, 24 September 1940, *ibid.*, p. 398.
76 Memorandum by the Prime Minister on the Munitions Situation, 3 September 1940, *ibid.*, p. 368.
77 PMAust to PMUK, 29 September 1940, *ibid.*, p. 509.
78 PMUK to PMAust, 2 October 1940, *ibid.*, pp. 569–70.
79 PMAust to PMUK, 4 October 1940, *ibid.*, p. 571.
80 Former Naval Person to President, 4 October 1940, *ibid.*, p. 397.
81 Prime Minister to Foreign Secretary, 4 October 1940, *ibid.*, p. 532.
82 CRS A981, item Defence 74A.
83 GGNZ to SSDA, 19 October 1940, *NZ Docs*, III, pp. 211–12.
84 Gillison, I, p. 144.
85 CRS A981, item Defence 74A.
86 Gillison, I, p. 144.
87 Churchill, *The Second World War*, II, p. 424.
88 Gillison, I, p. 144.
89 Casey to External Affairs, N.A. 22/4/47, Notes of Commander Burrell.
90 Memorandum WPD 4175–15, cited in M. Matloff and Edwin P. Snell, *Strategic Planning for Coalition Warfare* (Washington 1965), p. 25.
91 Memorandum for the Secretary, Op-12-CTB, 'PLAN DOG', 12 November 1940, cited in Kittredge MS, pp. 253–64, A–9505.
92 CRS A2682, item II, *Advisory War Council Minutes*.
93 'Betty to Bob', ser. 044212, Office of the Chief of Naval Operations, 16 November 1940, cited in Kittredge MS, p. 272, A–9505.
94 N.A. 22/4/47, Notes to Commander Burrell.
95 Casey to External Affairs (358), 20 November 1940, *supra*.
96 14/31/72/5, Record of a Meeting Held at the Admiralty on 22 November 1940, cited in Kittredge MS, pp. 276–8, A–9505.
97 *Ibid.*
98 PMUK to First Lord and First Sea Lord, 22 November 1940, Churchill, *The Second World War*, II, p. 544.
99 N.A. 22/4/47, Notes of Commander Burrell.
100 PMUK to SSFO, 27 November 1940, Churchill, *The Second World War*, II, p. 545.
101 J. Connell, *Wavell: Scholar and Soldier* (London 1964), p. 296.
102 PMUK to PMAust, 13 December 1940, Churchill, *The Second World War*, II, p. 483.
103 GGNZ to SSDA, 14 December 1940, *NZ Docs*, III, p. 214–15.
104 PMUK to SSDA, 15 December 1940, Churchill, *The Second World War*, II, p. 551.
105 PMUK to PMAust, 23 December 1940, *ibid.*, pp. 554–5.
106 PMUK to SSDA, 25 December 1940, *ibid.*, p. 557.
107 Dept of Defence Co-ordination, 16/1/41, British Policy in the Pacific (corrected copy).
108 PMUK to SSFO, 30 December 1940, Churchill, *The Second World War*, II, p. 489.
109 PMUK to COS, 6 January 1941, *ibid.*, III, p. 22.
110 *Ibid.*, p. 24.

111 *Ibid.*
112 PMUK to SSA, etc., 30 December 1940, *ibid.*, II, p. 561.
113 PMSA to PMUK, 8 January 1941, *ibid.*, III, pp. 28–9.
114 Connell, *Wavell*, p. 310.
115 PMUK to Wavell, 10 January 1941, Churchill, *The Second World War*, III, p. 30.
116 Gillison, I, p. 137.
117 *Ibid.*
118 Stacey, *Six Years of War*, p. 439.
119 B.U.S. (J) (41)2 British-United States Staff Conversations, 29 January 1941, Kittredge MS, pp. 300–2, app. B.
120 Grace P. Hayes, *The History of the Joint Chiefs of Staff in World War II: The War Against Japan*, Comnaveu Historical Study, MS, Microfilm Job No. E–108, p. 10.
121 Kittredge MS, p. 450.
122 *Ibid.*, p. 405.
123 PMUK to President Inonu of Turkey, 31 January 1941, Churchill, *The Second World War*, III, pp. 41–2.
124 The Australian figures were singularly accurate, in terms of actual Japanese strength deployed against the Empire. Total Japanese air strength in December 1941 was indeed nearer to 4,600 aircraft, but only 534 were committed to the campaign in Malaya and the Netherlands East Indies.
125 PMUK to Wavell, 12 February 1941, Churchill, *The Second World War*, III, pp. 64–7.
126 Connell, *Wavell*, p. 334.
127 G. Long, *Australia in the War of 1939–45: Greece, Crete and Syria* (Canberra 1953), p. 8.
128 Hasluck, I, p. 320.
129 Long, *Greece, Crete and Syria*, p. 8.
130 *Ibid.*, p. 18.
131 *Ibid.*, pp. 537–8.
132 CP 290/6, item 70.
133 Long, *Greece, Crete and Syria*, p. 15.
134 *Ibid.*, p. 15.
135 *Ibid.*
136 *Ibid.*
137 GGNZ to SSDA, 26 February 1941, *NZ Docs*, I, p. 242.
138 Long, *Greece, Crete and Syria*, p. 19.
139 SSFA to PMUK, 5 March 1941, Churchill, *The Second World War*, III, pp. 89–90.
140 PMUK to SSFA, 6 March 1941, *ibid.*, pp. 91–2.
141 Long, *Greece, Crete and Syria*, p. 9.
142 Connell, *Wavell*, pp. 332–3.
143 SSFA to PMUK, 7 March 1941, Churchill, *The Second World War*, III, p. 94.
144 Churchill, *ibid.*, p. 95.
145 GGNZ to SSDA, 9 March 1941, *NZ Docs*, I, pp. 257–8.
146 Long, *Greece, Crete and Syria*, p. 17.

147 ActPMAust to PMNZ, 11 March 1941, CP 290/6, Misc. Cables, 1937–43, CAO.
148 SSFA to PMUK, 7 March 1941, Churchill, *The Second World War*, III, p. 94.
149 PMUK to ActPMAust, 30 March, *ibid.*, p. 143.
150 Long, *Greece, Crete and Syria*, p. 37.
151 *Ibid.*, pp. 182–3.
152 These were of course not the only British aircraft engaged in the campaign in Greece. Total RAF strength in the Middle East amounted to 1,044 aircraft, many of which were obsolete and of which only 292 were assigned to combat duties. Most of these were apparently lost in Greece. (Churchill, III, p. 586.)
153 PMUK to Wavell, 28 April 1941, Churchill, *The Second World War*, III, p. 218.
154 Long, *Greece, Crete and Syria*, p. 208.
155 Freyberg to PMNZ, 1 May 1941, Churchill, *The Second World War*, III, p. 221.
156 Long, *Greece, Crete and Syria*, p. 209.
157 PMUK to PMNZ, 3 May 1941, Churchill, *The Second World War*, III, pp. 221–2.
158 Freyberg to PMUK, 5 May 1941, *ibid.*
159 Long, *Greece, Crete and Syria*, p. 209.
160 PMUK to CIGS, 22 April 1941, Churchill, *The Second World War*, III, p. 201.
161 PMUK to PMSA, 8 May 1941, *ibid.*, p. 594.
162 CIGS to PMUK, 6 May 1941, *ibid.*, pp. 336–8.
163 PMUK to CIGS, 13 May 1941, *ibid.*, p. 341.
164 Connell, *Wavell*, p. 460.
165 *Ibid.*
166 *Ibid.*, p. 462.
167 Long, *Greece, Crete and Syria*, pp. 328–9.

Chapter 9

1 Long, *Greece, Crete and Syria*, p. 320.
2 Gillison, *Royal Australian Air Force*, p. 158.
3 Kirby, *War Against Japan*, p. 525.
4 Files of the Governor, G50(9), COS 102.
5 See *Protocols signed at Paris on May 27 and May 28, 1941*, in *Documents on German Foreign Policy* (Washington 1962) ser. D, XII, *The War Years, 1941*, pp. 892–900; also Abetz to Ribbentrop, 11 June 1941, *ibid.*, pp. 1008–11.
6 B. Maugham, *Australia in the War of 1939–45, Tobruk and El Alamein* (Canberra 1967), p. 306.
7 Kittredge MS, pp. 349–50, A–17256, Record of Meeting of Prime Minister and Chiefs of Staff with United States Observers, 24 July 1941.
8 Maugham, *Tobruk and El Alamein*, p. 334.
9 PMUK to PMAust, 29 August 1941, in Churchill, *The Second World War*, III, p. 659.

10 PMUK to Auchinleck, 6 September 1941, *ibid.*, pp. 330–1.
11 Maugham, *Tobruk and El Alamein*, p. 348.
12 PMUK to PMAust, 11 September 1941, in Churchill, *The Second World War*, III, pp. 331–2.
13 PMUK to Auchinleck, 17 September 1941, *ibid.*, p. 332.
14 PMUK to PMNZ, 2 September 1941, *NZ Docs*, III, pp. 62–3.
15 Eggleston Papers, MS 432/9/1346.
16 *Ibid.*, MS 423/19/10. The Dutch had in fact three 6-inch gun cruisers, seven destroyers and thirteen submarines in commission, and one submarine refitting. It was indeed a small affair, but the Dutch submarines were the only units of Allied naval defences to inflict significant damage on the Japanese until the American victory at Balikpapan on 24 January 1942.
17 *Ibid.*, MS 423/19/11.
18 *Ibid.*, MS 423/19/8; 423/3/393.
19 *Ibid.*, MS 423/19/16; 423/9/1019.
20 *Ibid.*, MS 423/9/1438; 423/9/1349.
21 Sir Earle Page Papers, file 1 (a), no. 4.
22 Churchill, *The Second World War*, III, p. 147.
23 SSDA to GGCan, 19 September 1941, cited in Stacey, *Six Years of War*, pp. 440–1.
24 PMUK to PMAust, 14 October 1941, Churchill, *The Second World War*, III, p. 333.
25 PMUK to PMAust, 26 and 27 October 1941, *ibid.*, p. 335. The cables consist largely of recitals of the casualties, actual and potential, to which the Royal Navy was exposed during the completion of the relief.
26 CRS A2682, item II, Advisory War Council Minute 533, 16 October 1941.
27 L. Wigmore, *Australia in the War of 1939–45, The Japanese Thrust* (Canberra 1957), p. 102.
28 *Ibid.*, p. 103.
29 CRS A2682.
30 *Ibid.*
31 PMUK to PMAust, 26 October 1941, in Gill, I, p. 446.
32 PMUK to PMNZ, 3 November 1941, *NZ Docs*, III, p. 70.
33 PMUK to First Sea Lord, 22 September 1941, Churchill, *The Second World War*, III, pp. 678–9.
34 *The Times*, 11 November 1941.
35 CRS A989, item 44/801/1/67.
36 SSDA to PMAust, 11 December 1941, *NZ Docs*, III, pp. 110–11.
37 Wigmore, *The Japanese Thrust*, p. 164.
38 Casey to Roosevelt, 23 December 1941, *FRUS, 1941, The Far East* (Washington 1956), V, pp. 390.
39 Hayes MS, pp. 61–4.
40 Wigmore, *The Japanese Thrust*, p. 154.
41 CRS A2671, item 52/50, War Cabinet Agenda no. 436/1941.
42 PMUK to PMNZ, 6 January 1942, *NZ Docs*, III, p. 121.
43 Files of the Governor, G50 (13), COS 115, 10 January 1942.
44 SSDA to PMUK, 18 January 1942, PREM 3/187/1, 1246.

45 PMAust to PMUK, 23 January 1942, in Churchill, *The Second World War*, IV, pp. 50–1.
46 PMNZ to PMUK, 30 January 1942, *NZ Docs*, III, pp. 218–19.
47 Hayes MS, p. 89.
48 GGNZ to SSDA, 7 February 1942, PREM 3/63/10, 3613.
49 SSDA to PMNZ, 12 February 1942, in S. D. Waters, *Royal New Zealand Navy* (Wellington 1956), p. 285.
50 Wigmore, *The Japanese Thrust*, app. 5, Future Employment of A.I.F.: General Sturdee's Paper of 15 February 1942.
51 Churchill, *The Second World War*, IV, pp. 47–50.
52 See for example Stephen P. Cohen, *The Indian Army* (Berkeley 1971); H. Toye, *The Springing Tiger* (Bombay 1963).
53 Pownall Diaries, in *Sydney Morning Herald*, 14 November 1974.
54 See for example Kenneth Attwill, *The Singapore Story* (London 1959), for eyewitness accounts of looting and deserting by Australians in Singapore.
55 PMUK to PMAust, 20 February 1942, in Wigmore, *The Japanese Thrust*, pp. 450–1.
56 PMAust to PMUK, 22 February 1942, *ibid.*, p. 451.
57 PMUK to PMAust, *ibid.*
58 PMAust to PMUK, 23 February 1942, *ibid.*, p. 454.
59 PMNZ to PMUK, 28 February 1942, *NZ Docs*, III, pp. 232–3.
60 SSDA to GGNZ, 10 March 1942, *ibid.*, pp. 235–6.
61 PMNZ to PMUK, 15 March 1942, *ibid.*, pp. 241–5.
62 PMUK to PMAust, 30 March 1942, cited in D. McCarthy, *Australia in the War of 1939–1945, South-West Pacific, First Year* (Canberra 1959), p. 24.
63 PMUK to SSDA, 4 March 1942, Churchill, *The Second World War*, IV, p. 755.
64 Johnson to Hull, 7 April 1942, *FRUS, The British Commonwealth, The Far East*, pp. 628–9.
65 Alfred D. Chandler, jr, ed., *The Papers of Dwight David Eisenhower: The War Years*, I (Baltimore 1970), p. 273.
66 COS TS Decimal File, 1941–3, 381, sec. I.
67 PMUK to First Sea Lord, 17 May 1942, Churchill, *The Second World War*, IV, p. 770.
68 *Ibid.*, p. 323.
69 Churchill to Roosevelt, cited in Matloff and Snell, *Strategic Planning*, pp. 212–13.
70 CRS A816, item 14/301/239A.
71 PMUK to PMNZ, 25 July 1942, *NZ Docs*, III, pp. 253–4.
72 Curtin Papers, MS 4675 (17).
73 Maugham, *Tobruk and El Alamein*, p. 598.
74 *Ibid.*, p. 599.
75 Curtin Papers, MS4675 (19).
76 Maugham, *Tobruk and El Alamein*, p. 695.
77 C. Barnett, *The Desert Generals* (London 1960), p. 256.
78 Roosevelt to Curtin, 16 September 1942, in Gill, *Royal Australian Navy, 1939–42*, p. 106.

79 Maugham, *Tobruk and El Alamein*, p. 742.
80 PMNZ to PMUK, 20 November 1942, PREM 3/63/10, 3613.
81 *New Zealand Herald*, 5 December 1942.
82 PMNZ to PMUK, 5 December 1942, *supra*.
83 Curtin Papers, MS 4675 (44).
84 Kirby, *War Against Japan*, II, p. 356.
85 Evatt to Johnson, 24 February 1944, CRS A1608, item Y4/1/1.
86 Hayes, 'History of the Joint Chiefs of Staff', p. 484; Matloff and Snell, *Strategic Planning*, p. 111.
87 Hayes, II, p. 77.
88 *Ibid.*, pp. 78–9.
89 The Chargé d'Affaires, NZ Legation, Washington, to the Minister of External Affairs, 11 August 1943, R. Kay, ed., *The Australian-New Zealand Agreement 1944* (Wellington 1972), doc. 33.
90 Gill, II, pp. 466–8.
91 *Ibid.*
92 *Commonwealth Parl. Deb.*, 14 October 1943, vol. 176, p. 172.
93 Curtin Papers, MS 4675 (71).
94 HCNZ in Australia to External Affairs, 21 October 1943, Kay, *Australian-New Zealand Agreement*, doc. 35.
95 Curtin Papers, MS 4675 (87).
96 *Sydney Morning Herald*, 15 December 1943.
97 *Australian-New Zealand Agreement*, clauses 7, 15, 16, 26 and 27.
98 Johnson to Hull, 22 January 1944, *FRUS*, III, pp. 174–5.
99 Johnson to Hull, *ibid.*
100 Memorandum by Mr R. B. Stewart of the Division of British Commonwealth Affairs, 1 February 1944, *ibid.*
101 Watt to Hood, 29 February 1944, CRS A989, item 43/950/5/1.
102 Halifax to Eden, 22 June 1944, CRS A989, item 44/735/321/8.
103 PMUK to PMAust, 29 February 1944, cited in Long, *The Final Campaigns* (Canberra 1963), pp. 6–7.
104 PMAust to PMUK, 11 March 1944, *ibid.*, pp. 9–10.
105 PMAust to PMUK, 4 July 1944, *ibid.*, p. 15.
106 *Commonwealth Parl. Deb.*, 17 July 1944, vol. 179, p. 39.
107 Long, *The Final Campaigns*, p. 15.
108 Curtin Papers, MS 4675 (116).
109 Blamey to Curtin, 4 November 1944, cited in Long, *The Final Campaigns*, p. 395.
110 Eggleston Papers, MS 423/10/622.
111 Johnson to Hull, 14 November 1944, *FRUS*, pp. 198–9.
112 The Canadian 1st Infantry and 5th Armoured Divisions had been involved in the major fighting of the Italian campaign before being transferred to north-west Europe.
113 See for example Long, *The Final Camapigns*, p. 19, fn. 8; Gillespie, *The Pacific* (Wellington 1952), p. 110.
114 Minister of External Affairs, Canberra, to Minister of External Affairs, Wellington, 13 December 1944, N.A. 22/4/55.
115 'Appreciation on Operations of the AIF in New Guinea, New

Britain and the Solomon Islands', 18 May 1945, cited in Long, *The Final Campaigns*, app. 3, pp. 608–16.

116 *Ibid.*, p. 548.

117 *Ibid.*, p. 549.

118 *Ibid.*

119 *Ibid.*, p. 550.

120 VADPF Rawlings to CinC US Third Fleet, 1 October 1945, Defence of New Zealand and the Pacific Islands, N.A. 020/1/12.

121 See data compiled in H. Duncan Hall, *North American Supply* (London 1955); and H. Duncan Hall and C. C. Wrigley, *Studies of Overseas Supply* (London 1956).

122 Nicholson, *The Canadians in Italy*, p. 177.

123 *Ibid.*, pp. 564 and 470.

124 *Ibid.*, p. 681.

125 C. P. Stacey, *The Victory Campaign* (Ottawa 1960), pp. 641 and 276.

126 Dedman Papers, file 987/9/301, 13 August 1948.

127 House of Lords, *Parl. Deb.*, 17 March 1954, 5th ser., vol. CLXXXVI, p. 475.

Bibliography

A   PRIMARY SOURCES (UNPUBLISHED)

Private Papers
Curtin Papers, Australian National Library, Canberra.
Deakin Papers, Australian National Library, Canberra.
Dedman Papers, Australian National Library, Canberra.
Eggleston Papers, Australian National Library, Canberra.
Jebb Papers, Australian National Library, Canberra.
Novar Papers, Australian National Library, Canberra.
Page Papers, Australian National Library, Canberra.
Pearce Papers, Australian National Library, Canberra.
Saionji-Harada Memoirs, GHQ, US Armed Forces, Pacific, Far East
    Command, Military Intelligence Section, General Staff, Special
    Studies No. 161, Microfilm MS.
Seddon Papers, Alexander Turnbull Library, Wellington.

Documents
I   AUSTRALIA (COMMONWEALTH ARCHIVES OFFICE)
AA 1971/216, Records of the Council of Defence, 1935–1939.
CP 290, set 26, Miscellaneous Cables, 1937–1943.
CP 290/6, item 35, Cables, Letters and other papers to and from R. G.
    Casey.
CP 290/6, item 54, Cables re War Situation, mainly re Fall of France.
CP 290/6, item 70, Cables, etc., re Defence Conferences.
CP 290/9, item Bundle 1, War – 1941 – Cables from Mr Menzies.
CP 360/8, Vol. 4, Advisory War Council, Minutes.
CRS A461, A326/1/4, Prime Minister's Dept, Correspondence Files.
CRS A663, item 16/1/4, British Policy in the Pacific.
CRS A816, item 11/301/213, Defence II, Correspondence Files.
CRS A816, item 14/301/239A, Empire Cooperation.
CRS A816, item 19/301/437, U.K. – Defence (1935–1938).
CRS A816, item 52/302/135, Despatch Overseas of 2nd A.I.F.
CRS A981, item Defence 74A, Conference of Allied Governments, 1941.
CRS A981, item Great Britain 8B, Foreign Policy.
CRS A981, item Abyssinia – Italy 14.

CRS A981, item U.S.A. 15.
CRS A981, item Australian Foreign Policy 39.
CRS A981, item Japan 101.
CRS A989, item 43/950/1, U.S.A., Foreign Policy – General.
CRS A989, item 44/735/321/8, P.W.R. Far East and Pacific Post War Security Bases.
CRS A1608, item A41/1/1. International Situation 1939.
CRS A1608, item A45/2/1, War 1939. Second Australian Imperial Force.
CRS A1608, item C41/1/1, Resolutions of Supreme War Council.
CRS A1608, item SCO15, Prime Minister's Correspondence Files, SC Series.
CRS A1608, item Y4/1/1, Conference between the Prime Ministers of Australia and New Zealand.
CRS A2671, item 15/1939, War Cabinet Agenda, 1939.
CRS A2671, item 52/50, War Cabinet Agenda, No. 436/1961.
CRS A2671, item 55/1940, War Cabinet Agenda, 1940.
CRS A2671, item 96 and 97/1940, War Cabinet Agenda, 1940.
CRS A2671, item 114/1940, War Cabinet Agendum File, Air Co-operation with the United Kingdom.
CRS A2682, item Vol. II, Advisory War Council Minutes.
MP/729/2, File 1856/4/155, Strategic Position of Australia and New Zealand (1912).

2   NEW ZEALAND (NATIONAL ARCHIVES OF NEW ZEALAND)
G48, D.C.1, Defence of South-West Pacific.
G48, D.C.5, Possible Effects of German Demands for Return of Mandated Territories.
G48, D/6, Defence Conference, Wellington, April 1939.
G48, F/4, Notes on the Vulnerability of Australia and New Zealand.
G48, N/22, Naval, Defence of the Pacific (Australian Scheme).
G48, W/2, Despatch of New Zealand Expeditionary Force, 1914.
G50 (13), Chiefs of Staff 115, 1942.
G50 (9), Chiefs of Staff 102, 1940.
N.A. 020/1/12, Defence of New Zealand and Pacific Islands.
N.A. 5/4, Various: Arial [sic] Defence of New Zealand.
N.A. 5/4/2, Aerial Defence of New Zealand – Report of Air Chief Marshal Sir John Salmond.
N.A. 10/2, Correspondence . . . Relating to the Singapore Naval Base.
N.A. 22/4/7, Notes of Commander Burrell.
N.A. 22/4/50, Singapore Defence Conference.
N.A. 22/4/55, Australia-New Zealand Conference, 1944.
PM 156/1/1, Pt 1, Imperial Defence: General.
PM 156/6/18, Pt 1, Defence: CID A Papers.
PM 156/6/19, Pt 6, Defence: CID B Papers.
PM 201/11/1, United Kingdom: Defence: General.

PM 201/4/85, Pts 1–5, United Kingdom, External Relations, Japan.
PM 264/2/7, Pts 11–12, China, External Relations, Japan.
PM 455/7/1, Pts 1–3, Singapore, Defence.

3   QUEENSLAND (QUEENSLAND STATE ARCHIVES)
COL/31, Letter Book of Letters to the Governor, 1873–1878.
COL/92, Agent-General to Secretary of State for the Colonies.
GOV/11, Confidential Despatches from Secretary of State.
GOV/14, Report of the 1897 Colonial Conference.
GOV/21, Secret Papers in connexion with Military Matters received from the Secretary of State for the Colonies and Various Persons, 1898–1902.
GOV/22–27, Governor's Despatches to Secretary of State for the Colonies, 1859–1878.
GOV/35, Confidential Despatches for the Secretary of State for the Colonies.
PRE/21, Premier and Chief Secretary's Department, Correspondence and Associated Papers Relating to the Naval Defence of Queensland.

4   UNITED KINGDOM (PUBLIC RECORD OFFICE)
AIR 9/12, Notes on the History of the Employment of Air Power.
CAB 19(32)2, Singapore Naval Base.
CAB 19/33, First Report of the Dardanelles Commission.
CAB 21/369, Imperial Defence, Annual General Review, 1933.
CAB 21/397, Cabinet: Registered Files: Defence of Australia, 1935.
CAB 21/495/32, Committee of Imperial Defence, Chiefs of Staff Sub-Committee, COS 793.
CAB 21/496/32, *ibid.*, Ismay to Harding, December 13, 1938.
CAB 21/497/72, Imperial Defence, General Annual Review, 1939.
CAB 21/874, Consultations with the Dominions.
CAB 23/82, Cabinet Minutes, 50(35)2.
CAB 23/83, Cabinet Minutes, 15(36)1.
CAB 23/88, Cabinet Minutes, 23(37)2.
CAB 23/93, Conclusions of the Cabinet Meetings, 1926–39, 27(38)2.
CAB 24/476, C.P. (4)32, Minutes and Memoranda of the Committee on the Preparations for the League of Nations Disarmament Conference, 1931–2.
CAB 27/596, C.P. (8)35, Memo by C. W. Orde, January 7, 1935.
CAB 27/623, Foreign Affairs Committee Minutes.
CAB 32/9, Imperial Conference, 1923.
CAB 32/128, Imperial Conference, 1937.
CAB 53/29, Chiefs of Staff 539 (JP).
CAB 65/1, War Cabinet Minutes, 4(39).
CAB 65/1, War Cabinet Minutes, 8(39).
D.O. 114/66, League of Nations: Sanctions: Discussions with Dominion Governments.

D.O. 114/67, *ibid.*

D.O. 114/94, League of Nations: Czechoslovakia.

F.O. 371/6674, Correspondence with Dominion Governments: Anglo-Japanese Alliance.

F.O. 371/19108; J1711/1/1, Confidential Print of May 9, 1935.

F.O. 371/19120; J3292/1/1, Minutes of Meeting of Dominion High Commissioners at the Foreign Office, July 29, 1935.

F.O. 371/19127, Cabinet Conclusions, No. 1, (42/35).

F.O. 371/19129; J4565/1/1, UKHCAust to SSDA, August 28, 1935.

F.O. 371/19129; J4578/1/1, Minute by Thompson, August 27, 1935.

F.O. 371/19129; J4329/1/1, Memorandum on 1st Meeting of Committee of Five in Geneva.

F.O. 371/19130; J4538/1/1, Minute by D. R. Garran, September 5, 1935.

F.O. 371/19131; J4434/1/1, GGNZ to SSDA, September 5, 1935.

F.O. 371/19132; J4670/1/1, Telegram No. 82 from U.K. Delegation in Geneva, September 9, 1935.

F.O. 371/19137; J5234/1/1, Report of Meeting in Geneva between the Heads of the Delegations from the U.K., the Dominions, and India, September 17, 1935.

F.O. 371/19145; J5992/1/1, Circular Telegram from SSDA to Dominion Prime Ministers.

F.O. 371/20155; J493/7/1, Record of Meeting between Hoare and Dominion High Commissioners, December 25, 1935.

F.O. 371/21172; R3892/135/22, Meetings of Ministers held at Downing St on de jure Recognition of Italian Conquest of Ethiopia.

PREMIER 3/187/1, 1246, Secretary of State for Dominion Affairs to Prime Minister, United Kingdom, 1942.

PREMIER 3/63/10, 3613, Prime Minister United Kingdom to Governor-General of New Zealand, 1942.

5   VICTORIA (VICTORIA STATE ARCHIVES)
Defence Department, File 00/10105.

B   PRIMARY SOURCES (PUBLISHED)

Private Papers

Blake, R. (ed), *The Private Papers of Douglas Haig, 1914–1919* (London 1952).

Chandler, Alfred D. jr (ed), *The Papers of Dwight David Eisenhower, The War Years*, I, (Baltimore 1970).

Dilks, D. (ed), *The Diaries of Sir Alexander Cadogan, 1938–45* (London 1971).

Hancock, K. and van der Poel, J. (eds), *Selections from the Smuts Papers* (Cambridge 1966).

Harvey, J. (ed), *The Diplomatic Diaries of Oliver Harvey, 1937–1940* (London 1970).

James, R. R. (ed), *Chips: The Diaries of Sir Henry Channon* (London 1967).

Leutze, J. (ed), *The London Observer: The Journal of Raymond E. Lee* (London 1971).

Morison, Elting E. (ed), *The Letters of Theodore Roosevelt*, 8 vols (Cambridge 1951–4).

Patterson, A. Temple (ed), *The Jellicoe Papers*, 2 vols (London 1968).

Pickersgill, J. W. (ed), *The Mackenzie King Record, Vol. I, 1939–1944* (Toronto 1960).

Documents

I   AUSTRALIA

Parliamentary Papers, 1901, *Naval Defence of the Commonwealth.*

Parliamentary Papers, 1901–2, *Contingents (Australian) in China.*

Parliamentary Papers, 1903, *Colonial Conference 1902.*

Parliamentary Papers, 1903, *Naval Defence of the Commonwealth.*

Parliamentary Papers, 1906, *Report of the Director of the Naval Forces on the Naval Defence of the Commonwealth of Australia for the Year 1905.*

Parliamentary Papers, 1906, *Military Forces of the Commonwealth, Minute upon the Defence of Australia by Major-General Hutton.*

Parliamentary Papers, 1907, *Report of the Director of Naval Forces on the Defence of the Commonwealth of Australia for the Year 1906.*

Parliamentary Papers, 1908, *Naval Defence, Further Correspondence between the Commonwealth Government and the Admiralty, in Regard to the Naval Defence of Australia.*

Parliamentary Papers, 1908, *The Defence of Australia by Colonel H. Foster, together with Remarks Thereon by Capt. W. R. Creswell, Naval Director.*

Parliamentary Papers, 1909, *Defence: Correspondence Regarding a Conference between the Representatives of His Majesty's Government and the Governments of the Self-Governing Dominions on the Subject of Naval and Military Defence.*

Parliamentary Papers, 1912, *Naval Defence of the Empire.*

Parliamentary Papers, 1923–4, *Summary of Proceedings of the Imperial Conference.*

Parliamentary Papers, 1923–4, *Report of the Inspector-General of the Australian Military Forces.*

Parliamentary Papers, 1924–5, *Report of the Inspector-General of the Australian Military Forces.*

Parliamentary Papers, 1926–8, *Report of the Inspector-General of the Australian Military Forces.*

2   CANADA
Department of External Affairs, *Documents on Canadian External Relations, 1919–1939*, 3 vols (Ottawa 1970).
Riddell, Walter A. (ed), *Documents on Canadian Foreign Policy, 1917–1939* (Toronto 1962).

3   FRANCE
Ministère des Affaires Etrangères, *Documents Diplomatiques Francais, 1911–1914*, 25 vols (Paris 1929–54).

4   GERMANY
Lepsius *et al.* (eds), *Die Grosse Politik der Europäischen Kabinette, 1871–1914*, 40 vols (Berlin 1922–7).
U.S. Dept. of State, *Documents on German Foreign Policy, 1918–1945*, 18 vols (Washington 1949–64).

5   NEW SOUTH WALES
Votes and Proceedings, 1854, *Report from the Select Committee on the Volunteer and Yeomanry Corps Bill.*
Votes and Proceedings, 1881, *Report of the Intercolonial Conference.*
Votes and Proceedings, 1885, *Australian Contingent for the Soudan.*
Votes and Proceedings, 1885–6, *Colonial Naval Defences.*
Votes and Proceedings, 1885–6, *Naval Defence of Australia.*
Votes and Proceedings, 1900, *Administration of the Military Department.*
Votes and Proceedings, 1901, *Contingents to South Africa.*

6   NEW ZEALAND
Appendix to the Journals of the House of Representatives, 1885.
Dept of Internal Affairs, *Documents Relating to New Zealand's Participation in the Second World War*, 3 Vols (Wellington 1949–63).
Kay, Robin L. (ed), *Documents on New Zealand External Relations, Vol. I, The Australian-New Zealand Agreement, 1944* (Wellington 1972).

7   QUEENSLAND
Votes and Proceedings, 1865, *Statistics of the Volunteer Corps.*
Votes and Proceedings, 1878, *Queensland Defences – First Progress Report and Second Progress Report.*
Votes and Proceedings, 1882, *Report on the Defence Force.*
Votes and Proceedings, 1884, *Special Report of the Commandant upon the Volunteer Force of the Colony.*
Votes and Proceedings, 1890, *Remarks of Colonial Defence Committee on Major-General J. B. Edwards's Report on proposed Organisation of the Military Forces of the Australasian Colonies.*

8   SOUTH AUSTRALIA

Parliamentary Papers, 1890, *Remarks by the Colonial Defence Committee on Major-General Edwards's Report.*

Parliamentary Papers, 1895, *South Australian Naval Forces – Report by the Commandant for Year 1893–4.*

Parliamentary Papers, 1897, *Memorandum re the Conference of Premiers in London and Report of the South Australian Naval Commandant.*

9   UNITED KINGDOM

Butler, J. R., Woodward, E. L., *et al.* (eds), *Documents on British Foreign Policy, 1919–1939*, 45 vols (London 1946–72).

Gooch, G. P. and Temperley H. (eds), *British Documents on the Origins of the War, 1898–1914*, 10 vols (London 1927–38).

Naval Records Society, *Documents Relating to the Naval Air Service* (London 1972).

Naval Records Society, *Policy and Operations in the Mediterranean, 1912–14* (London 1970).

Parliamentary White Papers, *Report of the Select Committee on Colonial Military Expenditure, together with the Proceedings of the Committee, Minutes of Evidence, etc.* (1856).

Parliamentary White Papers, *Select Committee on Naval Estimates (1888) 3rd Report.*

Parliamentary White Papers, *Cmd. 8561, Imperial War Conference. Selections from Minutes of Proceedings and Papers laid before the Conference.*

Parliamentary White Papers, *Cmd. 2083, Singapore Naval Base, Correspondence with Self-Governing Dominions and India.*

Parliamentary White Papers, *Cmd. 2769, Imperial Conference 1926. Appendices to the Summary of the Proceedings.*

Parliamentary White Papers, *Cmd. 3718, Imperial Conference 1930. Appendices to the Summary of the Proceedings.*

10   UNITED STATES

Dept. of State, *Foreign Relations of the United States, Diplomatic Papers, 1940, Vol. III, The British Commonwealth, the Soviet Union, the Near East and Africa* (Washington 1958).

Dept. of State, *Foreign Relations of the United States, Diplomatic Papers, 1941, Vol. IV, The Far East* (Washington 1956).

Dept. of State, *Foreign Relations of the United States, Diplomatic Papers, 1944, Vol. III, The British Commonwealth* (Washington 1965).

War Office, *Report of the Military Board of Allied Supply* (Washington 1924).

11   VICTORIA

Papers Presented to Parliament by Command, 1884, *Annexation, Federation and Foreign Convicts.*

Defence Department, *Printed Papers (Naval) 1885–1908.*
Papers Presented to Parliament by Command, 1889, *Inspection of Colonial Forces by an Imperial General Officer.*

Parliamentary Debates
Australia, House of Representatives.
Canada, House of Commons.
New Zealand, House of Representatives.
United Kingdom, House of Commons and House of Lords.
Victoria, House of Representatives.

Official Histories
Agar-Hamilton, J. W. I. and Turner, L. C. F., *Crisis in the Desert* (Cape Town 1958).
Bean, C. E. W., *The Story of Anzac, Vol. I* (Sydney 1921); *The Story of Anzac, Vol. II* (Sydney 1924); *The A.I.F. in France, 1916* (Sydney 1929); *The A.I.F. in France, 1917* (Sydney 1933); *The A.I.F. in France, 1918* (Sydney 1942).
Collier, B., *The Defence of the United Kingdom* (London 1957).
Cutlack, F. M., *The Australian Flying Corps* (Sydney 1923).
Du Cane, H., *The German Official Account of the War in South Africa, March 1900 to September 1900* (London 1906).
Ehrman, J., *Grand Strategy, Vol. V* (London 1956); *Grand Strategy, Vol. VI* (London 1956).
Falls, C., *Military Operations in France and Belgium* (London 1940).
Gill, G. Hermon, *Royal Australian Navy, 1939–1942* (Canberra 1957); *Royal Australian Navy, 1942–1945* (Canberra 1969).
Gillespie, Oliver A., *The Pacific* (Wellington 1952).
Gillison, D., *Royal Australian Air Force, 1939–1942* (Canberra 1962).
Hall, D. O. W., *The New Zealanders in South Africa, 1899–1902* (Wellington 1949).
Hall, H. Duncan, *North American Supply* (London 1955).
Hasluck, Paul C., *The Government and the People, 1939–1942* (Canberra 1952); *The Government and the People, 1942–1945* (Canberra 1970).
Howard, M., *Grand Strategy, Vol. IV* (London 1973).
Jones, H. A., *The War in the Air* (London 1937).
Jose, A. W., *Royal Australian Navy* (Sydney 1928).
Kirby, S. W., *The War Against Japan, Vols. I–V* (London 1957–8).
Long, G., *Greece, Crete and Syria* (Canberra 1953); *The Final Campaigns* (Canberra 1963).
Macandie, G. L., *The Genesis of the Royal Australian Navy* (Sydney 1949).
Matloff, M., and Snell, Edwin P., *Strategic Planning for Coalition Warfare* (Washington 1962).

Maugham, B., *Tobruk and El Alamein* (Canberra 1967).
Milner, S., *Victory in Papua* (Washington 1957).
Nicholson, G. W. E., *The Canadians in Italy* (Ottawa 1955).
Ross, J. M. S., *Royal New Zealand Air Force* (Wellington 1955).
Scott, E., *Australia During the War* (Sydney 1936).
Stacey, C. P., *Six Years of War* (Ottawa 1955); *The Victory Campaign* (Ottawa 1960).
Waters, S. D., *Royal New Zealand Navy* (Wellington 1956).
Waters, W. H. H., *The German Official Account of the War in South Africa, October 1899 to February 1900* (London 1904).
Wigmore, L., *The Japanese Thrust* (Canberra 1957).
Wood, F. L. W., *The New Zealand People at War* (Wellington 1958).

C   SECONDARY SOURCES (UNPUBLISHED)

Anderson, D., 'Queensland's Colonial Defence Policies, 1866–1878', unpublished thesis, University of Queensland.
Ayling, Caroline A., 'Australian Attitudes towards Europe between the Two World Wars', unpublished thesis, University of Queensland.
Bittner, Donald F., 'The British Occupation of Iceland, 1940–1942', unpublished thesis, University of Missouri-Columbia.
Bright, Charles B., 'Britain's Search for Security, 1930–1936', unpublished thesis, Yale University.
Carmichael, D. G., 'Australia and the Italo-Ethiopian War, 1935–1936', unpublished thesis, University of Queensland.
Hayes, Grace P., 'The History of the Joint Chiefs of Staff in World War II: The War Against Japan', Comnaveu historical study, on deposit at the Operational Archives Division, Department of the Navy, Washington Navy Yard.
John, Douglas B., 'The Debate on British Air Policy', unpublished thesis, University of Kentucky.
Kittredge, Tracy B., 'United States – British Naval Cooperation, 1940–1945', Comnaveu historical study, on deposit at the Operational Archives Division, Washington Navy Yard.
Millar, T. B., 'In Case They Were Needed: The Story of the Victorian Colonial Defences from 1836 to 1900', unpublished thesis, University of Melbourne.
O'Rourke, T., 'Problems of Queensland Defence, 1878–1901', unpublished thesis, University of Queensland.
Papp, Nicholas G., 'The Anglo-German Naval Agreement of 1935', unpublished thesis, University of Connecticut.
Rudoff, Robin M., 'The Influence of the German Navy on the British Search for Naval Arms Control, 1928–1935', unpublished thesis, University of Tulane.

Sissons, D. C., 'Attitudes to Japan and Defence, 1890–1923', unpublished thesis, University of Melbourne.

D   SECONDARY SOURCES (PUBLISHED)

Articles

Chanady, A. and Jensen, J., 'Germany, Rumania and the British Guarantees of March–April 1939', *Australian Journal of Politics and History*, XVI (1970), pp. 201–17.

Cowburn, P., 'The British Naval Office and the Australian Colonies', *Royal Historical Society of Australia Journal*, 54 (1968), pp. 1–19.

Crowley, James B., 'A Reconsideration of the Marco Polo Bridge Incident', *Journal of Asian Studies*, XXII (1963), pp. 277–92.

Dedman, John J., 'Defence Policy Decisions before Pearl Harbor', *Australian Journal of Politics and History*, XIII (1967), pp. 331–43.

de Ward, H. A., 'Admiral Percy Scott and the Gunnery of the British Navy', *United States Naval Institute Proceedings*, 56 (1930), pp. 815–20.

Fitzhardinge, Verity, 'Russian Naval Visitors to Australia, 1862–88', *RAHS Journal*, 52 (1966), pp. 129–58.

Gill, G. Hermon, 'The Origins of the Royal Australian Navy', *RAHS Journal*, 45 (1959), pp. 140–50.

Griffin, David E., 'The Role of the French Air Force, The Battle of France, 1940', *Aerospace Historian*, 21 (1974), pp. 144–53.

Haight, J. MacVickar, 'Franklin D. Roosevelt and a Naval Quarantine of Japan', *Pacific Historical Review*, XL (1971), pp. 203–26.

Haydon, A. P., 'South Australia's First War', *Historical Studies Australia and New Zealand*, XI (1964), pp. 222–33.

Hooper, M., 'The Naval Defence Agreement 1887', *Australian Journal of Politics and History*, XIV (1968), pp. 52–75.

Imlah, A. M., 'British Balance of Payments and Export of Capital 1886–1913', *The Economic History Review, Second Series*, V (1952–53), pp. 208–19.

Kermer, R., 'Russia, the Straits and Constantinople', *Journal of Modern History*, I (1929), pp. 400–15.

Knox, B. A., 'Colonial Influence on Imperial Policy, 1858–66', *Historical Studies Australia and New Zealand*, XI (1964), pp. 61–79.

Livermore, Seward W., 'The American Navy as a Factor in World Politics', *American Historical Review*, LXIII (1957), pp. 862–79.

Louis, W. Roger, 'Australia and the German Colonies in the Pacific', *Journal of Modern History*, XXVIII (1966), pp. 407–21.

MacCallum, D., 'The Early "Volunteer" Associations in New South Wales and the Proposals in the First Quarter of the Nineteenth Century', *RAHS Journal*, 47 (1961), pp. 352–67; 'The Alleged

Russian Plans for the Invasion of Australia, 1864', RAHS *Journal*, 44 (1958), pp. 301–21.

McCarthy, J. M., 'Australia and Imperial Defence: Co-operation and Conflict, 1918–1939', *Australian Journal of Politics and History*, XVII (1971), pp. 19–32; 'The Defence of Australia and the Empire Air Training Scheme, 1939–42', *AJPH*, XX (1974), pp. 326–34; 'Australia: A View from Whitehall, 1939–45', *Australian Outlook*, 28 (1974), pp. 318–31.

MacLean, Guy R., 'The Canadian Offer of Troops for Hong Kong, 1894', *Canadian Historical Review*, XXXVIII (1957), pp. 275–83.

Meaney, Neville K., 'The British Empire in the American Rejection of the Treaty of Versailles', *Australian Journal of Politics and History*, IX (1963), pp. 213–34; 'A Proposition of the Highest International Importance', *Journal of Commonwealth Studies*, V (1967), pp. 200–13.

Melgund, Lord, 'The Recent Rebellion in North-West Canada', *Nineteenth Century*, 102 (1885), pp. 312–27.

Nish, I., 'Australia and the Anglo-Japanese Alliance, 1901–11', *Australian Journal of Politics and History*, IX (1963), pp. 201–12.

Penney, Barbara, 'The Age of Empire', *Historical Studies Australia and New Zealand*, XI (1963), pp. 32–42; 'Australia's Reactions to the Boer War – a Study in Colonial Imperialism', *Journal of British Studies*, VII (1967), pp. 97–130.

Poynter, J. R., 'The Yo-Yo Variations: Initiative and Dependence in Australia's External Relations, 1918–23', *Historical Studies Australia and New Zealand*, XIV (1967), pp. 231–49.

Richardson, H. W., 'Retardation in Britain's Industrial Growth', *Scottish Journal of Political Economy*, June 1965, pp. 125–37.

Sales, Peter M., 'W. M. Hughes and the Chanak Crisis of 1922', *Australian Journal of Politics and History*, XVII (1971), pp. 392–405.

Schuyler, Robert L., 'The Recall of the Legions: A Phase in the Decentralization of the British Empire', *American Historical Review*, XXVI (1920), pp. 18–36.

Scovill, Elmer B., 'The RAF and the Desert Frontiers of Iraq, 1919–20', *Aerospace Historian*, 22 (1975), pp. 84–92.

Spinks, Charles N., 'The Termination of the Anglo-Japanese Alliance', *Pacific Historical Review*, VI (1937), pp. 321–40; 'The Background of the Anglo-Japanese Alliance', *Pacific Historical Review*, VIII (1952), pp. 319–40.

Stacey, C. P., 'Canada and the Nile Expedition of 1884–1885', *Canadian Historical Review*, XXXIII (1952), pp. 319–40; 'John A. MacDonald on Raising Troops in Canada for Imperial Service', *Canadian Historical Review*, XXXVIII (1957), pp. 37–40.

Taylor, G. P., 'New Zealand, the Anglo-Japanese Alliance, and the 1908 Visit of the American Fleet', *Australian Journal of Politics and History*, XV (1969), pp. 57–76.

Trainor, L., 'British Imperial Defence Policy and the Australian Colonies, 1892–6', *Historical Studies Australia and New Zealand*, XIV (1970), pp. 204–18.

Watt, D. C., 'The Anglo-German Naval Agreement of 1935', *Journal of Modern History*, XXVIII (1956), pp. 155–75.

Williams, M. J., 'The Treatment of German Losses on the Somme in the British Official History', *Journal of the Royal United Services Institute*, CXI (1966), pp. 22–32.

Books

Amery, L. S. (ed), *The Times History of the War in South Africa, 1900–1902* (London 1905); *My Political Life* (London 1965).

Balfour, M., *The Kaiser and his Times* (London 1964).

Barnett, C., *The Desert Generals* (London 1960); *The Swordbearers* (London 1963); *The Collapse of British Power* (London 1972).

Bonham-Carter, V., *Soldier True* (London 1963).

Braisted, William R., *The United States Navy in the Pacific, 1909–22* (Austin 1971).

Brogden, S., *The Sudan Contingent* (Melbourne 1943).

Cassar, George H., *The French and the Dardanelles* (London 1971).

Chisholm, C., *A Handbook of Commercial Geography* (London 1916).

Churchill, W. S., *The World Crisis* (London 1933); *The Second World War*, Vols. I–V (London 1949–54); *Secret Session Speeches* (London 1946).

Clinard, Outen J., *Japan's Influence on American Naval Power, 1897–1917* (London 1960).

Connell, J., *Wavell: Soldier and Scholar* (London 1964).

Cook, Brown, Berger (eds), *Imperial Relations in the Age of Laurier* (Toronto 1969).

Cruttwell, C. R. M. F., *A History of the Great War* (Oxford 1934).

Deakin, A., *The Federal Story* (Melbourne 1963).

Dignan, D., *New Perspectives on British Far Eastern Policy, 1913–19* (Brisbane 1969).

Divine, D., *The Blunted Sword* (London 1964).

Doyle, A. Conan, *The Great Boer War* (London 1903).

Eayrs, J., *In Defense of Canada* (Toronto 1965).

Essame, H., *The Battle for Europe, 1918* (London 1972).

Feiling, K., *The Life of Neville Chamberlain* (London 1946).

Gardner, B., *The Lion's Cage* (London 1969).

Gordon, Donald C., *The Dominion Partnership in Imperial Defense, 1870–1914* (Baltimore 1965).

Guinn, P., *British Strategy and Politics, 1914 to 1918* (Oxford 1965).

Hankey, M., *The Supreme Command* (London 1961).

Hart, L., *Through the Fog of War* (London 1968).

Higham, R., *Armed Forces in Peacetime: Britain, 1918–1940* (London 1963); *Britain's Imperial Air Routes, 1918–1939* (London 1961).

Higham, R. (ed), *A Guide to the Sources of British Military History* (London 1972).

Horne, A., *To Lose A Battle* (London 1970).

Howard, M., *The Continental Commitment* (London 1972).

James, H., *English Hours* (New York 1960).

Johnson, D. H., *Volunteers at Heart: the Queensland Defence Forces, 1860–1901* (Brisbane 1972).

Kindleberger, C. P., *Economic Growth in France and Britain* (Cambridge 1964).

Kittredge, Tracy B., *Naval Lessons of the Great War* (Garden City 1921).

Kruger, W., *Good-bye, Dolly Gray* (London 1959).

Langer, William L., *The Diplomacy of Imperialism, 1890–1902* (New York 1965).

La Nauze, J., *Alfred Deakin* (Melbourne 1963).

Lehmann, J., *The First Boer War* (London 1972).

Le May, G. H. L., *British Supremacy in South Africa, 1899–1907* (Oxford 1965).

Mahan, Arthur T., *Retrospect and Prospect* (New York 1968).

Marder, A. J., *From the Dreadnought to Scapa Flow*, 5 vols (London 1961–70).

Menzies, R. G., *Afternoon Light* (Melbourne 1967).

Middlemas, R. K., *The Diplomacy of Illusion* (London 1972).

Mosley, L., *On Borrowed Time* (London 1972).

Moore, W., *The Thin Yellow Line* (London 1975).

Nish, I. H., *The Anglo-Japanese Alliance* (London 1966); *Alliance in Decline* (London 1972).

Parkinson, R., *Blood, Toil, Tears and Sweat* (London 1973).

Penlington, N., *Canada and Imperialism, 1896–9* (Toronto 1965).

Pelz, Stephen L., *Race to Pearl Harbor* (Cambridge 1973).

Preston, Richard A., *Canada and Imperial Defense* (Durham 1967).

Roskill, S. W., *Hankey: Man of Secrets*, vol. III (London 1974); *Naval Policy Between the Wars., Vol. I, The Period of Anglo-American Antagonism, 1919–29* (London 1968).

Ross, A., *New Zealand Aspirations in the Pacific in the Nineteenth Century* (Oxford 1964).

Stacey, C. P., *Canada and the British Army, 1846–71* (London 1966).

Stanley, George F. G., *Canada's Soldiers* (Toronto 1960).

Taylor, A. J. P., *The Origins of the Second World War* (London 1963).

Terraine, J., *The Western Front* (London 1964).

Thorne, C., *The Approach to War* (London 1967).

Toye, H., *The Springing Tiger* (Bombay 1963).

Trevelyan, G. M., *Grey of Fallodon* (London 1937).

Turner, L. C. F., *The Great War* (Melbourne 1971).

Van Creveld, Martin L., *Hitler's Strategy, 1940–1* (Cambridge 1973).

Wade, M., *The French Canadians, 1760–1967* (Toronto 1968).

Walder, D., *The Chanak Affair* (London 1969).

Woodward, E. L., *Great Britain and the German Navy, 1898–1914* (Oxford 1935).

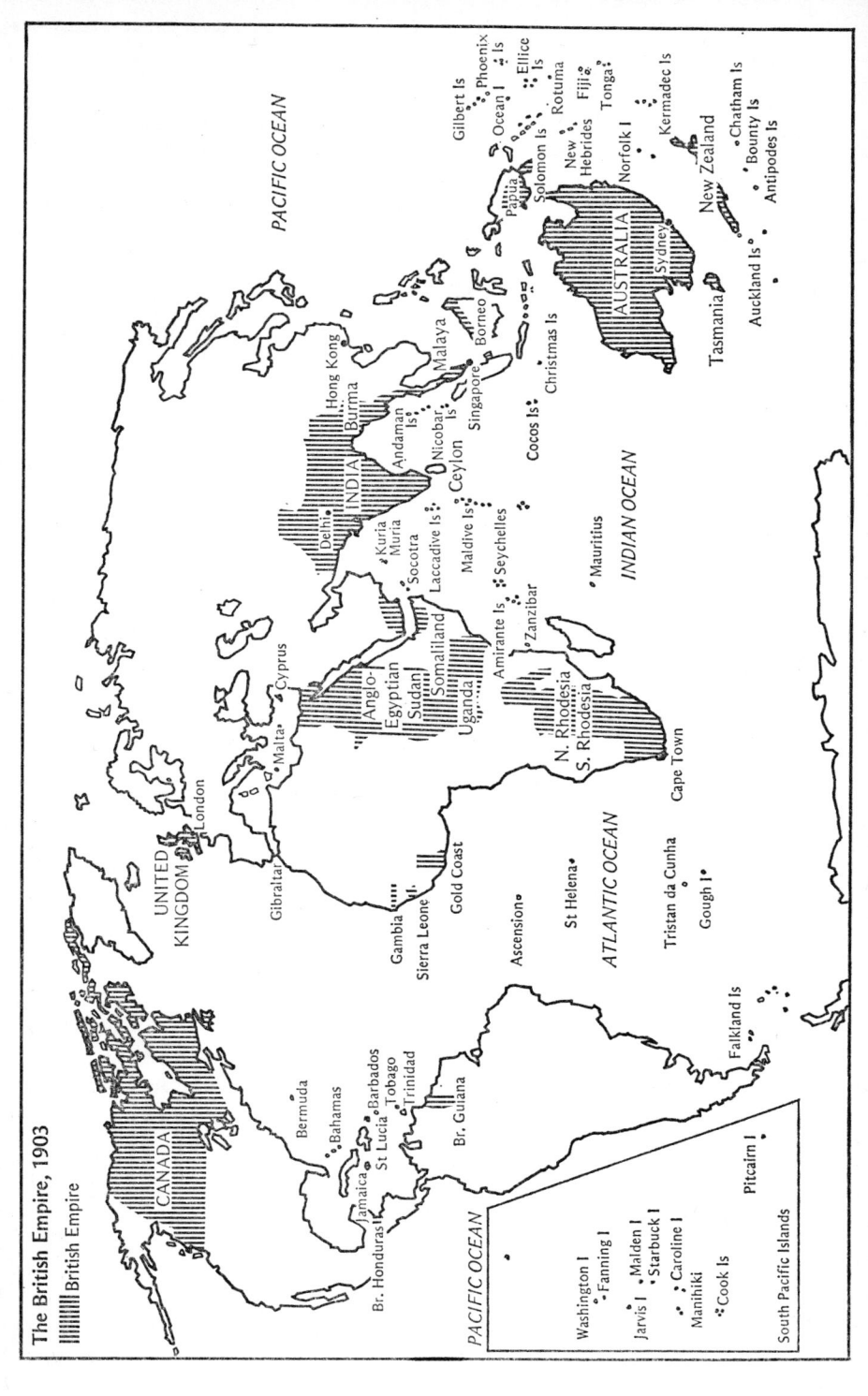

The British Empire, 1903

||||| British Empire

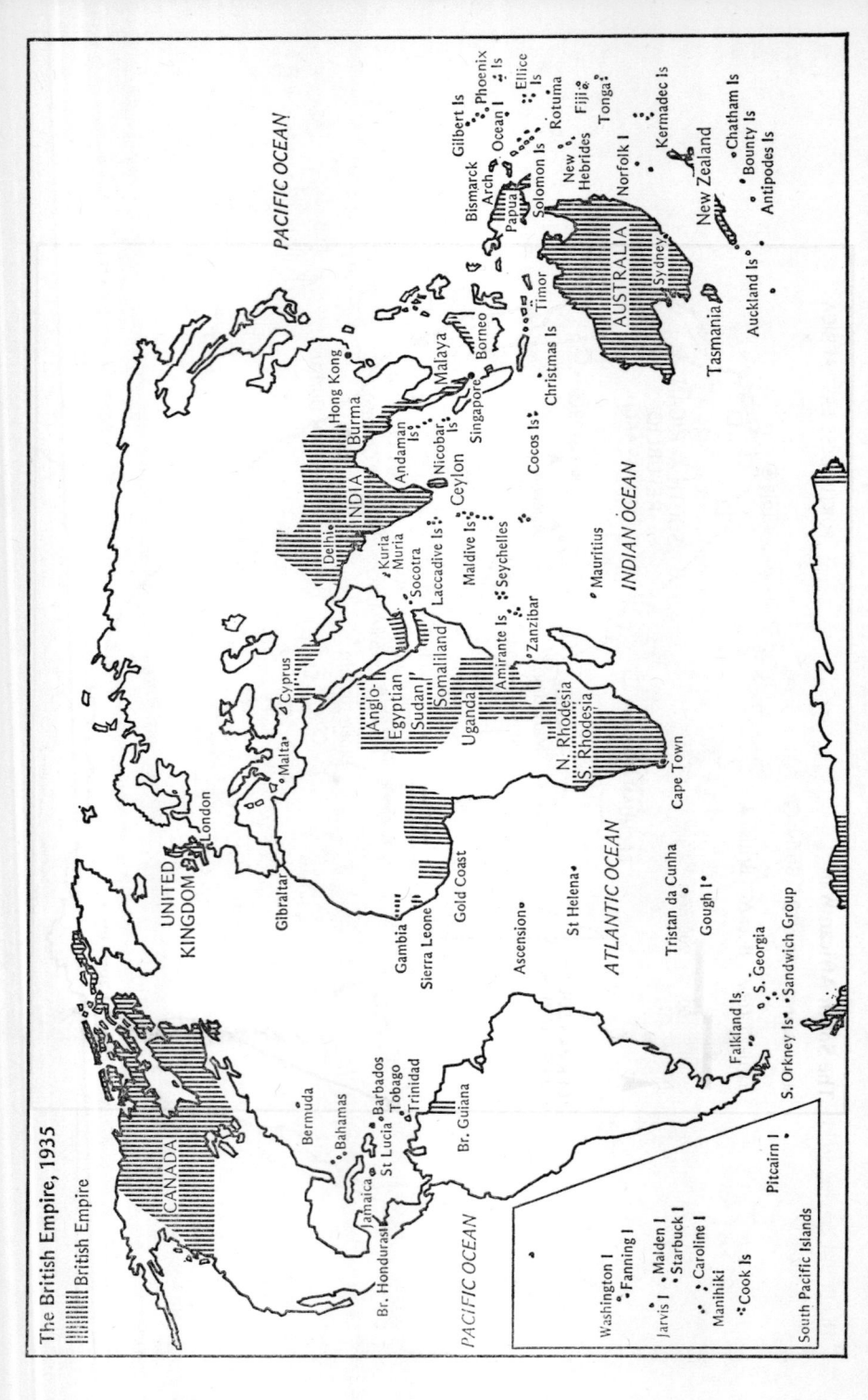

The British Empire, 1935

British Empire

PACIFIC OCEAN

Gilbert Is
Phoenix
Ocean I
Ellice Is
Rotuma
Fiji
Kermadec Is
Tonga
Chatham Is
Bounty Is
Antipodes Is
Bismarck Arch
Solomon Is
New Hebrides
Papua
Norfolk I
New Zealand
Auckland Is
AUSTRALIA
Sydney
Timor
Tasmania

Hong Kong
Burma
Malaya
Borneo
Singapore
Christmas Is
Andaman Is
Nicobar Is
Cocos Is
INDIA
Delhi
Ceylon
Kuria Muria
Socotra
Laccadive Is
Maldive Is
Seychelles
Amirante Is
Zanzibar
Mauritius

INDIAN OCEAN

Cyprus
Malta
Anglo-Egyptian Sudan
Somaliland
Uganda
N. Rhodesia
S. Rhodesia
Cape Town

UNITED KINGDOM
London

Gibraltar
Gambia
Sierra Leone
Gold Coast
Ascension
St Helena
Tristan da Cunha
Gough I

ATLANTIC OCEAN

Bermuda
Bahamas
Jamaica
Br. Honduras
Barbados
Tobago
Trinidad
St Lucia
Br. Guiana

CANADA

Falkland Is
S. Georgia
S. Orkney Is
Sandwich Group

PACIFIC OCEAN

Washington I
Fanning I
Jarvis I
Malden I
Starbuck I
Caroline I
Manihiki
Cook Is
Pitcairn I

South Pacific Islands

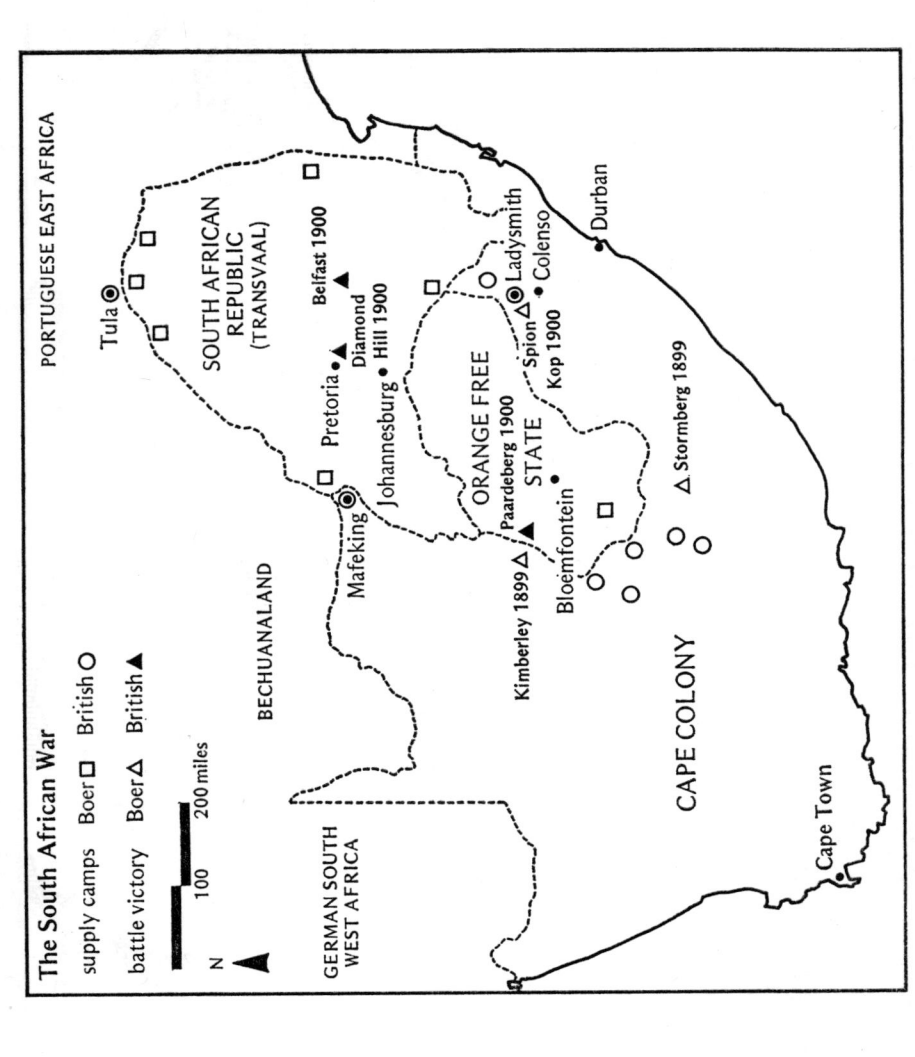

The South African War

supply camps   Boer ☐   British ○

battle victory   Boer △   British ▲

N ▲

100   200 miles

GERMAN SOUTH WEST AFRICA

BECHUANALAND

PORTUGUESE EAST AFRICA

Tula ◉

SOUTH AFRICAN REPUBLIC (TRANSVAAL)

Belfast 1900 ☐

Diamond ▲
Hill 1900 •

Pretoria •

Johannesburg •

Mafeking ◉

ORANGE FREE STATE

Paardeberg 1900 ▲

Kimberley 1899 △

Bloemfontein •

Ladysmith ◉
Spion △ Colenso •
Kop 1900

Durban •

△ Stormberg 1899

CAPE COLONY

Cape Town •

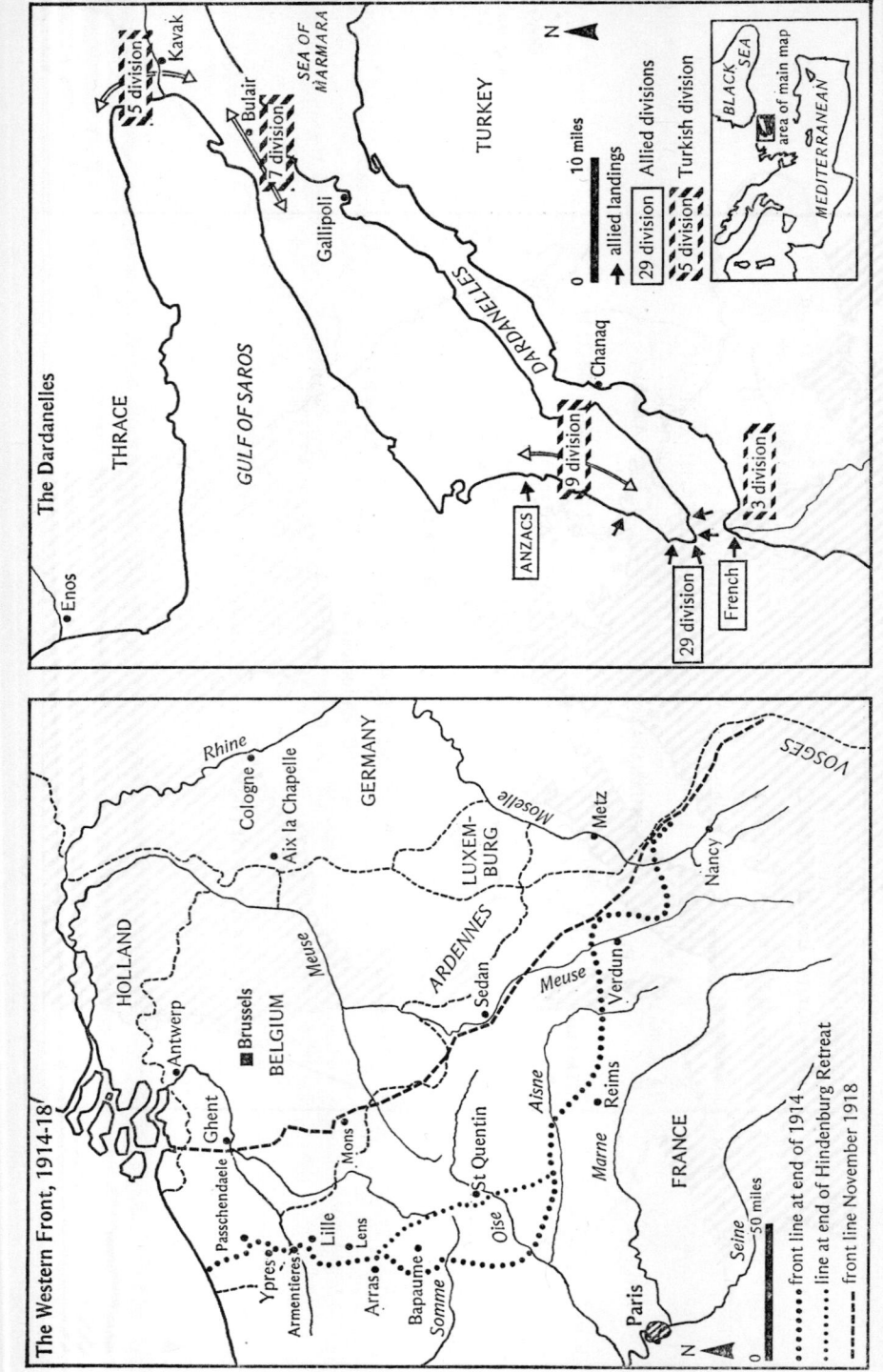

The Dardanelles

THRACE

GULF OF SAROS

SEA OF MARMARA

TURKEY

Enos

Kavak
5 division

Bulair
7 division

Gallipoli

DARDANELLES

Chanaq

9 division

ANZACS

29 division

French

3 division

N

10 miles

0

allied landings
29 division   Allied divisions

5 division   Turkish division

BLACK SEA

MEDITERRANEAN

area of main map

The Western Front, 1914-18

Rhine

Cologne

Aix la Chapelle

GERMANY

HOLLAND

Antwerp

Brussels

BELGIUM

Ghent

Moselle

Metz

LUXEM-BURG

ARDENNES

Meuse

Sedan

Meuse

Verdun

Nancy

VOSGES

Passchendaele

Ypres

Armentieres

Lille

Lens

Mons

Arras

Bapaume

Somme

St Quentin

Oise

Aisne

Reims

Marne

Paris

Seine

FRANCE

front line at end of 1914
line at end of Hindenburg Retreat
front line November 1918

N

0   50 miles

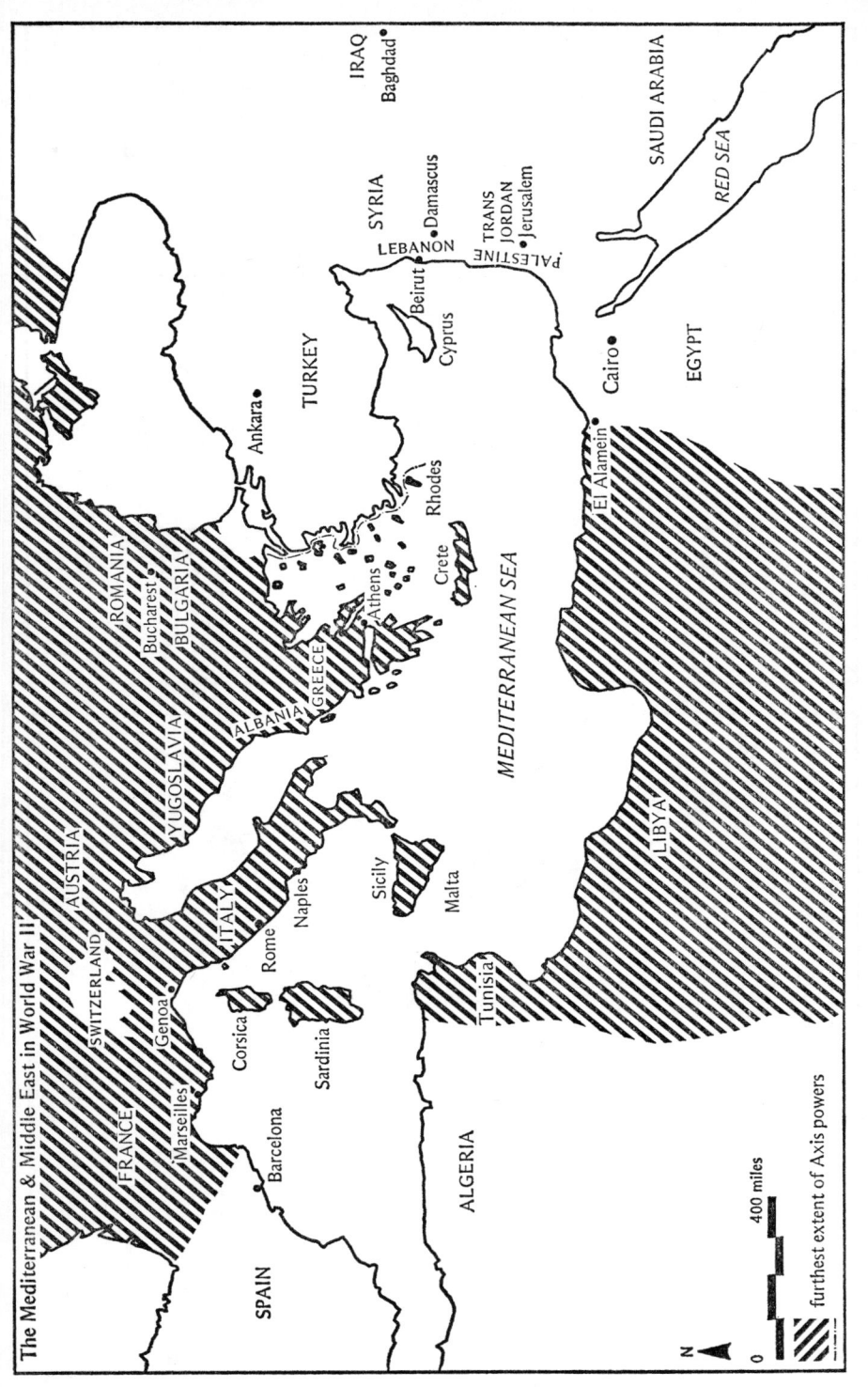

The Mediterranean & Middle East in World War II

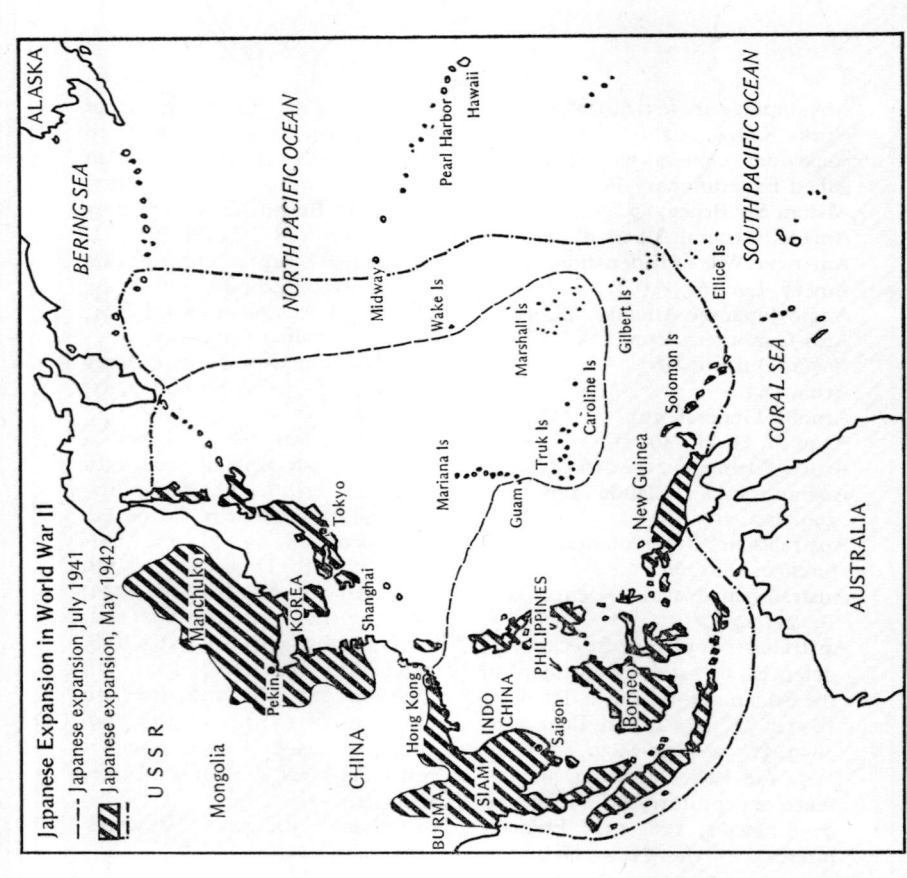

Japanese Expansion in World War II

--- Japanese expansion July 1941
▨ Japanese expansion, May 1942

ALASKA

BERING SEA

NORTH PACIFIC OCEAN

Pearl Harbor
Hawaii

Midway
Wake Is

Marshall Is

Gilbert Is
Caroline Is
Ellice Is

SOUTH PACIFIC OCEAN

USSR

Mongolia

Manchukuo

Pekin
KOREA

Tokyo

Shanghai

Mariana Is

Truk Is
Guam

Solomon Is

CORAL SEA

New Guinea

CHINA

Hong Kong

INDO
CHINA

PHILIPPINES

Saigon

Borneo

BURMA
SIAM

AUSTRALIA

Index

274 *Index*

Persia, 54
Philippines, 191
Piesse, Edmund L., 87
Plan Dog, 164, 166
Pleasant Island, 59
Poland, 141, 145–6
Port Arthur, 46, 47
Pownall, General Sir Henry, 197, 217, 221
Pratt, Sir John, 102

Queensland Defence Force, 8, 9

Rabaul, 82, 195
Ransome, Sir Arthur, 109–10
Rawlings, Admiral, 216
Rawlinson, General Sir William, 69
Repington, Colonel, 91
Rhodes, Cecil, 31
Richardson, Dr, 3
Riel, Louis, 10, 14
Rimington, Colonel, 40
Roberts, Lord, 32–3, 35, 39
Rommel, General, 178, 181, 195, 201, 202, 203, 205
Roosevelt, Franklin D.: on threat from Japan, 123; and Canada's entry into World War II, 143; supplies arms to Britain, 150, 152, 154, 155; Churchill asks for American squadron to be sent to Singapore, 162; Australia asks for help, 204; advises that 9th Division should be left in Middle East, 205; Curtin accuses of abandoning Empire in Far East, 206; at Pacific War Council, 207, 208; meets Churchill and Chiang Kai-Shek at Cairo, 209
Roosevelt, Theodore, 47
Royal Air Force (RAF): decline between world wars, 93; and Singapore base, 97; strength, 99, 105, 118, 127, 154; RAF training establishment refused by Canada, 125–6; Greek campaign, 180, 182–3; in Iraq, 180; Coastal Command, 99, 121
Royal Australian Air Force

(RAAF): Britain unable to supply aircraft, 116; limited capabilities of, 121; tries to buy Hudsons from United States, 132; strength, 132, 138, 192; Britain rejects expeditionary force, 144–5; sent to Singapore, 160; acquires Fairey Battles, 163; Pownall on, 197
Royal Australian Artillery, 29
Royal Australian Naval Reserve, 60
Royal Australian Navy (RAN): establishment of, 8, 52, 56–7; World War I, 58–9, 81, 82, 83; Jellicoe on, 85; naval rearmament, 93–4; strength, 138–9; alerted for World War II, 140–1; in World War II, 146, 163, 192, returns to Australia, 203
Royal Canadian Dragoons, 40
Royal Canadian Naval Service, 81
Royal Horse Artillery, 181
Royal Marines, 64
Royal Navy: strength, 1, 23–5, 45, 53, 95–6, 99, 138; and defence of Australia, 10, 16, 17, 19, 21; defence of South Africa, 18; imperial defence, 21–2; Australia's contribution to, 44, 50, 51; World War I, 65, 67, 79; rearmament after World War I, 84–5, 86; Australia opposed to any disarmament of, 100; Greek campaign, 180, 183; Japanese attack in Bay of Bengal, 200; China Squadron, 23, 96, 138; East Indies Squadron, 138, 155; Fleet Air Arm, 99, 104, 105, 121, 122; Royal Naval Air Service, 99, 104; Royal Naval Division, 64
Rumania, 62, 145
Rupprecht, Crown Prince, 68, 70–1
Russia: Crimean war, 7; naval squadron visits Australia, 9; possibility of war with Britain, 45; naval strength, 45, 46, 54; attacked by Japan at Port Arthur, 46–7; possibility of attack on India, 48; territorial agreement with Britain, 49; secret agreement with Japan over Mongolia, 56; World War I,